LIVING ON THE EDGE

LIVING ON THE EDGE
The Realities of Welfare in America

Mark Robert Rank

COLUMBIA UNIVERSITY PRESS
NEW YORK

1/96

Columbia University Press
New York   Chichester, West Sussex
Copyright © 1994 Columbia University Press

Library of Congress Cataloging-in-Publication Data
Rank, Mark R.
Living on the edge : the realities of welfare in America / Mark
Robert Rank.
p.   cm.
Includes bibliographical references and index.
ISBN 0–231–08424–2
1. Welfare recipients—United States—Interviews.   2. Public
welfare—United States.   I. Title.
HV91.R36   1994
362.5'0973—dc20   93–22818
CIP

Casebound editions of Columbia University Press books
are printed on permanent and durable
acid-free paper.
Printed in the United States of America
c 10 9 8 7 6 5 4 3 2

CONTENTS

LIST OF FIGURES

LIST OF TABLES

ACKNOWLEDGMENTS

This book has been a long time in the making. Gathering information and data, doing research, and analyzing and writing have taken place over a ten-year period. Inevitably, the success of a project of this size depends not only on the efforts of its author but also on the assistance and advice of many along the way. I have been truly fortunate in receiving such help from colleagues, staff, and friends.

Both Marvin Cummins and Shanti Khinduka have provided considerable institutional support and resources within the School of Arts and Sciences and the School of Social Work at Washington University. Their generous help has been invaluable. In addition, two summer faculty research grants from the School of Arts and Sciences at Washington University allowed me to conduct and analyze the in-depth interviews with welfare families. Paul Voss, along with Doris Slesinger and Elizabeth Thomson, offered support, encouragement, and guidance at the University of Wisconsin. James Gallagher and Ron Haskins were instrumental in furnishing me with a one-year fellowship at the Frank Porter Graham Child Development Center at the University of North Carolina that enabled me to focus my energies upon this project.

The assistance of Paul Green and John Verberkmoes allowed me the entrance to the welfare system necessary to my research. Their help and cooperation were absolutely vital to this work. Equally vital were the efforts of Eleanor Cautley, who was superb in working with me to conduct the in-depth interviews. If ever there was an ideal colleague to have on a project, Eleanor was it. Several students and staff members, including Elsie Glickert, Jacklyn Henkin, Kathie Laird, Sylvia Rothberg, Joan Russ, Teresa Sweeney, Adele Tuchler, and Scott Ward transcribed the interviews or provided other valuable assistance.

When I required help with computer problems, Robert Jamieson, Kathryn Jobe, Steve Middlebrook, and Gary Stephens addressed my questions. And William Olbrich helped me locate specific government publications and historical documents.

A number of colleagues read earlier versions and sections of the manuscript; I sincerely appreciate their many valuable suggestions. These colleagues include Bert Adams, Peter Adler, Rebecca Blank, Andrew Cherlin, Larry Davis, David Ellwood, Claude Fischer, Leonard Green, Robert Haveman, Thomas Hirschl, Saul Hoffman, Edward Kain, David Klein, Thomas Lasswell, Michael Sherraden, Ruth Sidel, Donald Tomaskovic-Devey, Nancy Vosler, and Gautam Yadama. In addition, I have had helpful conversations with Nancy Amidei, Steve Brodbeck, Catherine Chilman, Donald Cox, Virginia Ellis, Margaret Feldman, Debra Freed, David Gillespie, David Guilkey, Sandra Hale, Larry Hamlin, Joel Myerson, Eric Plutzer, Ronald Rindfuss, and Donald Strickland.

I have also benefited considerably from stimulating, thought-provoking interactions with my students pertaining to the ideas in this book. These exchanges emphasize the importance of viewing both research and teaching as interactive, symbiotic processes.

Portions of chapter 5 have appeared in *The American Sociolog-*

ical Review (vol. 54, no. 2, 1989), and *Journal of Marriage and the Family* (vol. 49, no. 1, 1987). In addition, portions of chapter 9 have appeared in *Social Service Review* (vol. 59, no. 3, 1985); *Social Forces* (vol. 66, no. 4, 1988); and *Poverty and Social Welfare in the United States,* edited by Donald Tomaskovic-Devey (Westview Press 1988).

I have been fortunate in receiving good advice about publishing from those in the trade, including Michael Aronson, Marquita Flemming, Sharon Panulla, Nancy Roberts, David Roll, Kathy Shaer, Henry Tom, Gladys Topkis, and Michael Weber. Dean Birkenkamp and Marlie Wasserman generously encouraged and supported this work. In addition, I received suggestions regarding the placement of my manuscript from Herbert Gans, Nathan Glazer, David Grusky, Donna Jablonski, Christopher Jencks, Sar Levitan, David Pittman, Bradley Schiller, Lawrence Summers, and Marta Tienda. I would also like to thank Nancy Mays at Washington University for her help.

The staff at Columbia University Press have provided excellent editorial support. Gioia Stevens, Sarah St. Onge, and Anne McCoy have all added considerably to the final product.

My family offered the wealth of emotional support and encouragement so important in any successful venture. I am grateful to my wife, Anne, and daughters, Elizabeth and Katherine; my mother and late father, Jean and Robert; my brother, Steve, and my father- and mother-in-law, Edward and Diane Deutch.

Finally, and most important, I would like to thank those women and men who opened their hearts, souls, and minds telling me their stories. Without a willingness to share their life experiences, this book simply would not have been possible. My utmost hope is that I have accurately and insightfully captured their experiences of living on welfare. I owe them no less.

1 INTRODUCTION

I'm not knocking the welfare program, because it's a lifesaver—it's there. Because you've got a roof over your head and you're not out in the street. But on the other hand, as far as my own situation is concerned, it's pretty rough living this way. I can't see anybody that would ever settle for something like this just for the mere fact of getting a free ride, because it's not worth it. I mean you only go around once. You should be able to enjoy some of it.

—*Fifty-one-year-old divorced mother on welfare*

1

S everal years ago, I received a telephone call from a local St. Louisian. He had read an editorial of mine in the Sunday newspaper, disputing some of the myths surrounding the welfare system. The caller was incensed. How in the world could I write such nonsense when everyone knew that most welfare recipients were black, on the dole for years at a time, living the good life, and so on. "But how," I asked "do you know that?" "Just look around!" he replied. He had no need for the data I used to argue my points; for him it was obvious that people on welfare were good-for-nothing parasites. The conversation went on for close to half an hour before I finally managed to get off the telephone. It was apparent I had struck a nerve.

Why was there so much anger with so little evidence to justify it? How had this man become so convinced that his viewpoint was correct? As bits and pieces of my research have come to the public's attention, I have encountered similar responses from individuals in various walks of life.

Recently I came across a more stunning example of such

attitudes. A member of the Milwaukee County Board of Supervisors proposed that the county government begin selling the organs of dead welfare recipients, even if they had not given their permission to do so. According to him, it would reduce the county's burial expenses. Furthermore, he noted, "If they can't help society while they're alive, maybe they can help it while they're dead" (*New York Times,* July 20, 1990). The idea was eventually dropped, but the fact that it was proposed and considered was an eye-opener.

For most Americans, the words *welfare recipient* evoke the image of a good-for-nothing freeloader who drives a Cadillac, uses Food Stamps to buy sirloin steak, or watches soap operas all day. It is a classic icon of American culture, routinely projected upon all who are receiving public assistance.

This book will challenge such images and beliefs. It will stand in sharp contrast to the stereotypes commonly attached to welfare recipients. It provides an opportunity to walk in the shoes of those whom so many of us quickly dismiss as parasites. In short, the purpose of this book is to provide a true sense of who these people are. Rather than the caricatures of neighborhood gossip, this book describes real people dealing with real problems and struggling daily with considerable effort and determination to survive.

I realize that shattering these stereotypes will be an uphill battle. They are used not just by our neighbors down the street but by those at various levels of political power as well. From president, to senator, to governor, to state legislator, one can hear the negative and distorted characterizations reverberate in the halls of power.

President Reagan often used anecdotes to paint welfare recipients as abusers of the system. When asked about the 1983 budget deficit, the president responded with "a story about an unnamed young man in an unidentified grocery who used Food Stamps to pay for a single orange, then bought a bottle of vodka with the change" (*Newsweek,* April 5, 1982).

In a more recent speech before the House of Representatives, Georgia Congressman Newt Gingrich declared that the core values of the welfare state and its programs "have the effect of protecting the criminal at the expense of the innocent. They have the effect of encouraging 12-year-old girls to have children [and of encouraging 15-year-old boys] to promiscuously impregnate girls" (*New York Times,* January 5, 1992). In discussing women on welfare, the president pro tem of the Missouri senate similarly declared, "People are saying these breeding factories have got to stop" (*St. Louis Post-Dispatch,* February 21, 1993).

The governor of California, Pete Wilson, noted after announcing his proposed 9 percent cut in the Aid to Families with Dependent Children program, "I am convinced they will be able to pay the rent, but they will have less for a six-pack of beer. I don't begrudge them a six-pack of beer, but it is not an urgent necessity." Wilson went on to say, "What you have in this budget when you cut the AFDC grant, you have prenatal care, you have programs that prevent drug use during pregnancy, you have preschool. You have a lot of things that are more important than a six-pack of beer or providing top dollar to a slumlord" (*Los Angeles Times,* January 12, 1991).

In Massachusetts, a state senator characterized his state's welfare program for able-bodied adults in this way: "General Relief goes to people who are urinating on the floor in the bus station in Brockton and throwing up. They take that $338 and go to the nearest bar and spend it" (*New York Times,* March 15, 1992). The legislator announced that he was not concerned how his comments might be received since welfare recipients do not vote.

During a debate on welfare, a Vermont state representative argued that the state's welfare program for families is responsible for child abuse. According to the representative, public assistance "creates child abuse as people lay around and do better on welfare than working" (*New York Times,* March 15, 1992).

And finally, in writing about the homeless and the poor, a former member of the Indiana House, Don Boys, characterized welfare recipients in the following way: "Many Welfare Mamas are, as the old-timers used to say, very 'fleshy,' sucking on cigarettes, with booze and soft drinks in the fridge, feeding their faces with fudge as they watch the color TV" (*USA Today,* December 10, 1985).

Countless other examples from all sections of the country, at various levels of political power, at every rank of social and economic position, and throughout our country's history could be given.[1] Yet clearly what is needed in this debate are not dubious assertions but rather honest attempts at understanding the actual circumstances of those living on public assistance. Rather than rhetoric and stereotypes, well-grounded evidence is mandatory for an intelligent understanding of this issue.

This book attempts to convey the realities, not the myths, of welfare recipiency. In some respects, the realities are much more troubling. Perhaps this is one reason we cling to our stereotypes. As Henry Haskins wrote in the nineteenth century, "The truth would become more popular if it were not always stating ugly facts."

This book presents those facts. It seeks neither to glorify nor to demean those who turn to public assistance but rather to provide an objective and clear accounting of the experience of living on welfare. It is a look into the world of welfare recipients—their problems, their strengths, their lives. My aim is to provide insight into this emotionally charged and critical issue.

Perhaps the key theme running throughout the book is that the welfare recipient is not that different from you or me—no better, no worse. Nevertheless, we Americans often view welfare recipients as somehow different from the rest of us: they live in inner cities, they have too many children, they are irresponsible and don't work hard enough; in short, they get what they deserve. The research findings in this book sharply contradict this viewpoint.

To be sure, some individuals do abuse the welfare system. And it is precisely these cases that quickly find their way into politicians' speeches, television talk shows, and individual perceptions. After all, some grain of truth can always be found in a stereotype. This book will demonstrate, however, that such cases constitute a very small fraction of the overall welfare population. Most welfare recipients want a better life for themselves and their children; they don't enjoy being on government assistance; and they persevere in the face of countless hardships and handicaps. Ultimately, they cling to the American dream despite the formidable odds against them.

I believe that this message is absolutely critical to the policy debate regarding the poor and public assistance. Our policy discussions should be based not upon how different the poor are from the rest of us but rather upon how much they have in common. Policies built on this assumption would be more effective and certainly less dehumanizing than the current system.

I am fully aware that in some circles my message will simply be seen as knee-jerk liberalism, or as left-wing rhetoric. Such conclusions would be an unfortunate mistake. Certainly political beliefs influence our thinking, including my own. To deny this would be absurd. However, the past fifteen years have taught me that much more important than political ideology is the necessity for the social scientist to be fair and objective. To do less is to lose one's credibility. Yet this does not mean that the social scientist should fail to have a viewpoint regarding his or her work. In fact, without such a viewpoint, research is often vacuous. The key is for such views to be well grounded in evidence that has been fairly, objectively, and insightfully analyzed. I believe that this book has been guided by that ideal.

A further goal that has shaped the writing of this book is an effort to communicate clearly and directly. Often times, social scientists muddy the waters with unnecessary jargon and cumbersome writing. As Howard Becker notes, too often such researchers try "to give substance and weight to what they wrote by sounding academic, even at the expense of their real meaning" (1986:7). There is simply no reason social scientists cannot write clearly and at the same time develop powerful and well-thought-out arguments. James Langford, director of the University of Notre Dame Press, put it succinctly in this description of his publishing mission: "We are interested in good writing, in people with something to say, in new approaches to old questions—in other words, in intellectual vitality—not in professional jargon, quaint obfuscation, or in manuscripts that offer neither light nor heat" (Parsons 1989:44). I hope the reader will find in this book a good deal of light and heat, some new approaches to old questions, and a minimum of professional jargon.

I have tried to communicate the experiences and lives of welfare recipients in terms both clear and discerning. In addition, I have allowed those whom I interviewed to express their thoughts and attitudes without lengthy reinterpretations. I feel that most people do an excellent job of expressing themselves and that readers will gain considerably more insight into the issues of poverty and welfare recipiency from hearing firsthand what welfare recipients experience. My job is to guide and represent fairly what those experiences and attitudes are.

Background

Few topics are more likely to spark a heated discussion on the streets of small-town America or the floors of Congress than the topic of welfare and welfare recipients. Such discussions have a long history. Since England's Poor Law of 1601, the government's role in aiding the poor has been vigorously debated.

William Graham Sumner wrote in 1881, "In truth, the human race has never done anything else but struggle with the problem of social welfare. That struggle constitutes history, or the life of the human race on earth." Three years later, Friedrich Engels noted, "The more civilization advances, the more it is compelled to cover the ills it necessarily creates with the cloak of love." Whichever view one accepts, social welfare, and specifically social welfare programs, constitute an important part of society.

Efforts to assist the poor have existed in the United States since the 1700s, but it was not until the Great Depression that public assistance programs were developed extensively on a national level. Included in Franklin Roosevelt's New Deal were the Social Security Act and the Federal Emergency Relief Act, both of which provided economic relief to millions. As Walter Trattner notes, with the Social Security Act, "the welfare state was born" (1989:268).

The issue of government assistance to the poor again came to the fore during the 1960s with the War on Poverty. During his 1964 State of the Union Address, Lyndon Johnson declared, "To help that one-fifth of all American families with income too small to even meet their basic needs, our chief weapons in a more pinpointed attack will be better schools and better health and better homes and better training and better job opportunities to help more Americans, especially young Americans, escape from squalor and misery and unemployment rolls where other citizens help to carry them" (*New York Times,* January 9, 1964). Various programs were developed or expanded in an attempt to attain that goal.

In contrast, the 1980s saw a sharp rejection of the concept of social engineering. The Reagan and Bush administrations viewed public assistance programs as causing more harm than good, undermining the incentives that move the poor out of poverty and into the economic mainstream (Glazer 1988). As Ronald Reagan often stated, "We fought the War on Poverty, and poverty won."[2]

Through all these ideological shifts, the poverty-stricken who rely on public assistance stay with us. Over thirty million Americans remain below the poverty line, many of them receiving some form of welfare assistance. Millions of Americans each year turn to the government for help. For some, that help will be temporary. For others, the stay on public assistance programs will be prolonged.

While editorials and commentaries appear regularly with regard to welfare recipients, we know relatively little about the lives of these people. For example, what is it like to live on public assistance for six months or a year? Surprisingly few studies have examined this basic yet important question. In addition, although numerous scholarly books and articles on poverty and welfare recipiency have appeared in the past fifteen years, their authors tend to rely on hypothetical examples of welfare recipients, secondary analysis, or philosophically based arguments. The poor themselves are consulted much too infrequently.[3] As Leslie Dunbar has noted, social science tends to treat "the poor like a foreign nation or refashions them into objects unlike us . . . [it is] a discipline that speaks mainly for the approval of other social scientists and of legislators, and seldom consults the poor themselves" (1988:18).

This book seeks throughout to address several broad questions. What are the underlying reasons for individuals being on welfare and in poverty? How do families adapt under such circumstances? What effect does welfare have on its recipients? What are the patterns and processes of key events (family change, employment, getting on and off welfare) among welfare recipients? How might public policy more effectively deal with the problem of poverty in the United States?

Further, this study goes beyond the existing research in several ways. First, few analyses have examined the entire process of welfare recipiency—that is, from applying for public assistance to eventually getting off the welfare rolls. Instead, the typical approach has been to focus on one aspect of welfare dynamics, such as length of recipiency.

Second, previous research on poverty and welfare recipients has primarily concentrated on families headed by women. Certainly, female-headed families with children constitute a significant proportion of the welfare population, but other types of families also receive public assistance, and information about these households has been limited. The recipients in this study include not only female-headed families but married couples, single men and women, and the elderly. The focus of this work is therefore considerably broader than much of the previous research, and more representative of the range of families that receive public assistance.

Third, much of the current debate regarding the poor has focused on what has been termed "the underclass." While the definitions vary somewhat, the label generally refers to those residing in inner cities of major metropolitan areas. These individuals are characterized as persistently poor, predominately minority, and largely dependent on welfare. Yet in spite of the vast amount of attention this group has received, its members constitute only a small percentage of the overall poverty population.[4] For example, Sawhill estimates that 7 percent of the entire poverty population, and only 15 percent of the black poverty population, resides in severely low income neighborhoods located in large urban areas (Sawhill 1988, 1989). What then of the remaining 93 percent of the overall poverty-stricken, or the remaining 85 percent of the black poverty population?

It is on this group that my book primarily focuses. Although some recipients in metropolitan inner city areas were sampled, the research was designed around a more representative sample of the overall poor population who are receiving welfare. This is not meant to undermine the importance and severity of the problems faced by those living in the inner city. They are formidable indeed. However, they are simply not representative of most people who are poor and on welfare. The reader should keep this observation in mind throughout the book.

Fourth, analyses of families on public assistance have tended to employ either a quantitative or qualitative methodology. Quantitative analyses have relied upon large-scale demographic and economic surveys such as the Panel Study of Income Dynamics (e.g., Duncan 1984; O'Neill et al. 1984; Bane and Ellwood 1986; Rank and Hirschl 1992). Qualitative research has generally been based on fieldwork and participant observation or on in-depth interviewing (e.g., Stack 1974; Sheehan 1975; Auletta 1983; Dunbar 1988; Anderson 1990). In contrast, this study combines in-depth interviews of and fieldwork on families receiving welfare, with a large longitudinal sample of welfare recipients. This blending of qualitative and quantitative data provides for a richer understanding of the lives of welfare recipients.

Finally, the study attempts to consider the experience of welfare recipiency within a larger theoretical context. Much of the previous research has been empirically driven, with a notable absence of broader theoretical concerns. In this book I focus not only on specific findings but also on the wider framework within which they reside.

Organization

The book is based on data gathered from 1980 to 1988 in the state of Wisconsin. The welfare system is quite decentralized and varies widely across states in terms of benefits, programs, and requirements (see chapter 2). For this reason, it is judicious to examine a single state rather than the nation as a whole. Furthermore, recent national reforms have been patterned largely on the system that exists in Wisconsin.

My focus throughout is on the general circumstances of receiving and living on public assistance, as opposed to a detailed analysis of the specific programs themselves. Although the particular programs are important, the analysis in this book is intended to be on a broader level. Over the long run, the specifics of these programs will change; the need for help from the government will persist. The basic findings in this book are intended to endure longer than the particulars of the programs themselves.

I used three complementary sources of data in the study. First, taped and transcribed interviews conducted with fifty families on public assistance detail a range of issues in chapters 3 through 10. Second, a statewide longitudinal caseload sample of nearly three thousand welfare households provides the basis for much of the quantitative analysis. Finally, fieldwork in the welfare system supplies firsthand knowledge of the workings of public assistance.

Both the interviews and the majority of the fieldwork were conducted in a single county chosen for its overall representativeness of Wisconsin's population. The primary city in this county is referred to throughout the book as "Ridgeton." A wide variety of professions and industries are found within the city itself. In addition, although the majority of Ridgeton's residents are white, a spectrum of ethnic and racial groups live in the city as well. Surrounding the city of Ridgeton are rural farmlands and small towns.

Figures, tables, and odds ratios are scattered throughout the chapters. Readers desiring more information about the manner in which the data were gathered and analyzed should begin with Appendix A, which provides a detailed accounting of the study methodology. Those interested in the full array of data used to generate the figures and odds ratios are directed to the supplementary tables in Appendix B.

Chapter 2 sets the stage for the remainder of the book by providing a brief historical background of social welfare in the United States, the structure of the current welfare system, and several of the dominant perspectives that have been applied to both the issues of poverty and welfare recipiency. Chapters 3 through 10 follow individuals and their families from the time they apply for public assistance to the period they eventually exit the welfare system. This examination of the day-to-day world of the welfare recipient—their daily routines and problems, beliefs and hopes, family dynamics, working experiences, and attitudes toward welfare—seeks to reveal as far as possible the entirety of the welfare experience. Throughout these chapters the names of recipients have been changed to protect their confidentiality.

Finally, chapter 11 interprets the major themes of the previous chapters from the broader theoretical context outlined in chapter 2. The book concludes with a chapter developing some general thoughts and observations concerning the issues of poverty and welfare recipients.

For all recipients, public assistance represents a last resort. The idea behind these programs is to provide the minimum resources necessary to sustain a daily existence. They allow for survival on a precarious edge. This book is about individuals and families who are living on that edge.

2 THE WELFARE DEBATE

A lot of people, I've heard, don't really need it. They're just too lazy to go and work. And that hurts the program for everybody. But I think for the majority—it's mainly hardships where they've really nowhere else to turn. And most of the people that I've known that do get help, it's just temporary, until they can get goin' on their own again.

—Thirty-six-year-old husband receiving Food Stamps

The debate surrounding welfare in the United States has been both long and heated. The concept of welfare tends to jar with the rugged individualism in which many Americans take pride (Gans 1988). Thus, while discussions about the role of the welfare state occur in most countries, they are especially vigorous in America. As Katz notes, "Nobody likes welfare. Conservatives worry that it erodes the work ethic, retards productivity, and rewards the lazy. Liberals view the American welfare system as incomplete, inadequate, and punitive. Poor people, who rely on it, find it degrading, demoralizing, and mean. None of these complaints are new; they echo nearly two centuries of criticism" (1986:ix).

Arguments tend to focus on the causes of welfare recipiency and poverty. Why do millions of Americans each year turn to public assistance programs for help? Likewise, why have over thirty million U.S. citizens annually fallen below the poverty line during the 1980s and 1990s (U.S. Bureau of the Census 1992a)? Such questions lie at the heart of the welfare debate.

This chapter reviews the background and development of social welfare programs in the United States, the structure of the current welfare system, and several of the dominant perspectives regarding the issues of both poverty and welfare recipiency.

Historical Background

Since the eighteenth century, the United States has provided limited forms of relief for the poverty-stricken, usually through churches, private charities, or local governments (for a more complete review of social welfare in the United States, see Katz 1986, 1989; Patterson 1986; Trattner 1989). Considerable debate existed in both the eighteenth and nineteenth centuries regarding the relative merits of "indoor" versus "outdoor" relief. Indoor relief provided support for the poor within institutions such as workhouses and almshouses. Outdoor relief did not require beneficiaries to reside in public institutions.

The Elizabethan Poor Law of 1601 marked the beginning of outdoor relief. Outdoor relief gained popularity during the seventeenth and eighteenth centuries, but by the nineteenth century this began to wane in both England and the United States. It was felt that outdoor relief encouraged pauperism. The rationale—supported by de Tocqueville in his lecture "Memoir on Pauperism," delivered in 1835—was that "giving relief to people in their own homes encouraged dependence, broke their spirit, corrupted their character, and made them feel entitled to a free livelihood from the state" (Handel 1982:127).

By the latter half of the nineteenth century, indoor relief had become the dominant legal method of providing for the poor in the United States, and it remained so until the Great Depression (Handel 1982). Virtually every county had a local almshouse. For the aged and disabled, the almshouse offered a refuge from the miseries of life; for the able-bodied poor, it represented order and hard work, a place to learn the lessons of respect and obedience (Handel 1982).

Throughout this period, it was commonly held that charity should be given out by private groups, not by the federal government, which was considered to have no direct role in aiding those in poverty. This concept radically changed with the onset of the Great Depression in 1929. Immediately before the Depression (in the spring of 1929), 2.86 million individuals were unemployed in the United States. By 1933, the number had reached 15 million. As competition for the remaining jobs intensified, wages and salaries fell. Banks and other financial institutions were in severe trouble, with some collapsing. The scope of the economic decline was unprecedented, with many "solid citizens" joining the ranks of the poor (Handel 1982).

Herbert Hoover, like his predecessors, was a firm believer that the federal government should play a limited role in aiding the poverty-stricken. It was not until late 1931 that he recognized the seriousness of the situation and began to advocate a more active role. However, the shift in policy was too late. Hoover lost the election in 1932 to Franklin Delano Roosevelt.

When Roosevelt gave his speech at the Democratic convention accepting the presidential nomination, he proclaimed, "I pledge you, I pledge myself, to a new deal for the American people." This New Deal represented a dramatic shift in America's social welfare policy.

A number of temporary work relief and emergency assistance programs were established during the first one hundred days of the Roosevelt administration. Never before had the federal government become involved in aiding its citizens on such a massive scale. The Federal Emergency Relief Act, the Civilian Conservation Corps, the Civil Works Administration, and the Works Progress Administration were but a few of the various programs and agencies established to deal with the Depression. The New Deal also introduced two concepts that represented a sharp break with previous policy. First, the federal government was to assume a large responsibility for social insurance. Second, it was seen as having a permanent role in public welfare. Both concepts came about in the Social Security Act of 1935.

The Social Security Act was arguably the most important piece of legislation produced by the New Deal. It established both social security and unemployment insurance, as well as the Aid to Dependent Children, Aid to the Blind, and Old Age Assistance programs.

During the 1940s and 1950s, the insurance and welfare programs that had been established under the Roosevelt administration changed little. However, by the early 1960s the issue of poverty was rediscovered, and a new interest arose in designing social welfare programs. While John F. Kennedy was campaigning for the Democratic presidential nomination in the spring of 1960, he encountered poverty-stricken families in West Virginia, and he stressed the issues of poverty, unemployment, and hunger in that state's primary election. Poverty quickly became an important issue in the Kennedy campaign.

As Handel (1982) notes, when the Kennedy administration took office in 1961, it began the first major effort in twenty-five years to advance a new concept of public welfare. The goal was not merely to provide cash assistance to dependent families but to prevent dependency in the first place and, where that failed, to rehabilitate the dependent. During his address to Congress on February 1, 1962, the president argued that the answer to the welfare problem was not just greater financial support to the poor but also the provision of services to enable the poor to climb out of poverty.

The policymakers in the Kennedy administration operated from several premises. First, there was a strong belief in the concept of human capital. It was felt that a major reason for poverty was the lack of skills, and therefore programs should be designed and implemented to remedy that lack (e.g., the Jobs Corps, the Neighborhood Youth Corps, etc.). A second premise was that among some low-income families a culture of poverty operated. Consequently, programs should also focus on instilling positive attitudes among the poor, preferably at an early age. In addition, programs were created or expanded to provide more coverage to those in poverty. The Food Stamp program was created, and the AFDC program expanded to allow states to include married couples whose head of household was unemployed.

At the time of Kennedy's assassination in November 1963, plans had been made, but not yet announced, to initiate a major push to eradicate poverty. For Lyndon Johnson, poverty became the right issue, for the right man, at the right time (Brauer 1982). It allowed him to continue the direction of the Kennedy policy, yet at the same time establish his own authority and identity. Furthermore, it was an issue about which he felt strongly.

In his State of Union address to Congress in January 1964, Johnson announced,

> This administration today, here and now, declares unconditional war on poverty in America, and I urge this Congress and all Americans to join with me in that effort. It will not be a short or easy struggle, no single weapon or strategy will suffice, but we shall not rest until that war is won. . . . Our joint Federal-local effort must pursue poverty, pursue it wherever it exists. In city slums, in small towns, in sharecroppers' shacks or in migrant worker camps, on Indian reservations, among whites as well as Negroes, among the young as well as the aged, in the boomtowns and in the depressed areas. Our aim is not only to relieve the symptoms of poverty, but to cure it, and above all, to prevent it.   (*New York Times,* January 9, 1964)

The president called for a wide range of legislative action including increased aid to Appalachia, youth employment legislation, wider Food Stamp coverage, the institution of a National Service Corps, broader coverage of minimum wage laws, and the creation of new jobs through tax reductions.

Following the declared war on poverty, Congress in 1964 approved the Economic Opportunity Act, which launched the broadest and most diverse federal social welfare effort since the New Deal. Programs focused on jobs, job training, and work for AFDC mothers. Various other programs that came into existence during this period included Medicare and Medicaid, Head Start, and the Elementary and Secondary Act, which provided federal funds to elementary and secondary schools based on the proportion of poor students in each local school district.

Both Kennedy and Johnson believed that poverty amidst plenty was intolerable and that the federal government had the responsibility and capacity to reduce or eliminate it (Brauer

1982). Both wanted programs with substance, based on research, that would work. And both emphasized that in the long run these programs would save money because they would eventually lead people out of welfare. Many of the War on Poverty programs also sprang from a philosophy of community action and community development. Programs attempted to involve poor individuals in devising strategies for attacking poverty. The principle was known as "maximum feasible participation" of the poor (for an analysis and critique of this approach, see Moynihan 1970). Community development approaches focused on rebuilding housing stock, encouraging the establishment of new businesses, and similar endeavors to transform inner cities into economically productive neighborhoods.

With the election of Richard Nixon in 1968, the Democratic hold on the presidency came to an end. The shift in policy toward social welfare was therefore something of a surprise.

During the latter half of the 1960s, the idea of a guaranteed income as a way to fight poverty gained increasing support. Simply put, if poverty is defined as a lack of money, then a guaranteed income is a straightforward way of dealing with the problem (Lemann 1989). All citizens are guaranteed a minimum level of annual income. Should they fall below this minimum, the government makes up the difference. Such a system has the advantage of standardizing government payments for recipients, simplifying the welfare system, and eliminating many of the middlemen associated with the welfare bureaucracy.

One of the chief proponents of this idea was Daniel Patrick Moynihan, who had been involved in the War on Poverty with Johnson and was now Nixon's advisor on urban affairs. When Moynihan proposed the Family Assistance Plan (the administration's attempt at a guaranteed income), he noted that it would eliminate tens of thousands of social workers from the federal payroll, at which the president's eyes lit up. For Nixon, the plan's virtues were obvious. It would permit the dismantling of many of the War on Poverty programs while addressing the problem of poverty in a more direct way. "The idea that this vast hodgepodge of government social programs could be consolidated into one simple grant appealed to Nixon's practical, rationalizing side" (Lemann 1989:66). In April of 1969, Nixon wrote to John Ehrlichman, "In confidence I have decided to go ahead on this program."

The Family Assistance Plan consisted of various income provisions, work provisions, and training provisions for those below the poverty line. It passed the House of Representatives in 1969 but was defeated in the Senate. A revised version met a similar fate in 1971. The Carter administration's attempt to reform the welfare system along the same lines, known as the Program for Better Jobs and Income, also failed to garner the support necessary for passage into law. Put simply, for the left, these various guaranteed income plans did not go far enough; for the right, they traveled too far.

Despite the failure of guaranteed income, both the number of recipients and the amount of money spent on social welfare programs increased substantially during the 1970s. While this expansion leveled off during the final years of the Carter administration, it was Ronald Reagan who sought to reduce the role that government had assumed over the previous fifty years.

Several basic themes underlined the Reagan philosophy. First, big government was to be avoided; instead, individual action, unhampered by government interference, was thought to spur an economy. (The budget and tax cuts of 1981 were consistent with this belief.) Second, the Reagan administration rejected the concept of social engineering that had dominated the design of social programs during the 1960s. Third, the Reagan philosophy was informed by a strong belief in the concept of federalism: that is, returning power and programs to the states (e.g., block grants), rather than centralizing them within the federal government.

As Glazer (1984, 1988) notes, these beliefs reveal an overall vision of how individuals overcome poverty: they do it on their own, and help from the government is likely to do more harm than good; after twenty years of major social programs, the underclass seemed as badly off as it ever was; social welfare programs provide incentives to remain in poverty; and, consequently, the government should stay as much as possible out of the individual's way. This vision led to programs being scaled back under the changes contained in the Omnibus Budget Reconciliation Act (OBRA) of 1981. Eligibility requirements were tightened, income provisions were lowered, and many work-related expenses were reduced or eliminated.

Reagan's philosophy on public assistance was clear in his 1986 State of the Union Address.[1]

> In the welfare culture, the breakdown of the family, the most basic support system, has reached crisis proportions—in female and child poverty, child abandonment, horrible crimes and deteriorating schools. After hundreds of billions of dollars in poverty programs, the plight of the poor grows more painful. But the waste in dollars and cents pales before the most tragic loss—the sinful waste of human spirit and potential.
>
> We can ignore this terrible truth no longer. As Franklin Roosevelt warned 51 years ago, standing before this chamber . . . "Welfare is a narcotic, a subtle destroyer of the human spirit." And we must escape the spider's web of dependency.

From 1986 to 1988, the Congress and the president had proposed various changes to the welfare system, with Senator Moynihan again playing a major role in the discussions. A compromise was finally reached in 1988 and signed by the president into law as the Family Support Act. The bill provided for 3.34 billion dollars' worth of funding for five years for services and training to help recipients locate jobs, allowing states flexibility in designing these services. It required single parents on welfare with children over the age of three to participate in job training, made it mandatory for states to provide AFDC to two-parent families, and required states to step up child support collections from noncustodial parents.

Many of the provisions in the bill were consistent with the overall Reagan philosophy. The president repeatedly reminded Congress that he would exert his veto power unless provisions tied various work requirements to welfare payments. Calling the new law a "message of hope to those in a life of dependency," Reagan said that this message included a demand from the citizens who pay the bills "that you will do your share in taking responsibility for your life and for the lives of the children you bring into the world" (*St. Louis Post-Dispatch,* October 14, 1988).

The Bush administration's attitude to poverty was consistent with the Reagan philosophy: individuals overcome poverty best on their own, along with the help of a strong economy. In addition, George Bush emphasized the importance of volunteerism from the private community, as well as the concept of empowering the poor through policies such as tenant management, school vouchers, and enterprise zones.

The attitude toward welfare remained similarly constant. Echoing the sentiments Ronald Reagan had expressed six years earlier, President Bush noted during his 1992 State of the Union address,

> Ask American parents what they dislike about how things are in our country, and chances are good that pretty soon they'll get to welfare.
>
> Americans are the most generous people on earth. But we have to go back to the insight of Franklin Roosevelt who, when he spoke of what became the welfare program, warned that it must not become a narcotic and a subtle destroyer of the spirit. . . .
>
> States throughout the country are beginning to operate with new assumptions: That when able-bodied adults receive government assistance they have responsibilities to the taxpayer. A responsibility to seek work, education, or job training. A responsibility to get their lives in order. A responsibility to hold their families together and refrain from having children out of wedlock. And a responsibility to obey the law.
>
> We are going to help this movement. Often, state reform requires waiving certain Federal regulations. I will act to make that process easier and quicker for every state that asks our help.

Indeed, during and since the Bush administration, states such as New Jersey, Michigan, Wisconsin, and California have modified the eligibility, requirement, and benefit structures of their welfare programs. These modified regulations primarily attempt to alter the behavior of welfare recipients by reducing, or occasionally increasing, their benefits if they behave in certain ways. Modifications implemented or being discussed include cutting benefits to a mother if her child drops out of school, freezing benefits if she has another infant while on welfare, restricting access to the General Assistance program, paying women on welfare to use the Norplant contraceptive, encouraging marriage by providing higher welfare benefits to couples, paying those who migrate into higher-benefit states at the levels of the state from which they came, and so on.

With the election of Bill Clinton, the philosophy toward the welfare system has remained fairly consistent with that of the Bush administration. During his acceptance speech at the Democratic National Convention in New York in 1992, Clinton stated, "We will say to those on welfare: You have the opportunity through training and education, health care and child care, to liberate yourself. But then you have a responsibility to go to work. Welfare must be a second chance, not a way of life" (Clinton and Gore 1992).

President Clinton's approach is largely compatible with the Family Support Act of 1988,[2] specifically, that the government will take some responsibility in providing services and training to help those on welfare get off the rolls, but individuals also have the responsibility of putting their lives back together in order to facilitate that goal. Like the Family Support Act, the Clinton approach stresses the importance of collecting child support, setting a deadline after which welfare recipients must work, and allowing states leeway in terms of experimenting with their programs. Finally, like the Bush administration, the Clinton administration has emphasized the concept of empowerment as a way of helping welfare recipients. This includes allowing recipients to accumulate more savings without being penalized, expanding the Earned Income Tax Credit, encouraging empowerment zones, and so on.

Without question, poverty and social welfare programs have changed in response to several ideological shifts over the past fifty years; nevertheless, the fundamental parallels among the visions of Franklin Delano Roosevelt, Ronald Reagan, and Bill Clinton are evident. Moreover, although there have been changes and modifications in the specific requirements welfare recipients must meet in order to obtain benefits, the general structure of the welfare system has remained largely intact since 1935.

Structure of the Current Welfare System

Jimmy Carter perhaps said it best when he described the welfare system in the United States as "a crazyquilt patchwork system stitched together over decades without direction or design." Unlike many of its Western European counterparts, the system is quite decentralized, its various programs administered on the local, state, and/or federal level. Programs and benefit levels vary from state to state, sometimes from county to county. AFDC and General Assistance payments vary widely across states, as does the extent of Medicaid coverage. Job training programs also differ considerably nationwide. The funding for these programs comes from both tax dollars and state and federal revenues.

Welfare programs can be divided into two broad categories: cash assistance programs and in-kind programs. In both cases, eligibility is means-tested: to qualify, a family's income and assets must fall below a certain level. Thus, these programs are aimed entirely at the poverty and near-poverty populations.[3]

There are three major cash assistance programs in the United States—AFDC, Supplemental Security Income (SSI), and General Assistance (GA). As noted earlier, AFDC began in 1935 under the Social Security Act. Today the program serves between four and five million families.[4] It is run on both the federal and state levels. Beyond a certain minimum, states are allowed leeway in terms of the amount of funds they allocate to the program. Depending on the amount contributed, the federal government supplies matching funds. This arrangement results in sizable discrepancies in benefit levels across states. In a number of Southern states, for example, the maximum monthly benefit allowed a one-parent family of three falls below two hundred dollars, whereas several Northeastern and North Central states offer maximum benefits over six hundred dollars per month.

To be eligible in all states, families must meet specific income and asset requirements, have at least one child under the age of eighteen, and have one parent absent due to death, desertion, divorce, incapacitation, or incarceration. Twenty-seven states also offer the AFDC–Unemployed Parent program, which provides aid to two-parent families with children under eighteen, where one parent is unemployed (in 1994, all states will be required to offer AFDC to two-parent families). In both programs, the grant amount is based on the number of children in the household and the income level of the parent(s). And for both programs, work and job training requirements exist, which vary widely from state to state.

The second major cash assistance program, SSI, was established in 1972 through amendments to the Social Security Act. The program federalized a variety of programs that had existed on the state level. SSI provides monthly cash payments to the needy aged, blind, and disabled. There are approximately five million participants in the program.

General Assistance is administered and funded primarily on the state and local levels. The extent of services varies, as do the types of recipients that qualify. It is primarily intended for those individuals who do not qualify for other programs (e.g., a single male) and is generally available on a short-term basis only. Approximately one million individuals receive General Assistance.

The other major category of welfare programs are those that are in-kind. These programs provide goods or services rather than cash. A major in-kind program is the Food Stamp program. It is federally funded and administered by the Department of Agriculture; consequently, benefits do not vary across states. Eligibility for the program is determined by income, assets, and family size. Families must be below 130 percent of the poverty line to qualify.[5] Recipients are given food coupons, which come in various denominations and may be exchanged for food products in grocery stores and supermarkets that choose to participate in the program. A family of four with no income would qualify for approximately three hundred dollars of Food Stamps a month. Between twenty and twenty-five million

people receive Food Stamps. Like all public assistance programs, the specific number of recipients varies from month to
month and year to year, depending on a number of factors,
such as the health of the economy.

Two other food-oriented in-kind programs are the Special
Supplemental Food Program for Women, Infants, and Children (WIC) and the Free or Reduced-Price School Lunch Program. The WIC program is designed to upgrade the nutrition
of low-income women, infants, and young children. Pregnant
women, women with newborns, and children under the age of
five receive food high in nutrients, such as eggs, juices, cereals
fortified with iron, cheese, and fortified formulas for infants.
The School Lunch Program provides free lunches for students
from homes with incomes under 125 percent of the poverty
line and reduced-price lunches for children from homes with
incomes between 125 and 195 percent of the poverty line.

By far the largest in-kind program in terms of federal expenditures is Medicaid, a health insurance program for the poor,
designed to cover hospital costs, visits to the doctor, nursing
home coverage, and so on. Up until its introduction in 1965,
medical care for the poor was primarily the responsibility of
state and local governments and private charity. Medicaid is a
combined federal and state program, with states exercising
broad administrative powers and carrying nearly half the financial burden. Income and assets determine eligibility for the
program. Families qualifying for AFDC automatically qualify
for Medicaid, as do virtually all individuals receiving SSI. At
this point, the program serves close to twenty-five million
people.

A final major group of in-kind programs comprises the
Housing Assistance programs, which provide subsidized housing for the poor. Public housing is one form of subsidized
housing; assistance is also available for low-income families
renting in the private market.

In all cases, public assistance programs—both cash and in-
kind—are intended only to provide a minimum subsistence,
not to enable individuals to escape poverty (O'Hare 1987). This
is consistent with the English Poor Laws, which held that

welfare benefits should not exceed the lowest paying job in a society. Only in Alaska do the combined benefits of AFDC and Food Stamps provide families with an income above the poverty level.[6] In all other states, families remain below the poverty line, sometimes by as much as 50 percent. Moreover, the real value of these benefits has been dropping over the past twenty years. Thus, surviving on public assistance in America is becoming increasingly difficult. Why then do individuals turn to the welfare system?

Explanations for Poverty and Welfare Recipiency

On one hand, the reasons for welfare recipiency are fairly straightforward. Lacking in economic resources, people turn to the government for help. But how do they arrive at this state? Why do they fall below the poverty line and therefore need public assistance? How might they escape such a predicament? These and other questions have perplexed social commentators for centuries.

Theories of poverty and welfare recipiency are as old as poverty and charity themselves. Hesiod of Boetia, in his poem "Works and Days," vividly portrays what poverty was like in early Greece, discusses its causes, and questions its justice. Biblical references to the poor and their condition are scattered throughout the Old and New Testaments. The debate continued through medieval and early modern times and was particularly intense in the nineteenth century (Hartwell 1986). Many of the theories in vogue today have existed for long periods of time.

The current debate on poverty and welfare recipiency can be divided into several broad perspectives. Ellwood (1987) divides it into three models—choice models, expectancy models, and cultural models. Kerbo (1983) discusses the cultural, situational, and structural views of poverty and welfare recipiency. Morris and Williamson (1986) discuss it in terms of motivational factors, ability-related factors, and structural factors. Based on this and other research and literature, this study considers explanations of poverty and welfare recipiency in light of three major criteria—individual, cultural, and structural. Within each of these lie several specific theoretical perspectives.

Individual Explanations

Individual explanations for poverty and welfare recipiency can be divided into two categories: (1) attitudinal/motivational explanations; and (2) human capital explanations.

Attitudinal/motivational explanations. Surveys suggest that were we to ask the typical man and woman on the street today why people are poor, they would probably say it has to do with individual motivation and/or attitudes.[7] For example, Kluegel and Smith (1986) replicated Feagin's (1975) earlier survey research on the perceived reasons for poverty. The results were highly consistent: a majority of those surveyed perceived lack of thrift, lack of effort, lack of ability and talent, and loose morals and drunkenness to be important reasons for poverty.

Likewise, respondents believe that individuals are on welfare, and remain on welfare, primarily because of insufficient motivation to exit from public assistance. In other words, such individuals are simply not working hard enough; were they to exert themselves, they would rise from the ranks of poverty and welfare dependency. George Gilder exemplifies this position in his book *Wealth and Poverty* (1981):

> The only dependable route from poverty is always work, family, and faith. The first principle is that in order to move up, the poor must not only work, they must work harder than the classes above them. Every previous generation of the lower class has made such efforts. But the current poor, white even more than black, are refusing to work hard.   (68)

Consequently, a person's attitudes and motivations are the critical factors in understanding poverty and welfare dependency. With sufficient effort and desire, people wishing to escape the chains of poverty will do so provided they work hard enough.

Human capital explanations. A second explanation attributes poverty and welfare recipiency to a lack of human capital—

training, education, experience, skills, and so on—rather than motivations and attitudes (Mincer 1958; Becker 1964). The labor market is conceptualized as a competitive system, in which wages are determined by supply and demand, as well as the resources or human capital that people possess. Those who do well in the labor market do so primarily as a result of the human capital they have acquired. Such people are in greater demand and hence enjoy brighter job prospects. Those living in poverty and/or receiving public assistance are lacking in human capital and therefore cannot compete as effectively in the labor market. The acquisition of greater human capital would enable them to exit from the welfare rolls.

According to this perspective, the way to reduce poverty and welfare dependency is to concentrate on upgrading individual skills. This might include ensuring graduation from high school, teaching people marketable trades, enabling them to acquire job experience, and so on. This premise underlies most job training programs directed at the poor, and, as mentioned earlier, many of the War on Poverty programs also operated from this premise.

Cultural Explanations

Rather than focusing on the individual, a second perspective emphasizes the culture in which individuals are raised as a dominant factor in affecting poverty and welfare status. Two major explanations fall under this perspective: (1) the culture of poverty argument; and (2) the social isolation argument.

The culture of poverty. The culture of poverty thesis arose from the ethnographic work of Oscar Lewis. His study *Five Families* (1959) examined lower-class Mexican family life, while a later work, *La Vida* (1966a), focused on Puerto Rican families residing in slum communities in both New York City and Puerto Rico. Based on these ethnographies, Lewis argued that a culture of poverty existed.[8]

Supporters of the culture of poverty theory contend that a set of values unique to the poor has arisen as a direct result of the experience of living in poverty (Moynihan 1965; Lewis

1966b; Glazer and Moynihan 1970). These attitudes and values include alienation, present-time orientation, and a sense of oppression (Curtis 1975). According to Banfield, the problem lies in "the existence of an outlook and style of life which is radically present-oriented and therefore attaches no value to work, sacrifice, self-improvement, or service to family, friends, or community" (1974:235). The actual day-to-day behavior of the poor is heavily influenced by these values. Much of it is deviant from the perspective of middle-class respectability and is highly dysfunctional for the poor themselves in that it works against their rising up and out of poverty. As Lewis argued,

> Once it [the culture of poverty] comes into existence, it tends to perpetuate itself from generation to generation because of its effects on children. By the time slum children are age six or seven, they have usually absorbed the basic values and attitudes of their subculture and are not psychologically geared to take full advantage of changing conditions or increased opportunities which may occur in their lifetime.   (1969:188)

Or, as Moynihan wrote with regard to black Americans, "Three centuries of injustice have brought about deep-seated structural distortions in the life of the Negro-American. At this point, the present tangle of pathology is capable of perpetuating itself without assistance from the white world. The cycle can be broken only if these distortions are set right" (1965:93).

From this perspective, then, welfare dependency is part of a cultural process in which children learn from their parents and from their surrounding environment that relying on public assistance, bearing children out of wedlock, dropping out of school, and so on, are acceptable behaviors (for example, see Sheehan 1975; Auletta 1983; Dash 1989). Consequently, the existing cultural process must change for welfare dependency to cease. A policy approach should not only focus on the individual but also on the transmission of cultural norms (for a more extended review of the culture of poverty argument, see Waxman 1983; Rainwater 1987; Steinberg 1989).

The social isolation explanation. William Julius Wilson offers a different perspective on the contribution of culture to poverty and welfare use, noting that the "key theoretical concept is not culture of poverty but social isolation" (1987:61). Wilson's theory is based on an analysis of the increasing problems found within inner cities and the reasons such problems have worsened over the past twenty years. Wilson deals with a specific group in poverty, those he terms "the truly disadvantaged." He argues that many of the problems found in the inner cities today are the result of concentration effects and social isolation. "The social transformation of the inner city has resulted in a disproportionate concentration of the most disadvantaged segments of the urban black population, creating a social milieu significantly different from the environment that existed in these communities several decades ago" (58). In addition, the inner city has become increasingly isolated from mainstream social behavior. As the black middle and working classes have left the inner cities, fewer positive role models are present in the community. The inner city has become more socially isolated, while at the same time experiencing a greater concentration of deviant behavior. "The communities of the underclass are plagued by massive joblessness, flagrant and open lawlessness, and low-achieving schools, and therefore tend to be avoided by outsiders. Consequently, the residents of these areas, whether women and children of welfare families or aggressive street criminals, have become increasingly socially isolated from mainstream patterns of behavior" (58).

Wilson repeatedly points out that the ultimate cause of inner-city conditions is not the culture itself but the social structural constraints and the lack of opportunities. Thus, "the key conclusion from a public policy perspective is that programs created to alleviate poverty, joblessness, and related forms of social dislocation should place primary focus on changing the social and economic situation, not the cultural traits, of the ghetto underclass" (137). Wilson further distinguishes his concept of social isolation from that of a culture of poverty by arguing that cultural traits are not self-perpetuating but rather adaptations to structural conditions. When structural conditions change, culture will change along with it (see Liebow 1967 and Stack 1974 for similar conclusions). Nevertheless,

Wilson acknowledges that a distinct culture exists in the inner city and that this culture fosters welfare dependency. Thus, while it may not be the ultimate factor, it does contribute heavily to Wilson's understanding of poverty and welfare recipiency.

Structural Explanations

Structural explanations for poverty and welfare recipiency assert that the causes are found within the structure of the economy, the society, or the welfare system itself. There are four major structural explanations: (1) Marxism; (2) dual labor market theory; (3) functionalism; and (4) the Big Brother argument.

Marxism. Marxism focuses on the economic structure of capitalism as the key to understanding poverty. Marx was primarily concerned with capitalist societies and the exploitative class relations within them.[9]

In feudal times, workers produced their own goods and bartered or sold them. Capitalism brought about a dramatic change: people began to work in settings other than the home (e.g., in a factory). Furthermore, they worked not for themselves but for the capitalists who owned the factories, who paid them wages in return for their labor. Marx argued that workers are not paid at rates that reflect the true value of what they produce. The difference between what they are paid and what the product is actually worth—Marx called this the surplus value—is what the capitalists take for their own profit. This, according to Marx, represents the exploitation of workers by capitalists. It is in the nature of capitalism for the owners of the means of production (e.g., factories, plants, etc.) to increase profits at the workers' expense:

> What then, is the general law which determines the rise and fall of wages and profit in their reciprocal relation? They stand in inverse ratio to each other. Capital's share, profit, rises in the same proportion as labour's share, wages, falls, and vice versa. Profit rises to the extent that wages fall; it falls to the extent that wages rise.   (Marx and Engels 1968:86–87)

As capitalism develops, it brings about a greater division of labor, which allows the capitalist to produce more goods with fewer workers, resulting in greater profits. Many of the remaining jobs become increasingly simplified, requiring fewer skills. This in turn makes individual workers more expendable, driving wages down even further. With a decreased need for workers and easily replaceable labor, more individuals are reduced to what Marx called the industrial reserve army. The soldiers in this army live much of their lives in or near poverty and are able to work full-time only during periods of boom or economic expansion. As Marx wrote, "Thus the forest of uplifted arms demanding work becomes ever thicker, while the arms themselves become ever thinner" (94).

According to Marx, then, poverty is simply inherent in the economic structure of capitalism—it is an inevitable by-product of the exploitation of workers by capitalists. To eradicate poverty, one must change the entire capitalist system.

Dual labor market theory. The dual labor market theory arose as a reaction against the perceived failings of human capital theory. Whereas human capital theory assumes that there is one labor market in operation, the dual labor market perspective posits the existence of two quite distinct markets that operate according to different rules. In the primary market, jobs are characterized by stability, high wages, good working conditions, a greater degree of internal job structure, and unionization (Gordon 1972). This market is limited to a certain sector of the private economy, called the core or monopoly sector. Firms within the monopoly sector tend to be large and capital intensive and to possess sizable and often international markets (e.g., the automobile industry, the defense industry, etc.). Within such firms, there exists what is called an internal labor market. Individuals from the outside can only enter this internal labor market at certain points, often the bottom rung of a career ladder. Jobs higher up the ladder are filled within the firm through promotion.

On the other hand, jobs in the secondary labor market are characterized as menial, having poor working conditions, and low wages. The secondary market exists primarily within what is called the peripheral or competitive sector of the private economy. Firms within the competitive sector tend to be small and labor intensive, with lower productivity per worker and more local markets. In addition, an individual's labor and skills can be easily replaced by another individual's. Examples include restaurants, gas stations, and grocery stores.

The determinants of earnings also vary between markets. In the primary market, earnings are affected by the worker's position in the career job structure, as well as seniority (O'Connor 1973). Wages in the secondary labor market are largely determined by market forces. Since workers in this market are generally considered homogeneous and have little union power, their wages are the product of supply and demand. Thus, differences in earnings are due primarily to the number of hours worked (Beck, Horan, and Tolbert 1978).

The dual labor market approach arose in large part to explain the persistent poverty of different social groups, persistent racial wage differences, and gender wage differences (see Hodson and Kaufman 1982). It argues that, for a variety of reasons (statistical discrimination, fewer skills, employers' perceptions of lack of commitment, etc.), women and minorities are more likely to begin their work careers in the secondary labor market. As Hodson and Kaufman note, "once workers enter the secondary market, they acquire unstable work histories" (1982:730). Employers in the primary labor market then use these histories as evidence that they are inadequate workers, and thus they are blocked from moving into the primary market (Bluestone 1970; Gordon 1972; Doeringer and Piore 1975). This in turn helps to perpetuate income inequality and poverty.

People are poor not because they are unemployed or do not participate in the economy but because of the way in which they participate in the economy. Because of the instability of jobs in the secondary labor market, workers in them often experience occasional unemployment and turn to welfare programs in order to survive lean times. In addition, these jobs often pay low wages, which workers may supplement periodically with benefits from public assistance programs. (See Cain 1976, Hodson and Kaufman 1982, and Sakamoto and Chen

1991, for a more extended review of the dual labor market theory.)

Functionalism. Functionalism has a long history in both the social sciences and sociology. Merton defined functions as "those observed consequences which make for the adaptation or adjustment of a given system; and dysfunctions, those observed consequences which lessen the adaptation or adjustment of the system" (1949:50). Functions can be both intended (manifest functions) and unintended (latent functions). For an institution or phenomenon to survive in a society, it must somehow be functional for that society. If it is not, it eventually disappears or is modified.

Using this perspective, Herbert Gans (1972, 1991) focused on the persistence of poverty in the United States. He argued that poverty serves a number of important functions for society in general and specifically that it serves important economic, social, cultural, and political functions for the affluent class. For example, the existence of poverty ensures that undesirable work gets done and creates a number of occupations and professions serving the poor (e.g., academics writing books about the poor); the poor can be identified and punished as deviants in order to uphold the legitimacy of dominant norms; and so on.

> My analysis suggests that the alternatives for poverty are themselves dysfunctional for the affluent population, and it ultimately comes to a conclusion which is not very different from that of radical sociologists. To wit: that social phenomena which are functional for affluent groups and dysfunctional for poor ones persist; that when the elimination of such phenomena through functional alternatives generates dysfunctions for the affluent, they will continue to persist; and that phenomena like poverty can be eliminated only when they either become sufficiently dysfunctional for the affluent or when the poor can obtain enough power to change the system of social stratification.
>
> (Gans 1972:288; for a similar interpretation, see Galbraith 1992)

The same structural constraints that keep people poor are responsible for their turning to welfare in order to make ends meet. In fact, some have even argued that welfare programs

themselves are functional for society and those in power because they placate the poor (Piven and Cloward 1971; Stack
1974; Block et al. 1987):

> It is clear that mere reform of existing programs can never be
> expected to eliminate an impoverished class in America. The
> effect of such programs is that they maintain the existence of
> such a class. Welfare programs merely act as flexible mecha-
> nisms to alleviate the more obvious symptoms of poverty while
> inching forward just enough to purchase acquiescence and si-
> lence on the part of the members of this class and their liberal
> supporters. As we have seen, these programs are not merely
> passive victims of underfunding and conservative obstruction-
> ism. In fact they are active purveyors of the status quo, staunch
> defenders of the economic imperative that demands mainte-
> nance of a sizable but docile impoverished class.
>
> (Stack 1974:127–128)

Such analysts point out that welfare programs tend to expand
during times of social upheaval precisely for this reason.

The Big Brother argument. A final structural perspective regarding poverty and welfare use is what Schiller (1989) has
labeled the "Big Brother argument." The emphasis here is on
the role of misguided social policies in exacerbating poverty.
Human nature is characterized as desiring the easiest way out
of difficult situations. In the case of poverty, welfare and charity create work disincentives. Individuals exert themselves less
when in dire straits because they know they can fall back on
the safety net of public assistance. As they become more accus-
tomed to receiving welfare, they eventually settle into the lifestyle. As de Tocqueville noted in his 1835 lecture to the Royal
Academic Society of Cherbourg, "Any measure which estab-
lishes legal charity on a permanent basis and gives it an administrative form thereby creates an idle and lazy class, living at
the expense of the industrial and working class. This, at least,
is its inevitable consequence, if not the immediate result"
(1983:113).

This argument has been used to explain what some have
called the counterproductivity of the War on Poverty programs. Charles Murray (1984, 1988) is the most widely cited
analyst working within this framework (in addition, see An-

derson 1978; Mead 1986, 1992; Working Group on the Family 1986; Kaus 1992). Murray points out that from 1964 onward, measures of poverty, employment, education, crime, and family structure have been deteriorating for low-income black families and that this coincides with the War on Poverty programs. Murray's thesis is that by violating several basic assumptions— people respond to incentives and disincentives; people are not inherently hard working; and people must be held accountable for their actions—these programs played on individuals' worst instincts, eventually trapping many into lives of poverty and welfare dependency, instead of helping them escape. It became easier (and economically more rational in the short term) from the mid-1960s onward to rely on welfare rather than to work at the minimum wage. As a result, Murray argues, it is the welfare system itself that is largely to blame for the fact that millions of Americans are currently in poverty.

From this point of view, the solution to the problem of poverty is to cut back substantially on social welfare programs and to ensure that work disincentives are minimized in the remaining programs. Governmental intrusion into private initiative must be curtailed so that people have no choice but to work themselves out of poverty. As noted earlier, the Reagan and Bush administrations largely adopted this perspective in explaining the use of welfare.[10]

While it is important to understand the varying perspectives used to explain poverty and welfare recipiency, it is also important to recognize the difficulty of definitively testing their validity within the confines of this study. For example, I cannot determine whether a dual labor market, a culture of poverty, or capitalism accounts for poverty and welfare recipiency. While insights will be present, I make no claim to have proved a particular theoretical framework. What I can claim, however, is to have examined the importance of a select number of individual, cultural, and structural factors in affecting the lives of welfare recipients. This in and of itself should be revealing. Simply establishing the general level(s) on which welfare recipiency is best viewed represents a sizable step forward in understanding and addressing the issue.

3 GETTING ON

I waited. I waited until the very last minute, until I probably was just about down and out. I think I probably called 'em up two or three times before I really wanted to go down there. And when I did, the guy on the phone told me that I'd better get down in a hurry. Because he knew the situation. And he knew that at that time I was tryin' to make it on the support I was getting for the children, that was only two hundred and twenty dollars a month. And that was pretty darn rough. It was just about impossible. I held out as long as I could. But you can only hold on so long. Then you gotta go down.

—*Divorced mother of two*

It was an unusually hot July afternoon when I entered the welfare office on Ridgeton's south side. This was the first of many offices I would visit. The building had been recently constructed, and was a long, one-story unit made of corrugated sheet metal. Passing through a set of glass doors, on the right was a receptionist, and straight ahead, an armed guard. To the left lay a large room with several tables and numerous chairs. A dozen or so people were awaiting their appointments. Decorating the walls were posters dealing with topics such as foster care, the need to avoid pregnancy, child support, elder abuse, and so on. The floors, walls, and ceilings wore a new coat of white paint.

Within rooms like this potential recipients begin their encounters with the welfare system, and it is here that this examination into the lives of welfare recipients begins. This chapter looks at the experience of applying for welfare, the circumstances leading to the filing of an application, and the background characteristics of those who enter the welfare system.

Applying for Welfare

Applying for public assistance is an arduous and complicated process.[1] Two components are described here—the procedure itself and recipients' reactions to the process.

The Application Procedure

Over the course of several months, I was able to visit a number of welfare offices and to observe the application process in a variety of settings. Social service offices differ quite dramatically in their atmospheres and physical environments. For example, a welfare office in a small rural town was located on a quiet street in a small white frame house. A receptionist and several social service workers were found inside. On a typical day, they might see five or six cases. The pace was relatively casual and relaxed. By contrast, an office situated in the inner city of a major metropolitan area reviewed hundreds of cases a day. It was located in what had been a five-story department store. The process was by necessity highly specialized. Individuals picked up their application forms at a window labeled New Cases. After completing the forms, they would return them back to the window and proceed upstairs to a color-coded waiting area. From there, names would be loudly called over a PA system, followed by curt instructions to report to door number one or door number two. Several armed guards patrolled the building.

Despite the physical differences, the two offices also shared many similarities in terms of the overall procedure of applying for public assistance. Many would-be recipients telephone or stop by the social service office in advance in order to schedule an appointment with an in-take worker; at that time, they also pick up informational material and application forms or make arrangements to have it sent to them. On the day they actually apply for assistance, they begin by approaching a reception window or desk. Their arrival being noted, they are given various application forms to fill out (if they have not done so already) and instructed to take a seat and complete the forms in the waiting area.

The form itself is made up of questions regarding each member of the household, asking about age, marital status, relationship to the applicant, education, disability status, and a variety of other demographic details. In addition, a large number of questions concern household assets, income, employment, expenses, and so on.

The length of time until an applicant's name is called varies from office to office, and from day to day, but is generally no more than fifteen or twenty minutes. During this period, people may talk quietly to whomever has accompanied them. They may read magazines or informational brochures. They may work on completing their application forms. Or they may simply sit pensively waiting for their appointments. In larger offices, an armed guard puts in an appearance every few minutes.

After this initial wait, the applicant's name is called, usually by the in-take worker who has been assigned to the case. The worker then leads the client back to his or her desk or some other office designed for the processing of information.

The next forty-five minutes to an hour are spent reviewing the items on the application form. Various questions require verification through documentation (birth certificates, rent receipts, marriage and divorce certificates, verification of medical expenses paid in the last four months, bank statements, paycheck stubs, titles for vehicles, and so on). Extensive verification is required to process each application. If any of the necessary documentation is not forthcoming, applications are held until such documents are provided.

Such scrutiny can be both intimidating and embarrassing. The social service workers I observed were generally aware of this and interacted well with potential recipients.[2] Each item on the application form was usually reviewed carefully. Assuming there is no need for further documentation, individuals are informed that their application will be processed and, should they qualify, they may begin receiving public assistance within the next several weeks. At this point, clients ask any remaining questions before leaving.

Reactions to Applying for Welfare

For most Americans, receiving welfare represents a failure to provide for oneself and one's family (Kluegel and Smith 1986). It is thus a highly stigmatized behavior (this issue is addressed extensively in chapter 8). Most applicants typically felt two emotions when applying for public assistance—embarrassment and anxiety (in some cases, fear). For example, Angela Lewis, a twenty-six-year-old never-married mother was asked about her experience of applying for public assistance: "I felt embarrassed. I don't know, there seemed to be a lot of women there with a bunch of little kids, and a lot of guys standin' around with their hair uncombed. It was kind of embarrassing. So I really just sat there and hoped nobody would walk in that knew me, you know? That's the feeling I had." Similarly, a young, recently separated woman commented, "I didn't like it. I really didn't. I was swallowing a lot of pride to go do that because I was never on it before. My mom and dad never went on anything like that either. I was scared, and I was a little bit ashamed, I guess you could say."

The application requires extensive documentation and probing; when coupled with the negative images of welfare, this leads to considerable anxiety. Joyce Mills, a separated woman with three children, was asked about her feelings when she applied for public assistance.

> Scared (*laughter*). I'd never done that before, and I really didn't know what was going on. Then when I had to sign the paper work for absentee parent, it made me even more scared. It was something that I'd done on my own, for the very first time. I didn't feel like I was capable of doing it. Or if I had done the right thing to begin with. But once I did it, I did feel more comfortable. And boy it was such a great relief getting that six-hundred-dollar check so I could pay the rent.

The following discussion was with Cindy and Jeff Franklin, a married couple with two children.

> Q: What were your feelings, attitudes, thoughts, when you went down to the welfare office and applied for the medical assistance? What did you think at the time?

Cindy: We really felt bad. We felt bad.

   Jeff: We were really uneasy. I remember sittin' there with those mile-and-a-half-long forms.

Cindy: We felt like it was a shameful thing to be doing, basically. And I remember when the in-take worker was going over our form and wanted to know what our income had been for the previous month, and we said, it was something like two hundred and fifty dollars. And she looked at us and she said, "Uhh, this can't be right, you couldn't live on this." And we said, "That's right, that's why we're here!" (*Laughter.*) I think we felt grateful that it was there. But it was a real blow to our pride. We had all kinds of . . . I mean . . . the way the public generally views welfare people, we had a lot of those same views. And it was really a hard thing for our pride to put ourselves in that position, and join that category of people.

Many of the applicants I observed repeatedly emphasized that they intended to remain on a program for a short period of time and/or that they would be finding a job in the near future. For most, it was indeed a hard thing to "join that category of people."

Circumstances Leading to Welfare Use

On one hand, the reasons for using welfare programs are straightforward: lacking economic resources, people turn to public assistance to seek relief. Yet how and why have they arrived at such a state of economic hardship?

While economic deprivation is common across all households, the specific circumstances leading to welfare use differ by family type. We examine these circumstances for female-headed families, married couples, single heads of households, and the elderly.

Female-Headed Families

Much has been written about the feminization of poverty (McLanahan and Booth 1989; Sidel 1992). Key to this issue is the detrimental economic effects upon women of separation/ divorce (Weitzman 1985) or single parenthood (Edelman 1987). For these women, it is largely changes in household structure that precipitate welfare use.

When asked why they had turned to public assistance, many female heads of households mentioned either a divorce or a separation that had caused severe economic distress. Often they had limited job experience and skills at the time of the separation. Most of the women interviewed could see no other choice but to turn to the welfare system, which they saw as a stopgap solution until they got back on their feet.

Marta Green is typical of this pattern. Originally from Honduras, she moved with her American husband to the United States in her late teens. Married for seven years, Marta was in her mid-twenties at the time of her divorce. During her marriage, she had stayed at home to care for her three daughters. Consequently, at the time of the separation, Marta had few job skills. She talked about the effects of the divorce upon her economic situation, "I didn't have any money left. And my husband had changed all the accounts. I didn't have any access to money. The kids came back to me without clothes. They were with nothin'. And I didn't have anything. Just my old car. And my things packed in the car. So that was the circumstances. I didn't have any money left." She went on to say,

> To me my divorce and the breaking up of my house was a crisis. I had everything. Everything I needed, you know, like electrical knives. That probably doesn't sound like much to you. But I did have all my utensils in the kitchen. And then, I come to an empty place, like we came here. We didn't have a frying pan. We didn't have a plate, a cup, or anything.
>
> When you get married you get everything in the bridal shower. And in the wedding you get stuff. And then little by little, before the kids come, you get things that you need, so you're all set up. But when we moved here, I had to buy the bed for

my kids because we were sleeping on the floor. That's money from the same grant, from welfare. But I could not buy that bed with the money left in one month. I had to save three-and-a-half months before I got the bed. And then there's things like the bed sheets and pillows and pillow cases. This is a crisis to me. It is. And then you come into the kitchen, and the kids want pancakes, and you don't have a frying pan.

For other female heads of household, and particularly for black female heads, the family structural change involves having a child out of wedlock. Much has been written about the unfavorable marriage market for low-income black women (e.g., Guttentag and Secord 1983; Wilson 1987; Jaynes and Williams 1989; Lichter, LeClere, and McLaughlin 1991; Hacker 1992), and indeed a much larger percentage of black women interviewed were not married when they had children.[3] An example is Ruth Miller. A long-term welfare recipient, she was asked why she began receiving public assistance in Chicago.

Well, I had two little bitty babies. And I was working at the time I got pregnant. So I tried going back to work when Stacy was about—say two months old. And the lady that I got to babysit for me just didn't come up to par for me. And with me having the two babies, one was just walking and one was an arm baby, I made the decision that it's best for me to try to be here with them. And I know they were taken care of like I would have wanted to be taken care of. So that's when I applied for aid.

For both white and black female-headed families on welfare, the economic downturn caused by changes in family structure is exacerbated by either the lack of or the low amount of child support payments from fathers. Furthermore, the majority of these households have only one possible wage earner, who often finds it difficult to participate in the labor force because of child care responsibilities and the relatively high cost of day care (see Bane and Ellwood 1989). And if a female head of household does enter the labor market, her earnings are likely to be lower (because of occupational segregation and fewer job-related skills) than those of her male counterparts. Taken together, these factors largely explain why female-headed families turn to public assistance.

Married Couples

For married couples, the circumstances leading to public assistance are quite different. Here the critical factor is the manner in which husbands participate in the labor market—that is, their jobs are unstable and/or low paying. Furthermore, such families may have a number of expenditures for child care, medical bills not covered by insurance, and so on. When few unanticipated expenses occur, and when work is plentiful, these families are able to live at or slightly above the poverty line. However, any misfortune may result in a major economic setback that leads married couples to seek assistance through various welfare programs.

An example is Jack and Tammy Collins. Married when they were eighteen, their first child was born shortly afterward, followed by five more. While Tammy has remained at home to raise the children, Jack has worked at various low-income jobs. Asked about the kinds of work he has done in the past, Jack replied, "You name it, I've done it. I started out cooking. I've been a janitor. I've been an auto mechanic. I drove a school bus for five years. I drove a semi coast to coast. I've worked in a foundry. I've worked in a shoe factory. I've worked in other factories, warehouses. I'll do just about anything."

I asked Jack about the problems in finding work.

> The main problem was findin' one with starting pay that's enough to really get by on. 'Cause even though this job [in a warehouse] is eight dollars an hour, it isn't enough. But a lotta jobs, you can't get anywhere near that to start. I started this job five years ago at five dollars an hour. It took me this long to get up that high. It's hard to just pick up and leave that. It's gotta be another job that's equal or more. An equal-paying job with better benefits would be great.

For the five years prior to our interview, Jack Collins has worked full-time at the warehouse. It pays just enough for his family to get by under normal circumstances. Yet when something out of the ordinary goes wrong, Jack and Tammy are likely to turn to public assistance to supplement their income. Now in their mid-thirties, they have been on and off welfare for fifteen years.

The married couples I interviewed fit the image portrayed in the various ethnographic studies of blue-collar families (Komarovsky 1962; Howell 1972; LeMasters 1975; Rubin 1976; Halle 1984). They live hard, working-class lives, just scraping by. Moderate increases in expenses and unstable, low-paying work occasionally lead them to rely on welfare to supplement their incomes.

Single Heads of Households

The circumstances leading single men and women to the use of welfare are quite different from those for female-headed families or married couples. The typical pattern for these individuals is that they have suffered from some type of illness, disability, or other misfortune that has sharply limited their abilities to support themselves.

Of the nine single heads of household interviewed, one was diagnosed as schizophrenic, another was experiencing severe seizure disorders, a third had had his left leg amputated, another had just gone through an alcoholic treatment program, one was in his fifties and had been laid off after twenty years with the same company, several suffered from drug addictions, and one man who had come to the United States from Cuba had had problems finding a job because of his difficulty speaking English. As a result of the above problems, these individuals have turned to the welfare system for economic assistance. Such assistance may be short term or, when the disability is severe, much more long term (see chapter 10).

Mike Thomas's story is typical. Mike had been jailed for burglary but had been allowed to go through an alcoholic treatment program as part of his sentence. When interviewed, he was residing in a halfway house. All residents were required to apply for Food Stamps in order to help defray the cost to the county. Before this most recent spell of welfare use, Mike had occasionally used Food Stamps for several months at a time when he experienced problems finding work. These problems were largely a result of his bouts with alcohol.

On the other hand, Susan Davis is likely to be on public assistance much longer. Four years prior to our interview, she had experienced multiple seizures during a ten-hour period. Since then, she has required constant medical attention, with a seizure occurring every few days. She describes how the original disability cost her her life savings: "And I had managed to save quite a lot of money at that point, which all went in about three days of intensive care when I became disabled. About twenty thousand dollars went (*whistles*)—goodbye! And nothing has irritated me so much as having lost that so fast . . . when it took me twenty-five years to put that amount of money away." Left with no savings and a severe incapacitation that precludes her from working, Susan is likely to remain on public assistance for a number of years (in her case, Food Stamps, Medicaid, Social Security Disability Insurance, and Housing Assistance).

The Elderly

The circumstances surrounding the elderly's use of public assistance are quite different from those of the previous three household categories. The noninstitutionalized elderly who turn to the welfare system tend to have fixed, limited incomes (primarily from Social Security) and fairly high expenses (largely medical). Such individuals simply cannot stretch their monthly Social Security checks far enough. Seventy-year-old Paula Okenfuss explained why she had applied for Food Stamps:

> I was living in an apartment, and my Social Security check wouldn't take care of the rent. The rent was so high. And I had my name in several places for apartments [referring to low-income housing], but you know there's a long waiting list on all of them. And so, when I paid three hundred and ten dollars rent out of a four hundred twenty dollar Social Security check, I had nothing left. Absolutely nothing. I had to have something

to live on! I was eating cornflakes. And that's one reason why I asked for Food Stamps.

Many of the elderly's medical expenses are not covered by Medicare, a prime example being nursing home care. Consequently, a large number of the elderly receiving Medicaid are nursing home residents (see table 3.1). In general most of the elderly on public assistance receive Medicaid.

Seventy-four-year-old John Renborn has had a heart attack, suffers from blindness in one eye, experiences difficulty in walking, and has a deformity in both of his hands. He describes why he applied for Medical Assistance six months prior to our interview: "Well, the reason for that is because I had to. I wanted some help. In September of last year I went blind in one eye. I don't know what happened. I woke up and went into the bathroom. I couldn't see nothing! So I got scared and I thought I was gonna go blind all together. That's when I went to the doctor up there in the University hospital. And that's when I went to an expert on medical assistance."

Background Characteristics

The figures and tables in this section provide information on the background characteristics of people entering the welfare system (those who have been on public assistance for six months or less). As noted in the introduction, for most of the numerical information discussed in this and other chapters, I rely on a longitudinal sample of approximately three thousand welfare households.

Figure 3.1 shows the overall composition of households recently entering the welfare system. These categories, by definition mutually exclusive, include: (1) households headed by unmarried women pregnant or with children (an earlier example of this type of family being Marta Green and her three children); (2) households headed by married couples with or without children (such as Jack and Tammy Collins); (3) households headed by unmarried men and women with no children (examples being Mike Thomas and Susan Davis); (4) households headed by men and women aged 65 and over, regard-

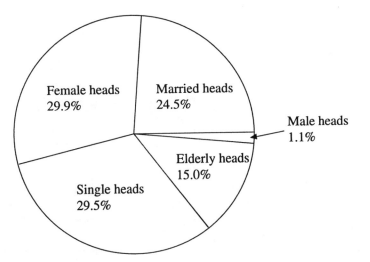

Figure 3.1 Household Composition of Recipients Entering the Welfare System

less of marital status (such as Paula Okenfuss and John Renborn); and (5) households headed by unmarried men with children.

As one can see in figure 3.1, only 1 percent of those households entering the welfare system are headed by males with children. Consequently, this category is simply too small to allow for any detailed analysis and is therefore not included in this or subsequent chapters. Approximately 30 percent of the remaining households entering the welfare system are headed by females, 25 percent by married couples, 30 percent by singles, and 15 percent by the elderly.

The bar graphs in figure 3.2 show the various combinations of welfare programs received by the four household categories. Most female-headed households receive AFDC along with Medicaid, and in many cases Food Stamps. Houses headed by married couples are fairly evenly distributed across the various program combinations, while virtually all singles receive Food Stamps and/or Medicaid. For the elderly, over 80 percent receive Medicaid only.

Demographic, household, and socioeconomic characteristics for those entering the welfare system are shown in table 3.1.

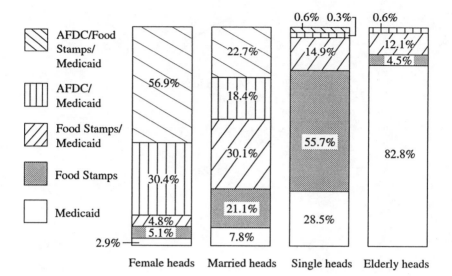

Figure 3.2 Program Percentages of Recipients Entering the Welfare System

Female-headed households are evenly divided among a major metropolitan county, other metropolitan counties, and non-metropolitan counties.[4] In addition, 70 percent are white, the vast majority are not incapacitated, and most are in their twenties or thirties. For married couples, nearly half live in nonmetropolitan counties, 86 percent are white, 9 percent of husbands are incapacitated, and most are in their twenties or thirties. Singles are fairly evenly divided across residential areas, 71 percent are white, 58 percent are male, 22 percent are incapacitated, and the majority are quite young—70 percent being under the age thirty. Finally, most of the elderly entering the welfare system are white, female, and incapacitated.

In terms of household characteristics, female heads tend to have either been never married or separated/divorced and to have between one and three children in the household; about half of such families have a child under the age of four. Married couples also tend to have between one and three children, and again slightly over half have a child under the age of four. For

TABLE 3.1
**Characteristic Percentages of Recipients Entering the Welfare System
by Household Type**

	Household Type				
	Female Heads	Married Couples		Single Heads	Elderly Heads
Characteristics		Wife	Husband		
DEMOGRAPHIC					
Region					
Major metropolitan	35.1	18.0	—	37.5	22.9
Other metropolitan	33.5	35.5	—	36.6	29.9
Nonmetropolitan	31.3	46.5	—	25.9	47.1
Race					
White	69.5	85.7	—	70.8	95.0
Black	23.5	3.6	—	22.4	2.2
Other	7.0	10.7	—	6.8	2.9
Sex					
Female	100.0	100.0	—	42.1	71.3
Male	—	—	100.0	57.9	28.7
Incapacitation					
Not incapacitated	96.8	96.5	90.6	78.2	42.2
Incapacitated	3.2	3.5	9.4	21.8	57.8
Age					
Less than 20	14.1	9.8	2.7	30.1	—
20–24	33.2	26.2	19.1	28.5	—
25–29	21.4	23.0	25.8	11.0	—
30–34	15.7	14.1	14.5	4.2	—
35–39	7.0	9.8	11.7	5.8	—
40–44	3.5	4.7	7.4	3.2	—
45–49	2.2	6.6	6.3	5.2	—
50–54	1.3	2.3	4.7	3.6	—
55–59	1.6	2.0	4.7	4.5	—
60–64	—	1.6	2.0	3.9	—
65–69	—	—	0.4	—	11.5
70–74	—	—	0.4	—	15.3
75–79	—	—	0.4	—	15.3
80–84	—	—	—	—	22.9
85+	—	—	—	—	35.0
HOUSEHOLD					
Marital Status					
Never married	37.7	—	—	72.9	10.3
Married	—	100.0	—	—	5.1
Separated/divorced	60.6	—	—	21.9	25.6
Widowed	1.6	—	—	5.2	59.0
Children					
0	11.5	13.7	—	100.0	99.4
1	39.3	27.0	—	—	0.6
2	30.0	30.1	—	—	—
3	11.8	15.6	—	—	—
4	6.1	8.2	—	—	—
5 or more	1.2	5.5	—	—	—

TABLE 3.1 (Continued)

Characteristics	Female Heads	Married Couples		Single Heads	Elderly Heads
		Wife	Husband		
Young child					
Under age 4	49.5	52.3	—	3.2	—
None under age 4	50.5	47.7	—	96.8	100.0
Living arrangement					
Home	98.7	99.2	—	93.2	25.5
Nursing home	—	—	—	4.2	74.5
Other	1.3	0.8	—	2.6	—
SOCIOECONOMIC					
Education					
Less than twelve years	41.2	46.7	44.3	47.3	84.1
Twelve years	47.6	43.0	44.7	35.6	12.4
More than 12 years	11.1	10.2	11.1	17.1	3.5
Employment					
Not employed	77.3	85.2	65.5	78.6	99.4
Employed	22.7	14.8	34.5	21.4	0.6
Monthly income					
$0	77.3	85.2	65.5	78.9	99.4
$1–249	2.6	4.3	7.5	6.5	0.6
$250–499	9.3	6.6	6.3	13.3	—
$500 or more	10.9	3.9	20.8	1.3	—

singles, most have never been married. The elderly tend to be widowed, with three-quarters residing in nursing homes.

Finally, looking across household categories, between 40 to 50 percent of recipients have less than twelve years of education (the exception being the elderly, for whom this percentage is 84.1), between two-thirds and three-quarters of the nonelderly are not employed, and those that are working tend to earn less than five hundred dollars a month (although 21 percent of husbands earned more than that amount).

These details regarding the background characteristics of the four major types of households entering the welfare system coupled with the earlier information concerning the circumstances leading to welfare use go far to clarify why households turn to public assistance and how their situations vary by household category.

4 DAY-TO-DAY LIVING

There's lots of nights that I go to bed and I lay awake and wonder how I'm gonna pay the bills. Because gas and electric is high. The telephone is high. And everything's going up instead of down. They keep everything up so high. It makes you wonder if you can make it through the month. When I take my check to the bank, I feel this way—I'm putting this check in the bank but it isn't gonna be my money. The bills are gonna have that money, not me.

—Elderly woman living on Food Stamps and Social Security

Public assistance programs provide a bare minimum on which to live. As discussed in chapter 2, they are not intended to raise a family's standard of living above the poverty line, only to provide limited assistance to particular categories of people. What is it like to live on welfare and in poverty on a day-to-day basis?

The Constant Economic Struggle

Perhaps most apparent when one listens to welfare recipients describe their daily lives and routines is the constant economic struggle that they face. This includes difficulties paying monthly bills, not having enough food, worrying about health care costs, and so on. The amount of income received each month is simply insufficient to cover all these necessary expenses. Having talked with dozens of families, having seen the daily hardships of recipients, having felt their frustrations and pain, I have no doubt that these families are indeed living on the edge.

This economic struggle is typified by the experience of Mary Summers. A fifty-one-year-old divorced mother, Mary and her two teenage daughters have been on public assistance for eleven months. She receives $544 a month from AFDC and $106 a month worth of Food Stamps. After paying $280 for rent (which includes heat and electricity), she and her daughters are left with $370 a month (including Food Stamps) to live on. This comes to approximately $12 a day, or $4 per family member. While this may seem like an implausibly small income for any household to survive on, it is quite typical of the assistance that those on welfare receive.

Mary turned to the welfare system because she had been unable to find work for two years (this in spite of a rigorous search for a bookkeeping or accountant's position, jobs she has held in the past). She comments, "This is probably about the lowest point in my life, and I hope I never reach it again. Because this is where you're just up against a wall. You can't make a move. You can't buy anything that you want for your home. You can't go on a vacation. You can't take a weekend off and go and see things because it costs too much. And it's just such a waste of life."

I asked Carol Richardson to describe what her day-to-day problems were. Having lived in poverty for most of her forty-five years—Carol and her five children have received welfare on and off for twenty years—she can be considered an expert on the subject: "Making ends meet. Period. Coming up with the rent on time. Coming up with the telephone bill on time. Having food in the house. It looks like we've got enough now. I got Food Stamps last month. Otherwise we would be down and out by now. It's just keepin' goin' from day to day. Carfare, busfare, gas money. . . ."

In chapter 3, Joyce Mills, described her feelings about applying for public assistance. At the time of the interview, she was no longer receiving AFDC. I asked her about her most pressing problems. Although she was working full-time in a clerical position, and although she was receiving eighty-one dollars a month from the Food Stamp program, she was clearly having a difficult time surviving economically:

I think it's just trying to make ends meet. I don't think I go out and spend a whole lot of money, not like I'd like to. I'd like to be able to fix the kids' rooms up nice and I haven't been able to. And if I do have the money, it's always something else that comes up. It's really frustrating. Then when I think, if my husband were not incarcerated and working with the job that he had, God, we could, both of us, be raking in very close to a thousand dollars a month. And it just makes me so mad. I've been juggling bills around trying to make ends meet. Now my muffler is off of the car and I gotta get that fixed.

I've been using that car very little since this happened this week. If it wasn't for this car, I would have had the money for Tommy's violin. And last night it just comes to a head, and I just released my tensions through tears. And thank God the kids were sleeping. It's so frustrating when you're trying to lead a normal life, but you can't do it. And then I was trying to think, "Well, if I get this in this month. If I can take so much out of this from the savings account. . . ." There was a time where I could have done that, but now I'm down to nothing. And this past check, it was down so low that I didn't have anything. I got paid and that week it was gone. It was all gone. So it was hard. I had to resort to borrowing.

Perhaps most revealing is her remark "It's so frustrating when you're trying to lead a normal life, but you can't do it." For many recipients, particularly those with children, this expresses in a nutshell their economic frustrations and the dilemmas they face.

Trying to lead a "normal" life under the conditions of poverty is extremely difficult. For example, Marta Green describes how not having a car for transportation severely restricts the kinds of activities she can do with her children, particularly during the wintertime.

In the winter we don't go anywhere. Because it's very hard without a car. I always had a car until last winter. It was very hard. Because we had to wait there sometimes twenty minutes for the bus. And with the kids and the very cold days, it's very hard. I only took them out last winter once, besides the Saturday afternoons that we go to church.

One Sunday, they had some free tickets to go to the circus.

And I only had to buy my ticket. They both had theirs free. The circus was at seven. And it was done by ten. And we were waiting for the bus until eleven thirty that Sunday night. In the middle of the winter. And then finally we started walkin' home. We walked all the way home. We made it home by twelve thirty. They were tired and almost frozen. And then I thought, this is it, no more. So we really don't go very much anywhere.

As a result of daily economic constraints, the diversions open to welfare recipients must be quite simple and inexpensive. Going for walks, visiting friends or relatives, playing with their children, watching television, and reading are the types of activities available to provide some enjoyment and diversion for recipients during their otherwise hard times.

Ironically, those who have the fewest economic resources often pay the most for basic necessities, frequently of inferior quality. Take Marta Green as an example. Without access to an automobile, Marta often shops at a small neighborhood grocery store that charges higher prices for food than do larger supermarkets. In addition, the selection and quality of food items are generally worse than the offerings of the large chains. Without a bank account, Marta has to pay to cash her government checks and to make other monetary transactions. Her winter utility bills also run higher because she cannot afford better-quality housing with improved insulation. This pattern has been found repeatedly among the poverty-stricken (Caplovitz 1963; Jacobs 1966; Beeghley 1989; Maital and Morgan 1992).

The hard times and daily problems are succinctly summarized by forty-six-year-old Alice Waters, who is on SSI as a result of cancer and whose husband died of emphysema: "Day-to-day problems? No money, that's number one. No money. Bein' poor. That's number one—no money."

The End of the Month

Food Stamp and AFDC benefits, received monthly, are usually not enough to provide adequately throughout a particular month. Many recipients find that their Food Stamps routinely run out by the end of the third week. Even with the budgeting and stretching of resources that recipients try to do, there is simply not enough left. Tammy and Jack Collins describe the process:

Tammy: Mainly it's towards the end of the month, and you run out of Food Stamps and gotta pay rent. Tryin' to find enough money to buy groceries. It's the main one.

Q: When that comes up, do you turn to somebody to borrow money, or do you just try to stretch what you've got?

Tammy: I try to stretch. And sometimes his ma will pay him for doin' things on the weekend for her, which will help out. She knows we need the money.

Jack: We collect aluminum cans and we got a crusher in the basement and we sell them.

Q: What happens when you run out of food?

Tammy: That's when his ma helps us.

Recipients often rely on some kind of emergency assistance, such as food pantries or family and friends, to help them through. As discussed in the next chapter, such networks provide an important source of support. Of the food pantries I visited, all reported that the numbers of people coming in for emergency food supplies increased dramatically during the last ten days of each month.

I asked Carol Richardson if she ran out of food, particularly at the end of the month.

Carol: Yeah. All the time.

Q: How do you manage?

Carol: We've got a food pantry up here that they allow you to go to two times a month. They give you a little card. And in between those times, we find other food pantries that we can get to. We've gone to different churches and asked for help all the time. And we get commodities at the end of the month. Cheese and butter. And then we usually get one item out of it, which helps an awful lot.

Borrowing from friends or relatives is another end-of-the-month strategy. We asked Rosa and Alejandro Martinez, an elderly married couple, about this. Rosa responded, "Sometimes we're short of money to pay for everything. We have to pay life insurance, mine and his. We have to pay for the car. We have to pay the light. And we have to pay the telephone. And there are a lot of expenses that we have to pay. And sometimes we can't meet them all. And between the month, I borrow, but I borrow from my friends to make ends meet."

Others deal with the financial squeeze at the end of the month differently. For example, Clarissa and John Wilson, a married couple in their thirties, rely on extra money from a blood plasma center to help them through. I asked them if they had bills which they are unable to pay.

Clarissa: Yeah, that's just frustrating. When you know that you can't pay your bills, and where are you gonna get the money to pay them. If you don't pay 'em, they're gonna always be with you. And that's just frustrating.

John: That's the main reason that we're always going to University Plasma. That's the main reason. To keep up . . . at least try to keep up, some of the bills. If the bills weren't a problem, we wouldn't go every week like we do.

Clarissa: Sometimes I don't see why we're gettin' the aid check because it still doesn't meet our needs—half of our needs. Maybe forty percent of it, I'd say.

In short, at the end of the month, the economic struggles that recipients face loom even larger. Even the basic necessities may be hard to come by.

A Set of Dominoes

For welfare recipients, there is little financial leeway should any unanticipated expenses occur. When nothing out of the ordinary happens, recipients may be able to scrape by. However, when the unexpected occurs (as it often does), it can set in motion a domino effect touching every other aspect of recipients' lives. One unanticipated expense can cause a shortage of money for food, rent, utilities, or other necessary items. The dominoes begin to fall one by one.

Unanticipated expenses include items such as medical costs and needed repairs on a major appliance or an automobile. During these crises, households must make difficult decisions regarding other necessities in their lives. I asked Cindy and Jeff Franklin to describe how they deal with these kinds of problems.

Cindy: Well, I think it's running out of money. (*Sighs.*) If something comes up—a car repair or (*pause*) our refrigerator's on the fritz. . . . We have enough money for a nice, adequate, simple lifestyle as long as nothing happens. If something happens, then we really get thrown in a tizzy. And I'd say that's the worst—that's the worst.

Jeff: Yeah, 'cause just recently, in the last month, the car that we had was about to rust apart. Sort of literally. And so we had to switch cars. And my parents had this car that we've got now, sitting around. They gave it to us for free, but we had to put about two hundred dollars into it just to get it in safe enough condition so that we don't have to constantly be wondering if something's gonna break on it.

Cindy: I think that sense of having to choose—the car is a real good example of it—having to choose between letting things go—in a situation that's unsafe, or destituting ourselves in order to fix it. Having to make that kind of choice is really hard.

When welfare recipients must make these types of choices, it is seldom because they have budgeted their finances improperly. Rather, they simply do not have enough money to begin with, often not enough to cover even the basic monthly expenses. Among the poverty-stricken, this is a major recurring problem. Public assistance programs help, but they just do not provide enough. Households are forced routinely to make hard choices among necessities.

One particularly difficult choice facing some households in

wintertime is choosing between heat or food—the "heat-or-eat" dilemma. A three-year study done by the Boston City Hospital showed that the number of emergency room visits by underweight children increased by 30 percent after the coldest months of the year. In explaining the results, Deborah Frank, who led the study team, noted, "Parents well know that children freeze before they starve and in winter some families have to divert their already inadequate food budget to buy fuel to keep the children warm" (*New York Times,* September 9, 1992). An underweight child's ability to fight infection and disease becomes even more impaired when that child is also malnourished.

Tammy and Jack Collins described earlier how they are pushed to stretch their food supplies and to juggle their bills, particularly at the end of each month. When asked about her children's needs, Tammy responded, "Their teeth need fixing. That's the worst. See, our insurance doesn't cover that. And we've got one that needs an eye checkup that we can't get in to get done because the insurance don't cover that." If they decide to get their children's teeth fixed or eyes examined, the Collinses know they will have to make some hard choices as to which bills not to pay or which necessities to forgo. The dominoes thus begin to fall.

Consequences and Effects

Much has been written about the negative consequences of poverty. The poor suffer from higher rates of disease and crime, experience more chronic and acute health problems, pay more for particular goods and services, have higher infant mortality rates, encounter more dangerous environmental effects, face a greater probability of undernourishment, and have higher levels of psychological stress (Schiller 1989). Chapter 6 focuses on the psychological consequences of living in poverty, while chapter 8 considers the impact of the stigma of welfare recipiency. In this chapter, however, the concern is the more obvious physical consequences.

As mentioned earlier, hunger is a real consequence of poverty. Many of the families I talked to admitted that there were times when they and their children were forced to go hungry and/or significantly alter their diets. Running out of food is not uncommon among those who rely on public assistance.[1]

A widow in her sixties, Edith Mathews lives in a working-class, elderly neighborhood. When she received forty-five dollars' worth of Food Stamps a month, they were not enough to provide an adequate diet (she was subsequently terminated from the program for not providing sufficient documentation). Edith suffers from several serious health problems, including diabetes and high blood pressure. The fact that she cannot afford a balanced diet compounds her health problems. She explains:

> Toward the end of the month, we just live on toast and stuff. Toast and eggs or something like that. I'm supposed to eat green vegetables. I'm supposed to be on a special diet because I'm a diabetic. But there's a lotta things that I'm supposed to eat that I can't afford. Because the fruit and vegetables are terribly high in the store. It's ridiculous! I was out to Cedar's grocery, they're charging fifty-nine cents for one grapefruit. I'm supposed to eat grapefruit, but who's gonna pay fifty-nine cents for one grapefruit when you don't have much money? But my doctor says that that's one thing that's important, is to eat the right foods when you're a diabetic. But I eat what I can afford. And if I can't afford it, I can't eat it. So that's why my blood sugar's high because lots of times I should have certain things to eat and I just can't pay. I can't afford it.

Similarly, Edith is often forced to reuse hypodermic needles to inject insulin. While she is aware that this could be dangerous, she feels she has little choice: "And then those needles that I buy, they cost plenty too. Twelve dollars and something for needles. For a box of needles. And you're only supposed to use 'em once and throw 'em away. But who could afford that? I use 'em over, but they said you shouldn't do that. Sometimes they get dull and I can't hardly use 'em. But I just can't afford to be buying 'em all the time. It's outrageous the way they charge for things."

Nancy Jordon was asked about not having enough food for

her three children. In her mid-thirties, Nancy had been receiving public assistance for two months. Her income from working as a cosmetologist was simply too low to survive on as a single parent. She explains that not having enough money for food has had physical consequences not only upon her children but upon her as well:

> *Nancy:* Well, as long as I got money. If not, I have to resort to other measures. It's a sad thing but a woman should never be broke because if she's got a mind, and knows how to use it, you can go out in the streets. Which is the ultimate LAST resort is to go to the streets. But at a point in a woman's life, if she cares anything about her children, if she cares anything about their lifestyle, they'll go. Matter of fact, some would go to the streets before they would go to aid.
>
> *Q:* Have you had to do that, in the past, to feed your kids?
>
> *Nancy:* A couple of times yes.

In addition to suffering from hunger, recipients may let health problems go unattended until they became serious, live in undesirable and dangerous neighborhoods, or face various types of discrimination as a result of being poor. But perhaps the most ubiquitous consequence of living in poverty and on public assistance is the sheer difficulty of accomplishing various tasks most of us take for granted: not being able to shop at larger and cheaper food stores because of lack of transportation and so paying more for groceries; having to take one's dirty clothing on the bus to the nearest laundromat with three children in tow; being unable to afford to go to the dentist even though the pain is excruciating; not purchasing a simple meal at a restaurant for fear it will disrupt the budget; never being able to go to a movie; having no credit, which in turn makes getting a future credit rating difficult; lacking a typewriter or personal computer on which to improve secretarial skills for a job interview. The list could go on and on.

These are the types of constraints experienced day in and day out by most of the people I saw and spoke with. The barriers facing the poor are often severe, apparent, and ongoing. They represent an all-pervasive consequence of living in poverty. Even the little things in life can become large. Recall Marta Green's difficulties when she took her children to the circus. Or consider the time the utility company shut off the Collins's gas: Tammy and Jack found that simply giving their children baths became a formidable task. Tammy explains: "They used to shut our gas off during the summer. And then I had no hot water for bathin' the kids. I had to heat it on the stove downstairs and carry it up to the bathtub. That was the worst times. I had an electric stove. I used to sit a big pan on top of it, and heat it."

For Cindy and Jeff Franklin, economic problems have turned what many of us would consider insignificant decisions into major quandaries.

Jeff: I mean there's times when I'm taking the bus, and I have to wonder can we really afford to take the bus this morning?

Cindy: Right now, today, we've got just over a dollar. And three dollars in food stamps. And that's all we've got till the end of the month, till the end of the month. That's fairly unusual because the car ate up so much money this month. Usually we manage our money better than that. But we really have to think. I mean, it's not just thinking about whether or not you can afford to go to a movie, but you have to think about can the kids and I stop and get a soda if we've been out running errands. It's a big decision, 'cause we just don't have much spending money.

Living in poverty and on public assistance is a harsh, ongoing economic struggle that becomes more acute by the end of the month. There is very little slack in the rope. When an unanticipated event leads to economic stress, entire lives suffer, domino fashion. Everyday life is complicated by a variety of negative physical consequences, including the difficulty of carrying out the most basic tasks. As Mary Summers commented at the beginning of this chapter, "This is where you're just up against a wall. You can't make a move."[2]

5 FAMILY DYNAMICS

That was one of my dreams when I was in school. Just being married and raising a family totally the opposite of what I grew up in. It became an obsession with me to do that. And I guess I overlooked a lotta things. That's why I was married so many times and it didn't work out. I stayed with my last two children's father as long as I did trying to hold on to that family structure. And willing to accept different things, just to keep that family structure. Just to keep them with their father, to keep the two of us together, which was a fight.

—Twice-divorced mother of three children

From childhood and adolescence, through marriage and raising children, and finally into old age, family relationships play significant roles in our lives. This chapter focuses on four different family experiences among welfare recipients: first, recollections of family background and upbringing; second, current family relationships: third, the likelihood and determinants of women giving birth while on welfare; and, finally, the probability of and causes related to marriage and divorce among welfare recipients.

Growing Up

We begin by exploring recollections of family background and upbringing.[1] Most of the recipients interviewed reported growing up in or around the Ridgeton area, the exception being black families, who often had been raised in Chicago or the South. The economic status of these households can best be described as working class. That is, families were able to keep afloat, but without much left over. Fathers tended to work in manual, blue-collar occupations, often holding down several jobs at once. Typical jobs included factory work, construction, and so on. Mothers often worked as well, especially when the children were in school, to provide extra income for the family.

An example comes from Colleen Bennett. Colleen and her husband, Ron, had gone on public assistance two months prior to our interview. She was asked about the kind of work her parents did when she was growing up.

Colleen: We were lucky. My dad was a drunk, but he could work two jobs. And so financially we were always . . . fine, or borderline. You know, we always had enough.

Q: What kind of work did he do?

Colleen: Construction. Road construction. He worked in warehousing, driving forklifts, or both. Or a combination of a gas attendant with one of the other jobs.

Q: And your mom worked also?

Colleen: Yeah. She works. She started working when I was three months old at the DNR [Department of Natural Resources]. And she's been there for twenty-one years.

A common response among recipients was that, although they seldom went hungry, there was not much extra. Hand-me-down clothes, furniture on its last legs, and leftovers stretched for days were often the norm. Yet few of these families received public assistance. Of the households we interviewed, only 18 percent recalled that their parents had collected any kind of welfare assistance.[2]

Many recipients also reported the presence of serious family problems during their childhood: alcoholism among parents, child and spouse abuse, family breakup, and so on. One-third of interviewees under the age of sixty-five revealed that one or both parents had suffered from serious alcohol problems. An example comes from Joyce Mills, who had recently separated from her husband as a result of physical abuse.

My mom and dad used to fight a lot. My dad was, I guess you could call him an alcoholic. He used to drink a lot. And from the very beginning, I cannot remember a moment where my mom and dad were not fighting. I would see pictures in the album of when they were dating. But yet it didn't look like mom and dad because they weren't fighting. But that was why my mom and dad divorced. Back then I didn't even know what was going on. But when she got back together with him again it was just so that my sister and I could have a father. And when I think back on it, that was the worst thing she could have done. Because things didn't improve. They were just as harsh as they were before she left.

Another example of severe family problems occurring during childhood comes from Nancy Jordon, who was quoted at the beginning of this chapter.

Nancy: I was born in St. Louis. We moved from there when I was four to East Moline. My mother remarried. It was a very horrible childhood. I felt that I was robbed of my childhood, from the point where we left St. Louis when my mother remarried. I was robbed of my childhood, and I was robbed of being a teenager. We've had a very abused home. I come from . . . a nightmare. And it took a long time for me to understand it. I don't know if I've yet to understand it.

Q: Can you tell me a little bit more? Are you talking about alcoholism, physical abuse, sexual abuse, emotional abuse?

Nancy: Physical abuse, sexual abuse.

Q: On the part of your stepfather, or other people like that?

Nancy: My stepfather and my mother. My older sister, her mind was halfway destroyed. And she still has got some loose balls up there now. But you know, it was just (*long pause*) very horrible (*sighs, near tears*). And back then I would run away from home. And all the agency would do was send me back. They chose to believe the parents. Or they chose not to deal with the problem, and just write it off. That's how I felt about it, they just chose to write it off (*spoken in a very depressed tone*).

When coupled with the tight economic conditions that most of their families faced, the childhoods of our interviewed sample can best be described as formidable. Perhaps, then, it is not surprising that many female heads and married couples reported having a child at an early age and/or marrying early, whether to escape family problems, because of a shortage of information, or for lack of alternatives. Typical ages for women at first birth were the late teens and early twenties. Often, pregnancies were accidental but nevertheless carried to term. Couples also tended to marry young, usually no later than their early twenties.

A young age at childbirth, together with constrained economic resources, foreclosed the possibilities of higher education for most recipients with children. For those without children, the likelihood of going on and completing college was slim given the lack of financial support from families. As a result, many began working full-time at an early age, typically sixteen, seventeen, or eighteen.

The childhood experiences of our sampled recipients closely resemble the recollections of the working-class families portrayed in Lillian Rubin's book *Worlds of Pain* (1976). Rubin writes,

> Thus, whether settled- or hard-living, most of the working-class adults I spoke with recall childhoods where, at best, "things were tight" financially. They recall parents who worked hard, yet never quite made it; homes that were overcrowded; siblings or selves who got into "trouble"; a preoccupation with the daily struggle for survival that precluded planning for a future. Whether they recall angry, discontented, drunken parents, or quiet, steady, "always-there" parents, the dominant theme is struggle and trouble. (48)

In short, these are childhoods in which life chances and options have been substantially reduced. The odds simply are stacked against such kids. Although some may become bankers or lawyers, most will not. The resources and support necessary to take such paths are largely unavailable. With few exceptions, these children will revisit as adults many of the struggles that their parents grappled with.

And indeed this is precisely what the prior chapter indicated. Most are confronting the same problems their parents faced. While many will leave the welfare system relatively quickly, they are likely to remain on a financial tightrope, one step away from public assistance. This process of class reproduction has been detailed in numerous studies, including Whyte (1943), Liebow (1967), Rubin (1976), and MacLeod (1987).[3]

Family Ties

There is a Spanish proverb that says, "An ounce of blood is worth more than a pound of friendship." Certainly this saying holds true among welfare recipients. In spite of the problems and difficulties of childhood, family ties are nevertheless an important source of strength and support.

I focus on three aspects of family ties. First, the demographic characteristics of households. Second, the care and raising of children. And, finally, the support available from the extended family.

Family Demographic Characteristics

The overall household composition of families on welfare is slightly different from the composition of households entering the welfare system (as shown in figure 3.1). Female-headed families and the elderly tend to remain on public assistance longer than do married couples or singles (this issue is discussed in greater detail in chapter 9). Consequently, a random sample of all recipients at any given time will tend to comprise more female-headed and elderly households as a percentage of the total. In table 5.1, 41 percent of the caseload sample of welfare households were female headed, 19 percent were headed by married couples, 18 percent by singles, and 22 percent by the elderly (less than 1 percent were male-headed families).

Family characteristics by these household types are shown in table 5.1.[4] Single and elderly households are quite small—79.8 percent of single heads and 93.8 percent of elderly heads have a household size of one. Household size for female-headed and married households is larger, averaging 3.2 and 4.5 individuals, respectively.

Not all households live in a home or apartment. This is most true for the elderly, where 81.2 percent reside in nursing homes. Twenty percent of singles are also institutionalized.

Turning to marital status, approximately 40 percent of female heads have never been married, while the bulk of the remainder are either separated or divorced. Roughly three out of four single heads have never been married, while 61.5 percent of the elderly are widowed.

Most female heads have one or two children in the household, while married couples have a slightly higher number of children. In both cases, approximately 40 percent of children in the household are under the age of six, and slightly less than 60 percent are between the ages of six and seventeen. Very few children living in the household are over the age of seventeen.

The table does not support the theory that large, extended families live together on welfare. Female-headed households average 3.2 individuals, and only 1.6 percent include three generations. However, as we will see, other family members do often live in the immediate vicinity.

Married households are somewhat larger, averaging 4.5 members; again, only 1.6 percent include three generations. Single and elderly headed households generally contain only themselves.

Raising Children

Welfare recipients share much the same frustrations and joys as other parents. Those interviewed spoke of the way their children have enriched their lives, mentioned disciplinary problems and other worries about their sons or daughters, and described

TABLE 5.1
Household and Family Characteristic Percentages by Household Type

Household Characteristics	Household Type			
	Female Heads	Married Heads	Single Heads	Elderly Heads
Household size				
1	2.6	0.2	79.8	93.8
2	34.9	9.0	7.9	4.8
3	29.8	22.1	3.6	0.7
4	16.3	26.1	2.8	0.5
5	8.1	19.2	2.4	0.0
6 or more	8.4	23.4	3.6	0.2
Average	3.2	4.5	1.5	1.1
Living arrangement				
Home	99.6	99.4	78.1	18.8
Nursing home	0.0	0.2	20.0	81.2
Other	0.4	0.4	2.0	0.0
Marital status				
Never married	39.7	—	73.8	13.8
Married	—	100.0	—	3.9
Separated	27.2	—	8.2	16.6
Divorced	31.4	—	12.1	4.2
Widowed	1.7	—	5.8	61.5
Number of generations in household				
1	3.8	9.6	97.2	98.0
2	94.7	88.8	2.8	1.8
3	1.6	1.6	—	0.2
Number of children				
0	3.9	11.6	100.0	98.7
1	41.8	23.2	—	1.2
2	29.5	26.9	—	0.0
3	14.2	19.0	—	0.0
4 or more	10.7	19.2	—	0.2
Average	1.9	2.3	—	—
Ages of children				
Less than 6	40.2	36.3	—	—
6–17	56.5	59.1	—	—
18 or more	3.3	4.6	—	—

their efforts to do what is best for their offspring together with their pride in their children's accomplishments. But along with these and many other topics relevant to parenting in general, welfare parents repeatedly raised several issues that appeared to be related to the experience of living in poverty.

Many parents discussed their frustrations over not being able to meet fully the physical needs of their children. These ranged from not having enough food on the table to not being able to keep up with the status symbols that other parents were able to provide for their children. The example of Marta Green is typical.

> Like the kids at school, they wear Nike tennis shoes. Name-brand tennis shoes. And then I go and buy them a five-dollar pair of tennis shoes. And they say, "Mom, no. We want the Nike shoes because my girlfriend, Emily, has them." And I say, "No, because for thirteen dollars I can buy shoes for both of you." And they get angry and they don't understand. But I try to talk to them. They are very good kids. They get upset for a little while and sometimes they cry, but after they get over it, I just talk to them and say, "Listen, this is the situation that we are going through. But we'll get over this. And in a couple of years, Mommy's going to buy you some nicer stuff. But right now we have to take it like it is."

Perhaps as a result, most recipients reported stressing to their children the importance of developing strong, independent lives of their own, particularly, of never having to rely on public assistance. This is reflected in the words of Donna Anderson, a forty-three-year-old separated mother of nine:

> I want them number one to be independent. And I want them to be honest. That's the main thing I demand from them. I can't stand dishonesty. Because I like to be able to say, "My kid's telling the truth." And I want them to be achievers. I want them to have certain things that they know they need to do in life. Instead of making up excuses why they can't do it. Like I tell them all the time, you *have* (*with emphasis*) to go to school. There's no way of getting out of that. You have to learn. This is the only way you're gonna learn. So that's basically all I want of them, is honesty, and to be independent one day. To work toward being independent and to be able to take care of themselves.

Parents emphasized to their children the importance of education as the means to achieving a strong, independent life. Ruth Miller, a thirty-eight-year-old female head of household with five children, explains:

I teach them that education is the best thing these days. As far as trying to drop out of school, we don't need that. 'Cause we're going to need the education in order to get us a good job. And they say they understand. They love going to school. My kids don't have a real problem with mischief. Sometimes they get out of hand, and we'll have a grade argument or whatever. But other than that, they understand that it's best to go to school. It's better than out on the streets, where you've got nothing to do, and you get lonely. You got no education. Can't get no good job. You gotta just take whatever they give you. They [*referring to her children*] don't want to be like that. They want to go to school, get a good education, and be assured they're going to get a job. And if they want to go to college, if I can see fit, I can send them to a college. So that's the way it is.

The dilemma facing many of these parents, as undoubtedly it was for their own parents, is the difficulty of promoting such goals for their children given their economic constraints. Like most families, the parents in my sample want what is best for their children. Their frustration comes from not being able to provide it.

Kinship Networks

Extended family ties are often an important source of strength and support for these households. Yet as we might expect, the amount of economic support that other family members can provide is rather limited given their own financial constraints. Furthermore (as chapter 8 details), some family members are hostile to the idea of their kin receiving public assistance. Nevertheless, recipients reported a fairly high degree of contact with relatives and a modest amount of shared resources.

Extended family contact was either face to face or by telephone. Often parents, siblings, and/or grown-up children lived in the immediate vicinity. Recipients reported being in touch with a relative an average of once a week; for some, this average was two to three times a week.

Valerie Jones is a thirty-year-old never-married mother of two who has been on and off the welfare system for nine years.

When interviewed, she was working as a cook in a fraternity house, while still qualifying for public assistance. How did she deal with troubles paying the bills? "Well, I have two sisters and two brothers here. So if they can help, they will. And then my aunt, she's in a good enough position and her husband. I kinda depend on my family if I need help. 'Cause if they need help, I'll do the same for them."

What about if she runs out of food? "If I don't have any food in my house, especially if the kids are here, my aunt will bring something. Or if I can get to my sister's house, I will raid their refrigerator (*laugh*)." For Valerie, such help was often the difference between getting by and a serious emergency.

The importance of family ties was also evident for Colleen Bennett and her husband. They lived in a rural area north of Ridgeton in a ranch-style house owned by Colleen's parents. She was asked about her family.

> We're all very close. We take care of each other if anybody has a problem. My husband and I have had financial problems on and off for years. And my brother recently lost his job. So when we have something where we can help them, we go ahead and give them a couple of dollars for gas in their car so they can find a job. 'Cause we know what it feels like when you don't have it. And then when we're low, they'll give to us. And nobody asks anybody to pay it back. It's like a running loan company.

These types of reciprocal exchanges are fairly common among the poor. As Carol Stack (1974) noted in her classic work on kinship networks in a low-income black neighborhood, they are an adaptive strategy for dealing with the uncertainties inherent in poverty. Being able to count on family members for support during troubled times helps people weather such spells.

Birthrates

Policymakers and the general public tend to assume that women on welfare have large numbers of children. In addition, many

contend that because benefits increase with the size of a household, women on welfare have a financial incentive to bear more
children.[5] For example, President Reagan's Working Group on
the Family, headed by Gary Bauer, observed, "Does the welfare system, particularly AFDC, give some women incentives
to bear children? Statistical evidence does not prove those sup-
positions; and yet, even the most casual observer of public
assistance program understands that there is indeed some relationship between the availability of welfare and the inclination
of many young women to bear fatherless children" (1986:35).
Several states have frozen or are considering freezing benefits
to women who have a child while on welfare for precisely
these reasons. Yet what does the evidence tell us? The longitudinal caseload data yields some surprising answers.[6]

Incidence and Determinants

Three separate questions are addressed with the numerical data.
First, what is the percentage and rate of women giving birth
while receiving welfare? Second, how do these rates compare
with those for the general population? And, third, what factors
increase or decrease the likelihood of childbearing among welfare recipients?

The likelihood of childbearing. Figure 5.1 graphically represents the percentage of women on welfare (aged eighteen to
forty-four) giving birth over the course of three years (for the
exact numbers and percentages, refer to table B.1 in appendix
B). The proportion of women giving birth during any six-
month interval is relatively stable at approximately 2 percent.
After one year on welfare, 4.58 percent of women will have
given birth, while 11.49 percent will bear children during a
three-year spell on welfare. The one-year overall fertility rate
for women on public assistance is therefore 45.8 per 1,000
women on welfare.[7]

Comparison with the general population. Information from the
Wisconsin Department of Health and Social Services (1981) and
the U.S. Bureau of the Census (1981) permits a comparison of
the fertility rates of women aged eighteen through forty-four

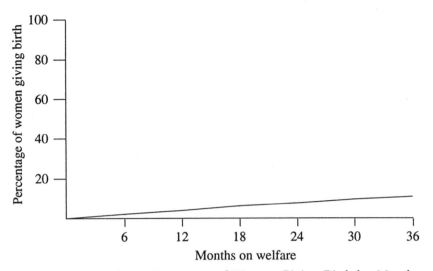

Figure 5.1 Cumulative Percentage of Women Giving Birth by Months on Welfare

in the overall population with those of women on welfare during the same period.

The overall childbearing rate in Wisconsin per 1,000 women was 75.3, and for the national population, 71.1. These rates are considerably higher than the one-year fertility rate of 45.8 for women on welfare. Consequently, contrary to the assumption that welfare encourages women to have children, quite the reverse appears to be true.

Yet to what extent do these results stem from differences across populations? Perhaps the demographic structure of the welfare population lends itself to a lower overall fertility rate. The key demographic differences between women on welfare and women in the general population (that can be controlled for) are race, marital status, number of children, education, and age. Women on welfare are more likely to be black, unmarried, have at least one child, possess less education, and be in their twenties when compared to women in the general population. What would the fertility rate for women on welfare be if they shared the same demographics as the general population? To find out, I standardized the welfare fertility rates for the na-

TABLE 5.2
Welfare Fertility Rates Standardized for Population Characteristics

Characteristics	Standardized for National Population Characteristics	Percentage Difference from National Rate[a]	Standardized for Wisconsin Population Characteristics	Percentage Difference from Wisconsin Rate[b]
Age	45.8	−35.6	48.3	−35.9
Children	50.2	−29.4	50.6	−32.8
Marital status	53.1	−25.3	53.3	−29.2
Race	37.1	−47.8	34.3	−54.4
Education	37.7	−47.0	36.3	−51.8

[a]The overall childbearing rate nationwide is 71.1 per 1,000 women aged 18 to 44.
[b]The overall childbearing rate in Wisconsin is 75.3 per 1,000 women aged 18 to 44.

TABLE 5.3
*Odds Ratios of Variables Predicting Childbearing
Among Women Aged 18 to 44 on Welfare*

Independent Variables	Odds Ratios
Demographic	
Not high school graduate	1.64★★★
Employed	1.15
Nonwhite	2.11★★
Age	1.49★★★
Household	
Number of children	0.50
Child under age 4	3.42★★
Married	1.31
Welfare variation	
Receiving all three programs	1.03
Lowered benefits	1.01
Length of welfare use	0.62★

★significant at the .05 level
★★significant at the .01 level
★★★significant at the .001 level

tional and Wisconsin population compositions.[8] The results presented in table 5.2 indicate that the fertility rates of women on welfare remain considerably below those of the national and Wisconsin populations. The lower overall birthrates among women receiving public assistance programs are therefore not an artifact of a more favorable demographic structure.

Determinants of fertility. What factors increase or decrease the probability of women on welfare bearing children? In order to address this, I have calculated what is known as a "logistic regression model" to examine how individual characteristics increase or decrease the probability of giving birth during any given six-month period. The odds ratios I obtained permit a straightforward evaluation of the magnitude of each variable's effect on the likelihood of giving birth (see table 5.3; refer to appendix B, table B.2, for the exact coefficients in the equation).

As an illustration, the odds ratio of 1.64 shown in table 5.3 for women not graduating from high school indicates that such women have a 64 percent greater probability of giving birth during a six- month interval than do women who have graduated from high school. This is true even after taking into account all the other confounding characteristics shown in the table (this is the concept behind what is known as a "multivariate model"). Thus, from the 2 percent chance of giving birth during a six-month interval shown in figure 5.1, the chances increase to approximately 3 percent. The significance level of .001 indicates that there is only a one-in-a-thousand chance that this is not true for the overall welfare population.

I used three sets of characteristics to predict childbearing among welfare recipients: demographic (education, race, employment status, and age), household (number of children, age of youngest child, and marital status), and variation in welfare programs (the number of programs received, before and after the lowering of benefits by the Omnibus Budget Reconciliation Act of 1981, and length of time on welfare).[9] Table 5.3 summarizes the results.

Several variables significantly affect the likelihood of childbearing among women on welfare: education, race, age, having a child under the age of four in the household, and length of welfare use. Women with less education, nonwhite women, older women, and women having a child under the age of four all have a greater probability of giving birth while on welfare.

Perhaps most interesting is the effect of the length of welfare use on fertility. The longer a woman remains on welfare, the less likely she is to give birth. Each additional year on welfare lowers the probability of giving birth by .62 to 1. Thus, controlling for confounding factors, rather than encouraging women to give birth, being on public assistance for longer periods of time actually reduces the rate of fertility.[10]

Reasons

Why is the rate of fertility among women on welfare relatively low? To shed some light on the potential reasons, I asked women about their experiences and their attitudes toward pregnancy and childbirth.

Twenty-nine of the fifty interviews were with a female household head or wife between the ages of eighteen and forty-four, with most women being in their twenties or thirties. Two women were pregnant at the time of the interview. The majority of women had borne one or two children.

None of the twenty-seven nonpregnant women were contemplating having a child in the near future, and only a handful were considering having more children in the long term. They clearly wished to avoid childbearing at this particular time in their lives. Several examples illustrate the underlying reasons behind this.

Marta Green, who had discussed the frustrations of trying to provide for her children, was asked whether she thought she would ever want to have any more children. She responded, "No. No. I don't think that I *ever* want to have another child. I think that will stop me from doing things that I want to do. And it won't be fair to me. It won't be fair for the new child. And it won't be fair at all for the two that I have."

Jennifer Smith, a never-married woman in her early thirties commented, "It's hardest to get by with one, let alone have another one just me by myself, ya' know. Tryin' to raise two."

Jill Nelson, a nineteen-year-old woman with one child, when asked if she had considered having any more children, replied, "Not quite yet (*laughter*). I kinda thought about, you know, the age difference. I don't want it to be real far, but I'm not quite ready for another kid, financially or . . . or mentally. I don't think I could handle two kids. (*Laughter*.)"

Finally, Cindy Franklin, whose comments about her economic frustrations appeared in the previous chapter, was asked why she was planning not to have a third child. She answered, "I suppose mostly, it has to do with me. Depression is a factor. I just don't know that I can handle more than this. And also, I want to get on preparing for my own career. And I don't want to have to go back to square one and raise a child, and stay home with it again."

These examples illustrate several of the predominate feelings and attitudes of the women that were interviewed. The economic, social, and psychological situations in which women on welfare find themselves is simply not conducive to desiring more children. Such women would appear to be motivated by cost-benefit considerations, but it is the costs that outweigh the benefits, not the reverse. Becoming pregnant and having a child are perceived as making the situation worse, not better. In addition, virtually all of the interviewed women expressed a desire to get off public assistance. Having an additional child was perceived as severely hampering that desire.

Denise Turner has four children, ages fourteen, twelve, ten, and eight. When asked whether the availability of welfare had had anything to do with her having children, she quickly responded,

> Nothing. I've read a lot of studies about that, and they're not true. No. It had nothing to do with it. You know . . . having a child is very traumatic. It's a very beautiful experience, but it's also very traumatic. And I suppose there are some women that just might have additional children to get an increase in money, but I would say that that's less than a very small percentage. Because you're committing yourself to anywhere from fifteen to twenty years of your life to that individual. You're taking nine months from the very beginning and doing all kinds of traumatic things to your body. So, no. That was not a consideration in having additional children.

Many of the pregnancies and births occurring to the interviewed women while on welfare had been accidental rather than planned. This is consistent with several of the predictors of childbearing summarized in table 5.3. Education and race are significant factors affecting the likelihood of childbearing, and both have also been shown in previous research to be highly correlated with an increased likelihood of unplanned births (Pratt et al. 1984). Angela Lewis, a never-married woman in her mid-twenties, was asked about her three pregnancies after her first child and whether she had wanted to have another. "Never. After that first time, my mom kept drilling into me about school and the importance of education and all. So that stuck with me all those years. And I always got pregnant through carelessness, you know. I kept saying, 'Well when I get married one day and settle down, and make sure my life is secure, then I'll have the children.' So that's why I always got the abortions."

The belief that women on welfare have a high fertility rate, so often implicitly accepted by social and policy analysts (e.g., Working Group on the Family 1986), is simply not supported by this analysis. In fact, women on welfare have a relatively low rate of fertility, with that rate dropping with years of recipiency.

Marriage and Dissolution

Policymakers have also been concerned about the effects of the welfare system on family structure. Some have argued that the welfare system encourages the formation of female-headed families (Bahr 1979; Murray 1984). Others have suggested that female-headed families create the need for welfare (Draper 1981; Darity and Meyers 1984). In this section, I examine the incidence of marriage and separation/divorce in the welfare population and the factors associated with these family compositional changes.

Overall Patterns of Marriage and Dissolution

Figure 5.2 charts the marriages and dissolutions of female heads of households and married couples over six half-year intervals. Slightly over 2 percent of female heads are likely to marry during any given six-month interval on welfare. The marriage rate for female heads during their first year on welfare is 5.49 percent, or 54.9 marriages per 1,000 women. This is below the national marriage rate of 102.6 per 1,000 unmarried women aged eighteen to forty-four, and 61.4 per 1,000 unmarried women aged fifteen and over during this period (U.S. Bureau of the Census 1991). Over the course of the three years examined, 13 percent of female heads of households married.

Approximately 3 to 5 percent of married couples dissolve their marriages during any given six-month spell on public assistance. The first year divorce/separation rate is 8.94 percent, or 89.4 divorces/separations per 1,000 marriages. This is substantially higher than the divorce rate of 22.6 per 1,000 married women aged fifteen and over in the general population during

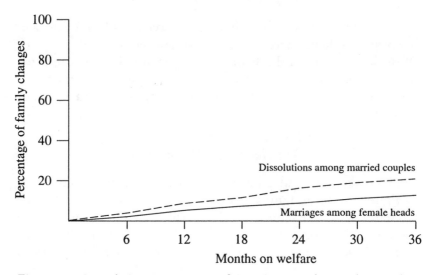

Figure 5.2 Cumulative Percentage of Marriages and Dissolutions by Months on Welfare

this period (U.S. Bureau of the Census 1991).[11] Finally, over the course of three years on welfare, an estimated 21 percent of couples will end their marriages (see tables B.3 and B.4 in appendix B for the exact numbers and percentages used to construct figure 5.2).

As this figure makes plain, the likelihood of a separation or divorce occurring among married couples in the welfare population is substantially greater than that of a female head marrying. Furthermore, the divorce/separation rate of married couples is much higher than the divorce rate for the general population, while the marriage rate for women on welfare is lower than their counterparts in the general population. These findings make sense in light of the uncertain and stressful conditions in which individuals in poverty find themselves.

Clarissa and John Williams had been married for only three months but were already experiencing severe strains when I interviewed them in their upstairs flat in a poor neighborhood of Ridgeton. As recounted in chapter 4, John and Clarissa often sell their blood plasma to tide themselves through the month. Clarissa was asked about the problems they faced: "We don't have the money. It makes us frustrated or mad with each other. We run out of things. We take that out on each other. 'Cause it makes you frustrated when you don't know where your next dollar's coming from. You just start in on money and it just brings on an argument." Later in the interview they elaborated:

John: When I'm out there, she's here. She don't know what I'm doing. And I'm trying to tell her that, and she's goin' on, "You're not doing this, you're not doing that." And that just makes me mad because I know what I'm doing.

Clarissa: Now that's our biggest problem. Money and that job. Him not having a job. Makes me frustrated. I'm paying all the bills. Taking care of everything. Even though he's on my grant. Which is nothing because they cut it. It just seems like I be doin' everything. That's a problem.

John: It frustrates me because I'm not working. I'm used to working.

This example illustrates the strains that many married couples in poverty experience every day. Such stress puts additional pressure on the relationship, which increases the likelihood of a separation or divorce. Indeed, a U.S. Census Bureau report indicates that poor two-parent families are approximately twice as likely to break up as are two-parent families that aren't poor. The report notes that the "stresses arising from low income and poverty may have contributed substantially to discontinuation rates for two-parent families" (1992c:29–30).

On the other hand, an example of a female head of household being unlikely to marry was Denise Turner. A thirty-seven-year-old never-married mother of four, Denise has been on and off welfare for the past fourteen years, often working as well. She was asked if she would like to be in a permanent relationship at some point in the future.

Sometimes yes, sometimes no. Sometimes I think about it and I say it would really be nice to have somebody that I could relate to. Somebody I could talk to and laugh with and share things with. And then it makes me sad that I don't. And then sometimes I look at it, and I say well I really don't have the time. . . .

You know, I think that if I had been more career minded when I was younger, I would not be in the position that I'm in today. So, at this point that's really what I'm moving to. I want a career! I want a job! I want to make some good money! The hell with everybody else! I will see you all later. I will find a man . . . on the other end. If not, that's just too bad. And I think that's what I'm moving towards. And I think I'm doing that out of survival reasons.

Again, it would appear that the conditions of poverty limit the options for such women. This is not to say that female heads on welfare do not marry. Indeed they do, as shown in figure 5.2. Nevertheless, poor women face very real constraints on their opportunities to cultivate the kinds of relationships that lead to marriage.

Factors Related to the Process of Marriage and Divorce

As in the earlier analysis of fertility, I used logistic regression equations to model and acquire odds ratios related to the processes of marriage and separation/divorce among welfare recipients (tables B.5 and B.6 in appendix B). Three sets of characteristics are examined—demographic, children, and welfare variables.[12]

Table 5.4 indicates that of the variables examined, only race is significantly related to marriage for female heads. Being white increases the odds of marriage by 60 percent over the odds for nonwhites. This finding is consistent with previous research demonstrating that the marriage market for black women is problematic. As Wilson (1987) has argued, black women, especially young black women, have access to a shrinking pool of "marriageable" (that is, economically stable) men. White women have not had to face this problem to the same extent.

Neither employment nor age are significantly correlated with

TABLE 5.4
Odds Ratios of Variables Predicting Marriage for
Unmarried Female Heads of Households on Welfare

Independent Variables	Odds Ratios
Demographic	
Employment	0.78
White	1.60★★
Age	1.05
Children	
Number of children	1.17
Child under age 4	1.30
Welfare variation	
Receiving all three programs	0.80
Lowered benefits	0.97
Length of welfare use	0.94

★significant at the .05 level
★★significant at the .01 level
★★★significant at the .001 level

marriage. Likewise, the number and age of children present in the household have no effect on predicting the likelihood of marriage.

As to the third set of variables, lowered welfare benefits resulting from the Reagan administration's cutbacks are insignificantly related to the likelihood of marriage. Likewise, female heads receiving all three programs (AFDC, Food Stamps, and Medicaid) are as likely to marry as their counterparts who receive public assistance through one or two programs. Finally, there is no evidence that being on welfare for an extended period of time significantly reduces or increases the odds of getting married. In short, the effect of welfare variation on the probability of marriage is negligible.

The second set of odds ratios (predicting divorce/separation for married couples on welfare) is shown in table 5.5. Two factors are significantly correlated with a change in family composition. A wife's employment increases the odds of a dissolution by 89 percent, a finding consistent with previous research (Adams 1986; Cherlin 1992). Employment may serve as a means for a woman to leave an unsatisfactory marriage. It may also reduce a husband's reluctance to end a marriage, knowing that his wife will be able to partially support herself. Or it may create further stress for a husband

TABLE 5.5
*Odds Ratios of Variables Predicting Dissolutions for
Married Couples on Welfare*

Independent Variables	Odds Ratios
Demographic	
Husband employed	0.87
Wife employed	1.89**
White	0.99
Wife's age	1.07
Children	
Number of children	1.46
Child under age 4	1.87*
Welfare variation	
Receiving all three programs	1.39
Lowered benefits	0.70
Length of welfare use	1.53

*significant at the .05 level
**significant at the .01 level
***significant at the .001 level

steeped in the traditional ideology of the male as the family breadwinner.

The second factor statistically correlated with separation/ divorce is the presence of a young child in the household, which significantly increases the likelihood of a marital breakup. This finding differs from analyses of divorce in the general population, which have shown that children at preschool ages deter divorce (Waite and Lillard 1991).

For married couples as for female heads, variation in welfare use does not significantly increase or decrease the risk of a change in family composition. Lowered welfare benefits, the number of programs received, and the length of time on welfare are all nonsignificant.[13]

In the analyses for both female heads and married couples, it would appear reasonable to argue that the conditions of poverty are more influential in affecting family formation than are the specific welfare programs per se. People in low-income families experience considerable tension and stress. These factors undoubtedly create problems in their lives. For married couples, these problems may lead to separation or divorce. For female heads, they may result in difficulties and constraints in finding a spouse. In either case, poverty, rather than welfare, is the more likely factor influencing the observed changes in family composition.

The issue of family dynamics among welfare recipients has been debated long and hard among policymakers. There is often an underlying fear that welfare contributes to the breakdown of the family: specifically that it encourages families to dissolve, women to have more children, extended families to crumble, children to follow in their parent's footsteps of welfare dependency, female heads not to marry, and so on (see Working Group on the Family 1986). The results presented in this chapter flatly contradict these assumptions.[14] For the vast majority of families, welfare does not appear to influence family dynamics (see Bane and Jargowsky 1988, Duncan, Hill, and Hoffman 1988, Duncan and Hoffman 1988, and Moffitt 1992 for a review of the literature and a similar conclusion).[15]

What does appear to be of utmost importance is the condition of living and growing up in poverty and hardship. In each of the familial experiences examined in this chapter, economic hardship has played a significant role.

To a large extent, welfare recipients follow in their parent's economic footsteps; however, this is not because children learn from their parents the easy life of welfare (indeed, most recipients' parents did not receive assistance). Rather, their educational and occupational opportunities have been severely limited as a result of parental financial constraints. Their scripts are too often written early on, resulting in formidable odds later in life.

This process is perhaps most cogently described in Elliot Liebow's study of streetcorner men in Washington, D.C.:

> Each generation does provide role models for each succeeding one. Of much greater importance for the possibilities of change, however, is the fact that many similarities between the lower-class Negro father and son (or mother and daughter) do not result from "cultural transmission" but from the fact that the son goes out and independently experiences the same failures, in the same areas, and for much the same reasons as his father. What appears as a dynamic, self-sustaining cultural process is,

in part at least, a relatively simple piece of social machinery which turns out, in rather mechanical fashion, independently produced look-alikes. The problem is how to change the conditions which, by guaranteeing failure, cause the son to be made in the image of the father.   (1967:223)

Like their parents before them, these children are constrained in what they can offer to their own offspring. During our interviews, parents repeatedly stressed their belief in the importance of education for their children and the desire that their children be independent. A better life is what they want for their kids. Yet their children's opportunities are likely to be as limited as theirs were. As this chapter has demonstrated, the key to understanding this and other dynamics within the family is not the influence of welfare but rather the conditions of poverty.

6 BELIEFS AND HOPES

Life is a fight. You get out of it what you put into it. You just have to keep fighting to get through things. Once you give up, then everything falls apart.　　　　　*—Twenty-six-year-old never-married mother of two*

It had been a long day when I arrived at Carol Richardson's apartment. She greeted me at the door, looking somewhat older than her forty-five years. As we talked, the hardships and struggles in her life became obvious. Yet something else was also quite clear: here was a woman who would not give up, who held on to her faith that things would eventually straighten out, that with enough time and effort she would be able to evade poverty. During our two-and-a-half-hour conversation, she often stressed her desire simply to get one step ahead of the game. As we finished the interview, I wished her good luck and headed home. Yet I could not stop thinking about the hopes and dreams that remain alive in even the most trying circumstances. This chapter explores those dreams and hopes.[1]

Beliefs

Time and again during the interviews, I would hear Carol Richardson's words echoed by others on welfare. While not all recipients held the same beliefs, the vast majority seemed to share largely similar views of the world and their responsibilities within it.

Life as a Struggle

For families on welfare, life is characterized by one word—struggle. As suggested in chapter 4, day-to-day problems are commonplace. Bills accumulate. Food may be in short supply. The rent is overdue. The list goes on and on. It is no wonder that recipients view life as something to survive.

Denise Turner was asked to characterize her family life.

> The only thing I can say, is that . . . it can be summarized in one word, and that's survival. That's what we're tryin' to do. We're tryin' to survive. And . . . I talk to a lot of people, and they say, "Well, hey, if you went to Ethiopia, you know, survival would be one thing. And that's . . . eating." But, damn it, I'm not in Ethiopia! You know. So I want a little bit more than just . . . having some food. Having a coupla meals. So, if I can just summarize it, in one word, it would be we're tryin' to survive. We're tryin' to stay together. That's my major concern, keepin' all my family together, my children together. And to survive.

Similarly a young husband, Dan Wilensky, summarized his philosophy of life: "For me, life is just basically a contest to see if you can survive. That's what life meant to me from way back when. It's just, for survival. To see who can survive and who can't. I happen to be one of 'em that has a good understanding about it. That hopefully I'll be able to survive like I did when I was younger."

I asked Carol Richardson how she felt life had treated her. She paused for a moment, leaned her head back, and began talking.

Carol: Oh *(pause)* good at times. Rough, umm . . . *(pause)*. That's hard really. I've had good times. I've had really, really sour times. Bad times where I figure nothing's gonna go right, I'm never gonna pull out of it. And then I've had really good times where everything goes fairly good. Everything is in fairly good shape. And there's peace and quiet for a while.

It's just a chart. (*Laugh.*) A mountainous chart of a lot of dips. You go so long and then all of a sudden you end up down there. And then you start climbing in and you just about hit the peak and all of sudden you end up down there again. You never quite make it to the top. And then once in a while, you just might for a little while sit up there on the mountain. Not too long. You don't stay up there. It's just the way everything is. I don't think anybody can really . . . at this day and age.

Q: Do you have any attitude or philosophy towards life at all? You know, the way you look at life?

Carol: Just keep hanging in there and try your best. Do the best you can with what you've got. And hope and pray that it works out. Like I said before you gotta have a lot of faith. That's helped me out a lot. I don't intend to sound overly religious or anything. But the good Lord, it's the only thing that's been keeping us going, on my part.

Q: So it's been a real source of strength?

Carol: Yes, it has. It really has (*softly*).

Q: Right now, what's your state of mind?

Carol: (*Voice over.*) Frustration! Let me tell ya, I just got done seeing a psychiatrist for stress and strain today so it's been building up. It's all the pressure right now. And, for the next, well until I get another job too, you know.

Q: So right now you feel pretty frustrated?

Carol: Yeah, I'm pretty frustrated. Landlord came over today too, so. . . . Disconnection notice on the phone. So we're not in good shape. We're at that pit right now. (*Laugh.*)

The day of our interview, Carol had found out she had lost her job. It was one more setback in a long series of hardships.

The same afternoon, I interviewed Cindy and Jeff Franklin.

A married couple in their late twenties, the Franklins lived in a pleasant house in a working-class neighborhood. Jeff was hoping to complete his degree at the university by the following year. Although their future was relatively bright, life was still seen as difficult. When I asked how they thought life had treated them, Cindy replied:

> (*Laughter.*) I was just thinking about that last night. 'Cause I saw, you know, the famous bumper sticker "Life's a bitch, and then you die" (*laughter*). And I thought to myself, well (*laughter*). I said, "Well, okay. This person thinks life's a bitch, and then you die." Woody Allen has come to feel that life is okay, and then you die. (*Laughter by all.*) How do I feel? (*More laughter.*) I guess I think life is pretty hard. And it has a number of compensations, and it's . . . it's difficult for me. It's difficult for me to overlook the hard part. And the depression plays a large factor here, because there are times when I simply don't . . . I'm not in control of my perspective. . . .
>
> Suffering is simply inevitably a part of life, of this life. And that there's no sense trying to deny that, or to live a life without it. So I guess I feel like I want to dedicate my life to the relief of suffering, as much as that's possible. The relief of suffering for others, and also relieving my own suffering and making my life as much worth living as I can.

For some families, specific hardships have shaped their attitudes. This was the case for Mike Abbot, a thirty-one-year-old husband who had suffered a serious back injury while on the job. As a result, he and his wife, Susan, were forced to rely on Worker's Compensation and Food Stamps.

> *Q:* Could you say how you think life has treated you in general?
> *Susan:* Good. Okay.
> *Mike:* Till the last year and a half. What did I do to deserve that? No! You get a little bitter, I do. (pause) You know, you worked all your life. Made a good home, good . . . (long pause), and everything, and then all of a sudden that happens. Something you had no control. I could see if you went out and blew it all. It

would be your own fault. Or, you know, somethin' like that. But somethin' you had no control over, you're bound to feel a little bitter about it. And it's been a lot of pain. I spent a lot of time in the hospital . . . Which isn't fun (pause) . . .

Q: Do you think you have a general attitude or philosophy about life, that you could summarize?

Mike: Keep on keepin' on. That's about it. It's the only thing you can do. You can't give up. You can't, you know, you can't change things. At least not in the position we're in. I could see if you were wholly okay you could change things. You could do somethin'.

Q: How do you think your attitude will change when you're able to work again?

Mike: I'm sure it'll change back to the way it was before. That may harp on that point, but you know, the money part has been the biggest shock to both of us.

Q: Right, well, that's been your standard of living.

Mike: Yeah, it changes your life! That's like if someone gave you a million dollars, you wouldn't live the same way you're livin' now. It's the same way if they take away thirty thousand dollars a year, you're not gonna live the same way you're livin' before. And it changes not only your lifestyle, but it changes everyone involved in your lifestyle. You know, your family.

A traumatic event also took its toll in the life of Joyce Mills, who was first mentioned in chapter 3. Her ex-husband was in prison for sexually assaulting the children. She was asked how life had treated her.

Hmm, okay, I guess (loud laughter). It could have been a lot better, I could have been born into the Rockefeller family or something (laughter). No, it's okay (laughter). I enjoyed it. The good parts were good. Now the parts that were hurtful (pause) should never of happened. I wish I could just rub out and start again. (Pause.) I've often wished that I didn't have the kids, only because of the mess that they found themselves in the middle of. But I love them dearly. I wouldn't trade them for the world. But I just wish that I could have prevented all of it, you know. A lot of the things that they have gone through, they should never in their entire life have been subjected to. But then again, you can't always tell what's gonna happen.

The belief that life is synonymous with struggle is perhaps best exemplified in Edith Mathews's passionate words about her life. Sixty-seven years old and diabetic, in chapter 4 Edith described her frustration about being unable to afford a proper diet. Her attitude toward life?

> But as far as the way life is today—you get up in the morning and you work all day long, and then at night you're tired, and you don't feel good. . . . And it seems like you just run circles. Everyday it's the same thing! Nothing, nothing better. All you got in your mind is bills. You get your check. You gotta pay your house payment. You gotta pay your gas and electric. You gotta pay your telephone bill. You gotta pay your boiler. The furnace is rusted out in this house so I have to get a new boiler and that costs a fortune. I have to pay forty-one dollars and forty-one cents every month for that. And then there's interest on it. And I've got insurance so that if somethin' happens to me it's automatically paid for. And then it's your insurance. I got some veteran's insurance, I pay that. And your groceries. And time you pay all of those bills there isn't anything left. If you wanna buy a piece of clothes there would be nothin' left. I got two pairs of shoes down at the Factory Outlet for five dollars. I was lucky (*slight laugh*) I got them (*laughs*). But uh . . . yeah, well I think it's just nothing very interesting. It's just the same old grind every day. It's kinda like a rat race. You go all day long and then at night you're tired, you go to bed, and then the next morning you get up, and you can start going again, working all day. And then there's nothin' coming in, only so much for the month. And it's mostly goin' out instead of comin' in.

Given the daily struggle just to keep going, living itself becomes an accomplishment. As one woman reflecting on her life remarked, "I guess it's not been terrible, I'm still here."

One Day at a Time

Families in poverty are forced to deal with the here and now; it is simply unrealistic for them to make long-range plans. This is reflected in the philosophy of Ruth Miller, a long-term welfare recipient, "I take one day at a time (*laugh*). One day at a time that's what I'm doing. 'Cause every time I make a plan, or doing something, you know, it always turns—always something a little different. One of the kids will get sick or somebody real close to me will get sick or something, something happens. So I said, from now on I just live one day at a time and see what happens."

This attitude was typical of many of the families interviewed. For example, Jennifer Smith lives in a small town with her twelve-year-old son: "Just . . . take each day at a time an' . . . Ya know, live day to day. That's all we do. Something comes up, take it just as it comes. That's all. There's gonna be problems. I know that (*laughs*)."

Janice Winslow, thirty-seven years old, separated, and the mother of three children, was asked about her philosophy toward life, "Lately it's been just live one day at a time. I seem to want to pile everything on top. And then I think well, wait a minute, just live one day at a time, and just work through one thing at a time. And just do it that way. Don't pile everything up on top of you, and worry about everything, that something could be worried about later on! Who knows, it may be ironed out by then."

For Alice Waters, a serious illness and operation led her to begin taking one day at a time. Although the doctors had given her only six months to live, she had somehow pulled through. There was strong conviction in her voice as she told me, "I thank God that I'm yet alive, because He could've took me on. I lost a good friend last year. Close friend. But He had mercy upon me, and He kept me here. So I just live one day at a time. I thank God for every day. And I live one day at a time. Our family were already a pretty close family before this happened, before I got sick, but my children are very close to me."

Fifty-five-year-old Joe Hall had been laid off work after

twenty years on the job. Throughout the interview, he stressed the importance and difficulty of finding work. The shock of being unemployed for an extended period of time had caused him to reevaluate his life.

> And then, I've always had a job . . . I always made pretty fair money (*sighs*). Well, I had twenty years with one company. So a person doesn't really think too much about it. This is your job. You go to work every day. You get paid and everything's pretty good. So for twenty years I didn't have too many kicks then, did I? Had it made and didn't know it, is what it amounted to. I figured after I got laid off, I'd find another job. But, rude awakening I got on that. If I was thirty years old there'd be no excuse at all (*small laugh*).

I asked him to describe his current state of mind. "Oh (*pause*), there's days I'd just like to can it. But then, you know you got other things goin' too. And I think living on a day-to-day basis. . . . Oh sure, you plan in the future, but how many of those plans ever come out? (*Laugh.*) When I was I young man I was gonna retire by the time I was forty-five. Yeah . . . did I ever (*laughs*). Things didn't work out the way I planned, but then again it coulda been a lot worse."

Finally, Chester Peterson had discovered two months prior to our interview that he had lung cancer. He had turned to Medicaid to help with the expenses. Was he depressed, hopeful, angry?

Chester: No, there's no sense in feeling depressed. I mean things happen, they happen; you can't do anything about it. And you just keep on goin' and get along as best as you can. You can't change anything, that's not possible (*laughs*).

Friend: His theory is one day at a time.

Chester: Right, that's all you can do. . . . I grew up with this idea that life is part of death. Everybody is gonna meet it some day, so why sit back here and worry about it. You can't twiddle your thumbs and say "Oh, I'm gonna die." Everybody knows that. You just go on and put it out of your mind. Do what you can. No sense in crying over it (*laughs*).

Keep Going and Believe in Yourself

A final belief shared by most welfare recipients is the importance of not giving in. Perseverance is viewed as essential: there is little left without it.

A haunting expression of this came from Mary Summers. A divorced parent in her early fifties, Mary was having difficulty finding employment in spite of extensive experience as a bookkeeper. She was asked about her current state of mind. After a long pause, she responded.

Mary: My own state of mind. . . . As long as you keep busy, and as long as you keep in contact with somebody and have something out there . . . a résumé, a phone call, or something . . . and you know that you have something going for you, you can retain your senses and your sanity. But I think if everything stopped, I don't know what would happen. Because there'd be . . . there'd be nothing to look forward to; there'd be just dead zone. It's just, it's a . . . it's a horrible thought. As long as you keep trying, and you keep something going for you, I think there's always . . . you keep your morale built up and your hopes high, and . . . (*pause*)

Q: So, in terms of being say, hopeful or depressed or angry, you'd put yourself more towards . . . ?

Mary: Well, I try to keep something going so I don't get to the depression stage and to the point where you just give up. Because you can't . . . you can't do that. You just gotta figure out some kind of a new angle so you don't.

Losing all hope is indeed a "horrible thought." To do so is virtually to die an early death. Carol Richardson elaborates: "We all have high hopes. Only ours haven't come, blossomed yet, more or less. But we're workin' on it. That's the main thing. Don't stop trying. Keep hangin' in there. Keep goin' at it. Well, I hope I can live up to what I'm saying (*laugh*). It's hard. Sometimes you just wanna crawl in a hole and give it all up and forget it. But you can't. I think about the rest around ya. No, you can' do that."

Part of not giving up is believing in oneself. Rather than taking a fatalistic view of the world, most welfare recipients feel that with time and effort they will improve their situations. Such views may seem incongruous from those who have experienced the numerous setbacks typical of poor households. Yet for these families, the spirit of optimism persists.

Janice Winslow lives in a neighborhood of rundown apartments and weather-beaten houses with a history of long-term poverty. She has been on welfare for five years. Nevertheless, her attitude toward life is "that you create your own life. I believe you create your own life situations and that you have control over your life. That you can and do have control over your life whether you acknowledge it or not, or whether you take that control."

The idea of believing in yourself to achieve success was voiced throughout the interview with Denise Turner. There was strong conviction in her voice as she said,

> And I always try to be positive in life. 'Cause I know it takes a positive mental attitude to be successful. So I said, "Well, hey, I may not have a lot of things, and I'm still on assistance, but I think I have a goal. I might not ever reach it, but at least I have a goal. Somewhere, something that I'm trying to accomplish." And I want to try to get as close to it as I can. And it's for that reason I'm positive . . . about my future, and my children. Their future is theirs.
>
> And that's another good thing about this country. . . . The avenues for success . . . are not limited to . . . just a few. I think the avenues for success are open up . . . to the majority of people in this country. Now, success to different people means different things. I don't mean to be a Howard Hughes . . . success. But I mean success in the respect that I'm able to stand on my own two feet and take care of my family. That's the kind of success that I think is open to me, and open to everybody in

this country. With a little bit of sacrifice, and a little bit of struggle. I think that everybody can accomplish that.

And so really, that's what myself and my family, that's what we're working towards. Being able to stand on our own feet. Being able to maybe even one day buy a house. Have our own home. And of course the children. No one is going to have everything they want. But some of the finer things in life so that they can be well-rounded children. They can be exposed to some cultural things. You know, 'cause it takes more to raising children than just sending them to school. And I would like to be able to have them be exposed to some culture. And then I can die and say that I had been a successful parent. And that's what we're trying, you know, to struggle towards.

When asked about a philosophy of life, the following responses were given in three separate interviews,

I basically . . . what I told you I wanted to instill in my kids. You're responsible for your behavior and what you do and what you get out of life. I mean (*emphatically*) you are directly responsible. You cannot depend on other people for everything. And, you can't depend on people to just give you things. It doesn't work that way. So that's just the way I think.

Even though you're on welfare, it's kinda what ya make it. Yourself. 'Cause if you want somethin' bad enough, you're gonna get it. That's how I look at it. 'Cause I've gotten a lot of things myself that I wanted. It might have taken me a *long time,* but I got it.

I . . . somewhat believe that you make your own . . . destiny. You make it yourself. If you're just gonna sit back an' let life go ahead, you're gonna miss out on a lot. Ya gotta make things happen yourself. At least for me.

Most recipients felt that while life may have treated them harshly, the only option available was to fight on and hope for a brighter future, believing that, with time and effort, particular circumstances might change for the better. Ultimately, the individual is seen as controlling his or her own destiny. Given the circumstances of poverty, taking one day at a time becomes a realistic coping strategy. It allows the individual to deal with daily problems, rather than becoming paralyzed in the face of the long-term task of economic upward mobility. Believing that one controls (to some extent) one's own destiny can also be seen as a coping mechanism. It implies that individuals can change their situations in the future. Whether that is true or not is beside the point; what is important are the hopes and beliefs. It is hope that often sustains those in the most difficult circumstances.

Hopes

As with beliefs, welfare recipients' hopes and dreams are molded—and sometimes destroyed—by the experience of living in poverty and on public assistance.

Getting One Step Ahead

The most common hope expressed by welfare recipients is getting out of debt, off welfare, and living a modest life—in short, getting one step ahead of the game, as Carol Richardson would say.

When asked what would be of help to her at the moment, a female head of household with two teenage daughters quickly replied, "Just to get outta debt. Be my biggest thing, my biggest concern. I never want to be rich. I never want to have a lot of money. I just want to be comfortable. I just want to be able to get up in the morning and think, 'Oh, I don't owe nobody anything.' It's the only thing I want."

Jennifer Smith is a thirty-three-year-old mother of one. At the time of our interview, she had been working on the assembly line at a plastics factory for the past four years. Although employed full-time, her income falls below the poverty line, qualifying her for Food Stamps and Medicaid. Her hopes for the future?

> I just hope things will be a lot better for us than how they are now. I know the economy is really bad. But, to a point. . . .
> See, they don't stop an' think of us as little people. Ya know,

we're considered . . . low-income people. They don't stop and think about the people tryin' to raise kids on their own. . . . I mean, he knows it [her employer]. But, they don't really care. I mean, that's your job. You do it. That's your pay. You get that. But I'm just hoping things will be a lot better in the years to come. I really couldn't predict what would happen or say what I would want to happen.

The desire for financial independence was expressed repeatedly by welfare recipients. As chapter 3 indicated, guilt and humiliation often accompany the need for welfare. Most recipients hope to sever their ties to the state.

An example was Marta Green. As she discussed in chapter 3, the dissolution of her marriage created serious financial problems, causing her to turn to public assistance. She talked about her hopes:

And the hope that I have is . . . (*sigh*) after I start workin', I'll pay the state back somehow. I keep track of everythin' I get from them. And I already know how much I received last year from them. And this year. And if my taxes are not enough, I put in something if I am able to, to the Red Cross, Salvation Army. And this is the hope that I have. To know that I do not owe anythin'. That if ever someone ask me, "Did you ever receive welfare?" I say, "Yes. But I paid back. It was a loan that I got." That's my hope, pretty much.

Dawn Plotsky, a nineteen-year-old single woman was asked about her hopes for the future.

(*Softly.*) For my future? (*Pause, then more loudly.*) Hopin' I can get to a point where I can . . . stand on my own two feet, an' . . . have a secure job, an' a nice place to live, an' say, "Yeah, I'm staying here." Maybe not the rest of my life, but at least for the next five, ten years, ya know. . . .

Where I can say I'm not . . . depending on everyone around me to . . . make it. I want to be more independent, on my own. Do it myself. Not that everybody can. You need a little help here and there, but . . . not as much as I'm gettin'. I can't . . . stand it. I hate to ask people for help anymore. I feel like I'm always asking.

The hope for financial independence pertains not only to welfare but to all of life. This is expressed by Denise Turner.

I think about trying to accomplish something. I'm getting older. My children are getting older. And I would like to have some kind of, maybe, Social Security . . . ready for me when I retire. I'm thinking about things like that. You know, because, hey, I'm not getting anything . . . Social Security-wise, being on assistance. And when I get older, I hope that my older years can be my better years. It's what my aunt always says. You try to live so that your older years are your better years.

See, when you're young, and I might be considered young, I can have assistance. I can have these certain things. But when I get older I wanna have something there for me without having to depend upon . . . the state. 'Cause I know they do old people terrible. They get it worse off than younger people on assistance. I mean, they be put into homes. They be mistreated. And if they don't have enough money, they get put out of homes. And it's really terrifying. That's what I really look at. You know, what's going to happen to me in thirty years?

That's why I'm out here workin'. Even if it's a little, little job. Even if it's paying minimum wage. Because then when I get to be sixty-five years old, I don't want to be mistreated. You know, when you're not as attractive. When your hearing goes. And this thing and that thing goes. And maybe you can't take care, you get incontinent. You can't take care of yourself. You'll be shuffled around from one senior's home to the next. I want to have something that I can put away, that I have saved . . . some Social Security put in so that I don't have to be mistreated. And that I don't have to be lookin' for my children to take care of me. 'Cause children may or may not take care of you. And I don't want to have to depend upon my children. My parents didn't depend upon me to take care of them. And I don't want to depend upon my children to take care of me.

It is interesting to contrast Denise's comments with those of Brenda Jackson, a seventy-seven-year-old woman who lives in a nursing home. Her desire for independence was strong despite her failing health. Brenda had been getting Medicaid but decided against it.

Q: Now, could you tell me, do you know what kinds of welfare assistance you're receiving now? Are you receiving medical assistance?

Brenda: No.

Q: No?

Brenda: (*Laughter.*) They want to know too much of my business and I told 'em forget it.

Q: I see. Okay.

Brenda: I don't . . . get nuthin' but Social Security. That's all I get. But these other organizations, I told 'em, I said no. We won't, I said. What if you want to know this and want to know that, you won't quit (*laughter*). And I said, don't come around here anymore. Because after all, they were goin' too deep in my affairs, and so I just told 'em forget about it, an' don't come back till I . . . I don't get no help from no organizations.

Nearly all welfare recipients hope to lead more comfortable lives in the future. Lives in which poverty no longer exists, in which financial independence is reestablished. As Jennifer Smith put it, "I'd like to . . . live comfortable. Not have to worry about so many things. (*long pause*) I'd like better things for him [her son]. I'd like to give him things that I didn't have when I was growin' up." I asked if there was anything else. "Well, better peace of mind. Better friends. Better surroundings."

Holding on to Dreams

Beyond the hope for economic independence, recipients are likely to hang on to special dreams. Though their chances of realization may be slim, these dreams are cherished, for they provide a temporary respite from the world of poverty and struggle. For some, dreams may be the only means of escape. Here are some of those dreams—from young and old.

We begin with twenty-two-year old Eddie Williams. A warehouse worker, Eddie had set his sights on something more than an ordinary nine-to-five job: he dreamed of making it big in the music industry, specifically, mixing and spinning records. His speech was filled with the jargon of the disc jockey. He was asked about his plans for the future.

> I'm gonna be doin' a lot of things when I get up there [referring to Chicago]. This is my first plan right now is to take over WQGN and Shakers. An' I'm doin' that right now. Every Saturday night you hear, "Hi, my name is Kid Ross, and here's another hot mix that (*sounding like a dj*) I jacked up exclusively on your ninety-one point nine radio, WQGN. So move out of the way on to Chicago. And (*in an exaggerated dj voice*) jack up the hall! Yeah, buddy, ain't I right." . . . And I wanna make my own records. As soon as I get this last equipment to go with my pieces, I'm gonna be makin' my own records like everybody else down in Chicago. Sixteen-year-olds makin' their own records.

It was strictly the big time and big money that Eddie was after. His dreams were of "jacking up" another tune on the Chicago airwaves; everything else paled in comparison.

Jim Duncan was living with his girlfriend in a rundown trailer court south of a busy overpass. The trailers were old, small, and very close together. An unpaved road ran through the court. Jim, twenty-three, had been very physically active until a car crash left him with a left leg so mangled that it had to be amputated and a severely damaged right leg and foot. After sixteen operations, the doctors would no longer perform surgery. Yet there was no self-pity in Jim's voice as we spoke. He was working hard at physical therapy and hoped to be able to walk with an artificial leg in the near future. His wheelchair stood in the corner of the room as he talked about his ambitions and dreams.

> That's another ambition. I always wanted to race motorcycles. I could've if I woulda had sponsors or more money. 'Cause I was good. I mean, I bought my first motorcycle an' . . . I was racin' with these guys from the motorcycle shops an' stuff. An' here I had a regular motorcycle, just bought from the show-

room floor an' theirs is all . . . built up an' modified an' everything like that. I drove motorcycles, like I said, all my life. I
even drove one like this an' I couldn't shift. Eleven hundred yet.
One of my friends has got one. An' he got on the back an' held
me up an' I climbed on the seat an' he put up the kickstand an'
put it in gear for me an' . . . took off. We went for a ride
around the trailer court an' stuff (*small laugh*). That was fun.
That kinda got me motivated where I could still do it.

For thirty-year-old Clarissa Wilson, a mother of four, employment had been one long series of dead-end jobs—working
in nursing homes, cleaning apartments, unpacking shoes in a
Sears warehouse, and the like. Her dream was to be a secretary
working downtown.

> Hopefully, I will have a better job and not on welfare. I always
> wanted to live glamorous (*laugh*) an' be a secretary until . . . I
> always dream about that. I never forget. I keep it in my mind.
> Or nurses' aide or secretary. Although sometime I be uptown
> on Third Street and I see the business women, you know,
> passin' by with their briefcase or . . . lookin' all nice an' glam-
> orous. Sometimes I say I wish I was a businessman.

She had spoken with obvious pride of wearing a uniform in
one of her previous jobs. It gave her respectability, she said.
Her dream was to find that respectability.

The American dream of owning a home was held by many
welfare recipients. Thirty-three-year-old Jennifer Smith was
one such recipient: "I would love to have my own home. I
really would. Even if I didn't get married, I'd still love to have
my own home. That is one dream I would like to fill. Buy
some land, an' just, have my house built. Maybe when I get
old an' gray I might just do that (*laughs*). But that would be
nice."

As fifty-five-year-old Joe Hall had earlier explained, being
laid off after twenty years on the job was quite a shock. Although fading, his dreams centered on getting his job back and
being able to own a cabin up north. Inside his mobile home, he
was asked to look into the future.

Joe: (*Very quietly.*) I don't know. Day-to-day basis right now (*long pause*). My big future outlook in life was when I retired, why I was gonna live in a nice little cabin up north on a lake. But it's still in my dreams. Maybe it'll happen, maybe it won't.

 Q: Are there any particular hopes that you do have for your future?

Joe: I wanna get outta the rut I'm in (*laugh*). Aw, I'm sure it's gonna work out eventually (*pause*). Back in my head I guess I'm thinkin' that Dairy Products will hire me back eventually. If they get into the special products an' stuff then I know I'd probably get back. But it might not be until next summer. And I gotta have somethin' before that. In fact I'm four months past when I'd thought I'd have a job. (*Very, very long pause.*) Maybe I'll hit that one today. You never know.

Finally, John Renborn spoke of his seventy-four years in Wisconsin. A Native American, he had lived through hardship. His wife had died of alcoholism, while a daughter was severely injured in an automobile accident. He had had a heart attack, tuberculosis, was nearly blind in one eye, and had difficulty moving. As we chatted across the kitchen table, I felt in him a strong sense of dignity in spite of his problems. His wish was to return to an earlier day, perhaps as a young man working in northern Wisconsin. Going back to work in the cranberry bogs was John's dream. His voice was filled with hope as he spoke,

John: Well, if I'm still able to get around, like I do now, I'm gonna go earn a few dollars from the cranberry company again. There should be a little pay, a little more than what they used to give many years ago. I guess they pay a little over three dollars an hour for just common labor.

 Q: Do you have any other hopes for the future?

John: That's the only hopes I have (*laughs*).

There were other dreams as well: owning a business, forming a rock group, moving closer to relatives, and so on. For each recipient, the dream was different. The hope, however, was the same: perhaps one day, the dream would become reality.

Little Left to Hope For

Although hopes and dreams existed for most, several recipients reported that they had little left to hope for. They had reached what Mary Summers had described earlier as "dead zone"—an area where dreams no longer exist, where burdens are all that remain.

This was the case for thirty-two-year-old Judy Griffin. She had severely injured her back while working in a warehouse. The injury dramatically changed her life.

> Well yeah, 'cause it affects a lot of things. 'Cause I don't know if I'm ever gonna be able to work. I couldn't even get a desk job right now because I can't sit for a long period of time. Stand, anything. And so it's affecting everything. Everything. And there's just a lotta things that I like to do that I can't do anymore. And when my daughter leaves home, what am I gonna do then! You know! I can't work. There's no help then. I'll probably be a bag lady. (*Frustration.*) What else is there? Nothing. (*Pause.*) So, it's a lot to think about.

Her frustration, anger, and despair built during the interview. They were released near the end of our talk.

Q: Is disability with SSI going to be an option for you?

Judy: No. Because if I've other income I'm not eligible for SSI. I applied for Social Security. An' because of my age I'm not disabled (*anger*). Nice, huh! I got three doctors saying (*hits table with hand*) that I cannot work! (*Emphatically.*) I got a letter back from Social Security. (*In tears.*) Well I should certainly be able to go back and do warehouse work [referring to the letter]. (*Long pause.*) I'll tell ya sumpin'. My mother had cancer for I don't know how many years. She was not able to work. I mean she had lung cancer. She had brain cancer. She had brain surgery. She went through hell to get SSI or Social Security. You know when she got it? About two months before she died (*in tears*). That's sad.

Finally, asked about her hopes for the future, she replied, "I don't know if I even have any. (*Depressed.*) I mean what's to hope for. You know I can't see where there is anything to hope for. (*Pause.*) Other than not being out on the street an' endin' up a bag lady after my daughter leaves. I'm hopin' maybe I'll even have one room! (*Tearfully.*) Who knows? (*Long pause.*) There's not really a whole lot ta hope for."

Mary Zimmerman was living in an elderly housing complex when I talked with her. It was obvious that she had led a hard life. Her only child was born when she was thirty-six, and her husband, who drank heavily, left four years later. She was forced to support her son by working several jobs. An injury at age sixty-two forced an early retirement. She was asked about her hopes for the future.

> I don't know. I guess I don't have any hopes. There isn't much to hope for. . . . There isn't much else to . . . well, what is there anymore? What kind of hope would there be? Ya know. (*Pause.*) Guess you hope it won't be any worse, no sickness, no nothing like that. I always worry about (sigh) having sickness, and being confined. That's not good either to think about. Especially when you're alone. . . . Well, you just have yourself. If you have family that's near you, it's different. But, like I say, ya just have to live from day to day. That's all.

For both women, one young and one old, hopes were hard to come by. The day-in and day-out struggles had finally left them with too many burdens and little else. Their dreams had long since been abandoned. While they are not typical of most welfare recipients, nevertheless such cases do exist. They show us what is left when all hope is gone: futility and despair.

Eternal Faith

Amid the struggles and adversity, some recipients expressed one ultimate hope and belief: a belief in a stronger power and a faith that their struggles will someday end.

For Alice Waters, that belief and hope was in God. The strength of her conviction was apparent in the following discussion.

Alice: Well, I'm hopeful. I'm not the type of person that can stay really depressed a long time. I can get depressed one minute and be okay the next minute, because I know God. I put all my hope, and confidence and trust, I put everything in the hands of God. And I know the Lord, and I know Him in the pardon of my sin right now. I know what He done for others, He can do it for me. And I know He's not gonna let anything happen to me. I know that God is gonna make a way. He made a way this far for me. He's gonna make a way out of no way. He's been good to me. And like I say, I know the Lord. He has did great things for me. When I was at the point of death, I know what He done for me. I depend upon the Lord. I just know that there is a God, and I know He's gonna take care of me. And I know someway, somehow I'm gonna come out! Someway, somehow. I might be depressed this minute, or down and out that minute, but someway, somehow God is gonna bring me out.

Q: So you basically are hopeful, that things eventually will work out?

Alice: (*Voice over.*) I had a hopeful, yeah I just—I just believe, you know, I tell my children . . . don't nothin' last. I used to tell 'em about the weather. I said it don't lasts forever. You know, it's gonna get better. (*Laughter.*)

Q: Right, it can't always storm. (*Laughter.*)

Alice: It can't always storm like that. You know, I told 'em, I said when I was comin' up, my mother used to say the storm of life is raging. And I said, it'll be better after awhile, the sun gonna shine! So that's the way I feel. I got turned down today on a house, but . . . You know, I feel like tomorrow's a brighter day ahead! I'm gonna tell you somethin', if it wasn't for me knowin' the Lord, I probably would just break down and cry all the time,

> an' everything, but . . . He's been so good to me. . . .
> Like I said, when I really, really, needed Him, He's al-
> ways there. He say I may not come when you want me,
> but I'll be right on time. And He's been right there, and
> I need the Lord, and He know I needs Him. And I'm
> not a person to sit up and bother God all the time—
> "Oh, Lord, I need you, oh, Lord"—I'm not that type
> of person. I pray, I say my prayers, and I talk to the
> Lord. Sometime I be in this house by myself, I say "Lord,
> I thank you just for this day." And, I'll go ahead about
> my business. He hasn't forgotten me. You know, He
> hasn't forgotten me.

Cindy Franklin spoke earlier in this chapter about her struggles. She perceived suffering as inevitable. Her hope and faith
lay in a world beyond.

> I guess I don't believe that this life is all there is. I believe that
> it's all in a larger context that we comprehend in part, but not
> entirely. And so I have a real hope that eventually after I die,
> that I will have a life where there isn't any sorrow, where there
> isn't any corruption. And there isn't mental corruption or phys-
> ical corruption. And I really look forward to that. And that
> hope really helps me to cope with the difficulties I have to deal
> with now.

The connection between suffering and hope is quite clear. As
Cindy states, her hope for a better world allows her to cope
with her current situation. These hopes are of obvious importance to welfare recipients, for they are sustaining in times of
trouble.

For Susan Davis, faith lay in receiving and giving support to
others. Although burdened with a seizure condition that required attendants twenty-four hours a day, she was determined
to contribute to the world. By sharing and feeling the needs of
her fellow human beings, she was able to rise above personal
despair. Susan was asked to describe her philosophy of life.

> (*Pause.*) I guess a probable, basic philosophy, is that as soon as
> you give up your self-will to something that's a little bigger,

then things are gonna straighten themselves out in terms of all of your life. Things all fall into place. It's sorta like this humongous puzzle. When you get the right puzzle piece in, it seems like everything else fits pretty rapidly. Or you have a lot more insight to that happening. And, when you first asked that, my first thing off the top of my head was to give you my weird sense of humor, "Life's a bitch, and then you die." (*Q and Susan laugh.*) And thought, well, no—that isn't really what I'm feeling now, because I really think that I've a lot more optimism about living in general. That there's a lot to give after you get your head in gear. It's taken me a long time to get my head in gear, unfortunately. I don't look with great pride on the fact that it's taken me as long as it has to begin to have that happen. I think as soon as you can feel, you can live.

The interview concluded with the following discussion.

Susan: But, I also believe in candle power for people. I don't know if you know about that American Indian tradition?

Q: No, I don't.

Susan: Which is that . . . white is for good energy. And when people had exams, I'll tell ya this—we used a torch power here. We had the torches goin'. Red is strength and courage. I have a green one over here, which is for healing. Blue is for tranquility. Yellow's for intelligence, and orange is for joy. And . . . I have the good energy one goin', I'll tell ya. One of my counselors has been involved in this whole yucky trial that's going on in Ridgeton. Not easy. Very, very difficult and trying. So, a lot of candle power. I have another friend who just became a lawyer, part of my support system—she's hoping to get a call-back on a job. So all the torch power's goin' into it, see. (*Susan and Q laugh.*) But those are the sort of things that happen when you develop a support system. You can think good thoughts for other people, and they for you. And . . . that's the way it works out. I think the more you're thinkin' of 'em, you care. And I tend to care about people, I think, pretty much. I try anyhow. (*Laughing.*) I feel for you because you're always having to say "yes, yes, yes." (*Q laughs.*) Don't you get tired at the end of the day just sayin' "yes"? Wouldn't you like to get in a dialogue half the time?

Q: Yes, I would.

Susan: (*Voice over, imitating Q, both Q and she laughing heartily.*) Yes, you can turn off the tape.

Q: Right. Yes, I think we're finished now. (*Still laughing—tape ends.*)

Characteristically, she insisted on giving us half a loaf of freshly baked banana bread to take home.

7 WORKING

> I feel better about myself when I'm working than when I'm not. Even if I had a job and every penny went to living from pay day to pay day, it doesn't bother me because I feel like a better person because I am going to work.
> — *Thirty-year-old never-married mother of two*

Welfare recipients, by definition, are not economically self-sufficient. While their circumstances differ across household type (as shown in chapter 3), recipients are either not employed or underemployed. Clearly, getting off welfare and restoring economic self-sufficiency are linked to locating and landing a job that pays a reasonable wage. Various aspects of this process are examined in the pages that follow.

Attitudes Toward Work

As reviewed in chapter 2, many policymakers believe that welfare recipients lack positive attitudes, particularly toward work (see, e.g., Gilder 1981). The attitudes expressed by the recipients I interviewed contrast sharply with this viewpoint. Welfare recipients repeatedly emphasized their desires to work, often regardless of the working conditions. As recounted in chapter 6, Judy Griffin had experienced a serious back injury while loading and unloading heavy goods in a warehouse. Her attitudes were typical: "Well, I dislike NOT being able to work at all. I mean, I'm used to doing work (*pounds hand on table*). Sure, I don't like every day I go to work. But I don't like sitting home every day. The first week is just wonderful, but after that, you know, you can have it. No, I'm not used to sittin.' That's hard." Variations on these sentiments were often expressed; the general attitudes toward work were strong and positive.

There are several reasons for such attitudes. First, working is seen as an important source of personal fulfillment. For example, Joyce Mills was asked about how she felt toward working.

> I like it. Now, there are times where I wish I could just stay home and not work. But yet, the time after I stopped working at the canning company, the time before I started working for Pioneer Insurance, I was really going buggy in the house. I wanted to do something. I was feeling, "Let me out of here." Because the only people that I was associating with, really, were my kids. And they're fine for awhile but after that you just want to go "Naaaaaaaa!" So when I got this job, I was really excited about it. And I still enjoy going to work.

Joyce had been receiving AFDC, Medicaid, and Food Stamps for a number of years. She was asked what had been her motivation for getting a job.

> I just needed to get out. I felt like I was on a rotten long vacation. And I was just getting antsy. The walls were closing in on me. My landlady said that she knew a lady who just sat home and did nothing but collect welfare checks. And God, she was able to afford just about anything you could think of. And she told me, "Don't work, or you'll jeopardize your check, you won't get that much." And you know I thought, "Gee, that sounds good, all this money and not work for it, you know." But yet I can't do that. After awhile I sort of feel like I've gotta do something. And to be able to work with a computer, now that's what I wanted to do before. And then they called me up and said that I had the job if I wanted it. That was great.

Similar were the attitudes of Chester Peterson. Chester, who was sixty-eight at the time of the interview, had been recently diagnosed with lung cancer, which forced him to leave his part-time job driving a cab. As he put it, "Well you gotta work. If you don't, you'd go out of your gourd. You gotta work. You can't just sit around and do nothing. That's the biggest problem [I have] right now, is sittin' around doing nothing."

Recipients also want to work because they believe working is simply part of what mainstream America is about and therefore idleness (or not working) is wrong. As Fred Block notes, the common assumption that, when everything else is equal, people will generally choose leisure over work, "vastly exaggerates the seductiveness of idleness; both historically and currently, work has a powerful attractiveness that is independent of any monetary reward. This attractiveness is rooted in the social meaning and social rewards that derive from participation in the world of work" (1987:129). This feeling was often expressed by interviewees. As Denise Turner said,

> I don't think there are too many people that dislike working, because it's like being an adult. If a person dislikes working, he's not a person that wants to be an adult. Because you're working. You're making money. It's your money. You're putting in your time, your skills. You have an opportunity for advancement. You know, if you want to live in this system, I don't see how anybody could say they don't like working. (*Pause.*) Because I like being an adult.

Alice Waters, whose remarks describing her faith in God were reported in the previous chapter, talked about her attitude toward work:

> I believe in a person going to work. I believe if you are physically and mentally able, you're able-bodied, you got the activity of your limbs, I believe that you should get out there and want to do something for yourself. My husband worked with emphysema. And I know if my husband could work with emphysema and go into a dusty, dirty mill for thirty-one years . . . I know if he could do it, the next one could do it too.

Related to this, and explored in greater detail in the next chapter, is the fact that recipients simply do not enjoy living on welfare. Typical are the sentiments of Wendy Nicholson, who had recently gotten off of AFDC: "I don't like just sitting around not having anything to do. And I like having my own money, not like when somebody's sending it to me so that I gotta live on a fixed income. You can only buy certain things, and go certain places, at certain times of the month. I like to go out, and I like to do things. I like to buy clothes, and I like nice stuff. And you know, AFDC just won't get it. So I prefer to work."

All in all—and contrary to the conventional stereotype—the overwhelming consensus among recipients was that working in the labor force constitutes an important and essential aspect of being an adult (for similar findings, see Goodwin 1972, 1983, and Lewis and Schneider 1985).

Work History

Virtually every welfare recipient interviewed in this study had a background of employed work. For some (e.g., recently divorced women with children), that history was limited; for others (e.g., married husbands), it was quite extensive. Yet in practically every case, recipients had had various experiences in the labor force, usually in a series of low-wage jobs, often in several different occupations that required either semi-skilled or unskilled labor and carried little status. As detailed in chapter 5, recipients' families often are unable to provide the opportunities and resources that make possible the acquisition of extensive human capital. The pattern of early work often adds to the constraints on further education and training.

The previous chapter introduced Eddie Williams, a young single male with dreams of going to Chicago and making it big in the music industry. His work history was in sharp contrast with those dreams. At the time of the interview, Eddie was working in a warehouse.

Eddie: I unload all the trailers and then load 'em up. I work out in the shipping area of the dock.

   Q: What kinds of jobs have you had before this one?

Eddie: I worked at the Tivoli theater as an usher for about six months. I worked at the car wash. I worked at East

Side Medicine Fairs selling cotton candy. I think I've done everything.

Q: How old were you when you had your first job?

Eddie: Thirteen

Q: What was that?

Eddie: I was working at International House of Pancakes. I was bussin' dishes.

Ruth Miller, whose strong views on the importance of education were detailed in chapter 5, talked about her work experience: "I worked at nursing homes. I worked at restaurants. Let's see, what else did I do? I worked at factories. I used to work at Spiegel. Then I worked at three or four different nursing homes. When I got pregnant with Stephanie, I was working at a nursing home. And I worked there for about two and half years. It takes a whole lot at nursing homes, dealing with them. I don't think I would want to do that again." Perhaps one reason for her insistence upon her children's education is related to the kinds of work she has done in the past.

I asked seventy-one-year-old Bill Schneider to recall the types of jobs he had held during his working years. At the time of our interview, Bill was living well below the poverty line and suffering from a number of medical problems. The work he had done had not allowed him to save much in the way of bank accounts or pensions. He began working on his father's farm.

I wanted to go to high school but my dad wouldn't let me because he had to have me home for the work. I wish I went to high school. I'd probably been sitting on top of the world today 'cause I liked school. If I'd a went to high school I'd a probably gotten a good job. Had some education anyway. (*Pause.*) But at that time, well it was hard times, you know, nineteen thirty-two, thirty-three. Hard to come by at that time.

I helped on the farm 'till I got married and that was in nineteen thirty-six. Then I worked at Smith creamery. It was a small creamery out in the country. Took in milk and they made butter and stuff like that. I worked there for four or five years I guess. Then I went to work in a grocery store. And I worked there for ten or twelve years. I clerked. . . . After I left there I think I went trucking. I worked for a fellow in Popular Bluff.

Had a bunch of trucks. I worked for him for, oh God (*pause*), quite a few years. Then when I left him I went driving Grey-hound. I drove Greyhound for two years. I wish I was still there. I just loved it. But my wife wouldn't let me stay there. Too much traveling. Was gone away from home too much. One time I was gone five weeks before I got home. . . . In a way I wish I woulda stayed there and got a pension. Christ . . .

I asked Bill about the last job he had held. He replied, "Driving cab in Ridgeton. But I had to quit that on account of my eyes goin' bad on me. And I had the cataract operation. (*Pause.*) Then I broke my hip after that. I was there many years. Twelve, thirteen years I guess."

There are, of course, exceptions to the pattern. For example, in chapter 6 Joe Hall described how hard it was for him to adjust to being laid off after working with the same company for twenty years (as a result of a decline in the farming indus-try, his job as electrical assembler was one of 430 eliminated out of a total of 500). Likewise, the work history of Susan Davis does not fit the above patterns. Prior to her epileptic seizures, Susan had worked as a teacher in New York City, as well as on a research project at New York University. Several other exceptions could be cited, but for the most part the pattern of working at a series of semiskilled or unskilled jobs was the norm.

Percentage Employed

Some recipients have a history of mixing work with welfare for most of the time they are on public assistance. The remain-der of the welfare population either does not work while on public assistance or does so only sporadically.[1] Table 7.1 pre-sents the percentages of people under age sixty-five who were employed while receiving public assistance. The percentages are categorized according to household type, and the analysis excludes all recipients listed as incapacitated or pregnant.

The top panel of the table shows the overall likelihood of employment at each of the seven longitudinal sampling points. During the first month, 28 percent of female heads, 37 percent of married males, and 28 percent of single heads were employed. These percentages remained approximately the same at the six- and twelve-month sampling points but declined at the eighteenth month. This corresponds to the OBRA changes discussed earlier that affected eligibility criteria and work incentives.

The second panel of the table shows the proportion of the employed who had been working six months prior to the sampling point. By far the majority of those who were working and on welfare had also been working six months earlier. For all three groups, approximately three out of four employed welfare recipients at any point in time were employed a half year earlier.

The bottom panel of the table reports the first observed spell of employment. Once employment occurred, cases were eliminated from the analysis. It is clear that the longer a recipient is on welfare and not working, the lower the probability of employment occurring. For example, 28.2 percent of female heads were employed during the first month. But by the sixth month, only 7.9 percent of those who had not worked during the first month were employed.

The table also reports the probability of working at least once during the seven sampling points in the columns labeled "Cumulative employment." Approximately 48 percent of female heads had worked during one or more of the seven months, while the corresponding figure for married males is 65 percent and 51 percent for single heads. Thus, roughly one out of two female and single heads of households on welfare was employed during at least one of the seven sampling points throughout the three years that recipients were followed. For married males, two out of three had been employed at least once during this period.

Overall, between one-quarter and one-third of welfare recipients are employed at any point in time. The percentages vary depending on the structure of the household. Married men are most likely to be working, followed by singles and then female heads.

TABLE 7.1
Employment Percentages by Household Type

Month	Female Heads		Married Males		Single Heads		Total	
	Employment	Cumulative Employment	Employment	Cumulative Employment	Employment	Cumulative Employment	Employment	Cumulative Employment
	Overall Employment							
0	28.2	—	36.9	—	27.5	—	30.3	—
6	27.9	—	36.5	—	29.1	—	30.0	—
12	27.5	—	43.0	—	28.4	—	31.0	—
18	20.1	—	35.5	—	19.1	—	22.8	—
24	18.0	—	32.8	—	20.0	—	20.6	—
30	15.9	—	26.0	—	22.7	—	17.8	—
36	13.1	—	36.0	—	15.8	—	16.7	—
	Percentage of Employed Who Were Employed Six Months Earlier							
0	—	—	—	—	—	—	—	—
6	79.3	—	75.8	—	67.4	—	77.1	—
12	72.9	—	77.1	—	76.2	—	74.4	—
18	75.8	—	80.0	—	75.0	—	77.3	—
24	70.9	—	77.5	—	66.7	—	72.5	—
30	75.0	—	88.9	—	60.0	—	77.6	—
36	74.2	—	65.6	—	100.0	—	72.2	—
	First Observed Spell of Employment							
0	28.2	28.2	36.9	36.9	27.5	27.5	30.3	30.3
6	7.9	33.9	14.7	46.2	13.1	37.0	9.9	37.2
12	8.0	39.2	12.0	52.6	9.1	42.7	8.8	42.7
18	4.8	42.2	9.0	56.9	4.0	45.0	5.3	45.8
24	4.3	44.7	8.5	60.5	5.3	47.9	4.8	48.4
30	3.3	46.5	2.6	61.5	6.7	51.4	3.4	50.1
36	2.2	47.7	9.1	65.0	0.0	51.4	2.7	51.5

Working Conditions

What kinds of jobs do welfare recipients find and what are their overall work environments like? In general, recipients work at jobs similar to those they held in the past—positions requiring semi-skilled or unskilled labor, paying low wages, lacking benefits, and usually part-time. The jobs held by those interviewed typically paid four to five dollars an hour and included janitorial work, cooking for a fraternity house, cocktail waitressing, unloading trucks at a warehouse, working as an attendant to an elderly couple, working in a factory, working as a cosmetologist, doing clerical work, housekeeping, working as a cashier, working for a relative's answering service, laying bricks, and laboring on a farm. In addition, recipients occasionally reported working at small, often one-time jobs such as doing a friend's laundry, baby-sitting, repairing a relative's car, and so on. This income was generally not reported.[2] Kelly McGrath explains: "There's people that baby-sit and get paid cash and don't report it. And they probably don't report that their family members are helping 'em. They wouldn't say, 'Yeah my mom gave me a hundred dollars last month.' I mean they just wouldn't do that because it's hard enough to survive on the aid. When you get extra, you don't want 'em to take it away from you. And that's what they do."

The work that recipients performed was often physically demanding. For example, Mike Thomas builds pallets used in trucking. It is piecework, and although Mike is in good shape physically, the work is nevertheless extremely demanding: "It's real physical. I really don't mind that too much. But it's just gettin' up and going to it all the time, you know. It's like I have to turn on the burners from seven thirty to four thirty everyday. So it takes a lot outta me. But I'm getting used to it. I try and just pace myself through it the best I can."

Recipients could expect little in the way of benefits. In most cases, there were none. For example, Jack Collins runs a warehouse for a commercial plumbing contractor. At the time of our interview, he and his wife Tammy were receiving ninety-six dollars in Food Stamps and had been receiving small amounts of public assistance on and off for fifteen years. Although the job pays more than most (eight dollars an hour), the benefits were lacking,

Jack: I've had one [vacation] week in five years, but I'm gettin' one this year. I'm lookin' forward to it.

Q: Do you have any sick days? Or is that unpaid like the holidays?

Jack: Oh no, we don't never. No sick days. We do get, like if there's a funeral, we'll get paid for the day to go to the funeral. There's no sick day. There's no holiday pay. No time and a half. No overtime.

Because so many welfare recipients lack human capital and experience, they are in a poor position to compete for decent jobs. Take the case of Ellen Harris, a forty-three-year-old mother of seven. At the time of our interview, she had recently reunited with her husband after a five-year separation. Ellen had had her first child at age seventeen (causing her to drop out of high school) and was married by age eighteen. Her history of employed work began when she and her husband separated. It included working as a maid, as a janitor, and in a laundry. When we spoke, she was taking care of an elderly couple, cooking, cleaning, grocery shopping, and attending to their overall needs. She worked approximately twenty hours a week, at four-fifty an hour, with no benefits. I asked her if not graduating from high school had been a problem in finding work. Her response: "I think if I was looking for a good job it would be. But for the type of work that I do, I don't think so. But I know if I was out to get a secretarial job, or anything like that, I think it would be a big problem. Because I know the first thing they look for is your high school." Limited in terms of what she is competitive for, Ellen's options are relatively few. She is likely to keep working at the types of jobs she has done in the past, characterized by low pay and no benefits.

Barriers to Working

Only one-quarter to one-third of welfare recipients work, and they generally work only part-time. Both of these facts cause considerable anger among the general public. True, anyone working full-time cannot receive much in the way of public assistance, so it is not surprising that many on welfare work less than forty hours a week. Still, the question remains, why do not more welfare recipients find full-time work and get off welfare altogether? The reasons are several.

First, the majority of welfare recipients (under age sixty-five) are either working or actively looking for work. As shown in table 7.1, approximately 30 percent of those receiving public assistance are employed. Many of these people would prefer full-time jobs but have been unable to find them. Other recipients are regularly looking for work or are receiving some kind of job training. Within the in-depth interview sample, 71 percent of households whose members were under age sixty-five were characterized by the head or spouse employed or actively looking or preparing for work. Such activity involves participating in job training programs, responding to want ads, attending technical college, or pursuing various other job-related activities (detailed below). Indeed, one of the requirements for continued eligibility in most public assistance programs is that able-bodied adults must actively look for work. But, like Ellen Harris, many recipients are lacking in human capital and consequently face stiff competition in the job market. As a result, it can often take a long time to locate permanent employment.

For the remaining one-quarter of recipients who are neither employed nor looking for work, what barriers are preventing employment? For some, physical injuries and other health problems are important factors. Previous chapters related the circumstances of Judy Griffin and Mike Abbot, who had both suffered severe back injuries while on the job. Susan Davis's epileptic seizures require her to have twenty-four-hour care. Jim Duncan lost one leg and permanently crippled the other in an automobile accident. Such physical problems make employment unlikely.

For others, particularly female heads of household with young children, the lack of affordable child care coupled with concerns regarding their children's upbringing, can present a major barrier to employed work. The dilemma is whether to pay a significant sum for child care in order to work at a low-paying job, lacking in benefits, or to stay at home with one's children and receive public assistance. Janice Winslow elaborates, "I don't think of myself as being unfortunate for being on AFDC. My choice was I could send the kids to day care, the babies, and go work and make about what I'm making now, if I made that much, once you pay for day care for three kids or two. That's just not much of a choice to make."

A related obstacle to working is that welfare benefits are often reduced by a dollar for every dollar a recipient earns. This is in effect a 100 percent tax rate.

For Denise Turner, choices are further limited by discrimination. Employed part-time, she has been looking for full-time work in the area of journalism where her training lies.

> This is an extremely racist city. And the racism is very subtle. It's very difficult for an intelligent black person to find anything of substance to do in this city. And that's one of my major problems that I'm encountering now.
>
> I have a job now which is paying minimum wage. Not using any of my skills. I'm working at a toy store. You know, I can do plenty of that. I can do plenty of waiting tables. And I can be at McDonald's and Burger King. But that is not what I want to do! And it's not gonna pay me to raise four children. To take anything that's gonna pay minimum wage, it's just not gonna work out. And I have discussed this with my case workers. And they say, "Hey, it's just not gonna pay you. It's not gonna work out for you." To get a job paying minimum wage is not gonna work out. And so getting a job is difficult. I don't even think there are any jobs here.

Raising the issue of what constitutes "work," Denise also questioned the idea that women with children who are not employed and on welfare are lazy.

> I mean if you got a family, what're you talkin' about lazy?! A woman is on it because she's got some children. And if she's at home and she's doin' for her family, how the hell is she lazy? In today's economy, when the family is not worth very much, it's called laziness. In a rural economy, the family had a higher priority. A woman's value and place in the family, being a homemaker, was considered much higher. So when she was in the family raising her children, she wasn't considered lazy. But

in today's economy a woman is considered lazy when she's at home taking care of her children. And to me that's not laziness. If she's doing a good job at that, she has to use a lot of skills. And she's putting in more than forty hours a week when she's taking care of her family. And that's not laziness! Let some of these men that work in the government, let some of them stay home and do that. They'll find that a woman is not lazy when she's taking care of her family.

Finally, a few people do appear half-hearted when it comes to working. A prime example is Scott Meyer, who was receiving eighty dollars a month in Food Stamps. Twenty years old, Scott was fired several times for using drugs on the job. He has been severely addicted to cocaine and has also dealt drugs. When interviewed, Scott was on probation. His probation officer had found him a job as a janitor. Without such pressure, Scott would probably not be working. He talked about when he was receiving General Assistance and Food Stamps: "It's easier than workin' for these low-paying jobs. If I wasn't on probation, I'd probably still be on welfare, 'cause it's easier. Two hundred and sixty a month. And I could still work for this dude paintin' and collect cash. So, I'd be doin' all right." He went on to say, "Yeah, I was kickin' back there for awhile. Why work if your rent's paid and you got all the food you need?" Asked if he would be working if he were not on probation, he answered, "I don't think so (*laughter*). I don't know if I could find a good job. I wouldn't be working in a minimum wage job."

Attitudes like Scott's were very atypical, but they do exist and represent yet another barrier to working.

Looking for Work

Welfare recipients tend to take two different approaches to locating employment. The first is to search the want ads in the daily newspaper while keeping an ear open for word-of-mouth leads. Joe Hall explains.

I get up in the morning, and I run her to work [his live-in companion]. I stop and get a newspaper. And I hit the want ads. . . . And then I start poundin' the beat. See what we can scare up for a job. I find that I have better luck looking for jobs in the morning hours. It just seems like the afternoons, the people are too busy to even talk to me. And I just go until about one o'clock in the afternoon, then knock it off and come home. Straighten up the house a little bit. Get a little more chow down and go pick her up and come home and stay here until the next morning. It's not much else to do. Or we can't afford doing anything else.

Most of my time is used up in lookin' for a job. And it has been for the last four months. In just looking for a job I've put on about ten thousand miles in four months on my car. That's a lot of miles. I just couldn't believe it. Maybe you hear somebody tell you, "Well, they're hirin' over here." And then bang, you jump into the car and you go and you get over there and, "No, we're not hirin'! Nothin' goin' on here." Just so many dead ends.

A second major approach is to participate in job training or job club programs, which many welfare programs require. I attended several of these. They advise recipients where to look for job openings and how to talk to potential employers on the telephone, help them learn how to articulate what their skills and talents are, put together résumés and fill out job applications, give them opportunities to hone their interviewing skills, and so on. Positive thinking is always stressed, as evidenced by the adages posted on the wall during one of the weeks I attended: "Before you say you can't, give it a try!" and "People who don't grow shrink. Stretch yourself!"

Carol Richardson describes job training.

First thing welfare did was say "You've gotta get a job." I says, "Great, that's why I came up here. Do you have any training programs?" And they put me right into the Job Club which helps you, shows you how to fill out a résumé, make your applications out. They help you find jobs, show you how to look through the paper, the telephone book. They've got several companies that send in, "We need so and so for such and such type of job." And if they feel you're competent and able to look into it, they give you the card to go check it out. You have to make so many appointments a day and you have to turn in so many applications a day. For somebody that really wants to get a job, it helps.

The problem with the above approaches is that employers often turn to classified ads or unsolicited applications only after all else has failed. Kathryn Neckerman and Joleen Kirschenman (1991) examined the hiring strategies of 185 Chicago-area firms to determine whether the approaches just described improved the inner-city black population's chances of finding employment. Their findings are also pertinent to the welfare population. Neckerman and Kirschenman found that "almost half of our respondents [the employers] said that employee referrals were their best source of qualified applicants, and it has become more common for employers to pay recruitment bonuses to employees whose referrals are hired. One respondent estimated that he hired 80 percent of all employee referrals, compared to only 5 percent of all applicants attracted by a newspaper ad" (437). They go on to note that "more than 40 percent of our respondents did not use newspaper advertising for their entry-level jobs, and those who did place ads often did so as a last resort after employee networks had been unsuccessful" (438).

Turning to the specific factors leading to employment, the odds ratios in table 7.2 itemize various characteristics associated with getting a job.[3] Clearly, greater human capital, along with fewer constraints, is associated with a higher probability of becoming employed. For all three household types, education is significantly and positively connected to finding a job. For example, female heads with a high school degree are 48 percent more likely to become employed than their counterparts without a high school degree. Being older also is positively related to employment for married males and single heads. On the other hand, having a child under the age of four and having larger numbers of children are both negatively associated with the chances of employment for female heads. Finally, receiving all three welfare programs reduces the likelihood of employment for both female-headed and married couple households, while lowered work incentives decrease the odds of employment for female-headed families. All these results are consistent with the conclusions suggested by the interviews.

TABLE 7.2
Odds Ratios of Variables Predicting Employment for Female Heads, Married Males, and Single Heads on Welfare

Independent Variables	Female Heads	Married Males	Single Heads
Demographic			
Age	1.02	1.05★	1.06★
High school graduate	1.48★★★	1.19★	1.24★
White	1.20	1.38★★★	1.06
Male	—	—	1.10
Children			
Number of children	0.61★	1.64★★	—
Child under age 4	0.65★★★	1.14	—
Welfare variation			
Receiving all three programs[a]	0.51★★★	0.61★★★	1.31
Lowered work incentives	0.66★★★	0.99	0.53
Length of welfare use	1.17	1.08	1.08

★significant at the .05 level
★★significant at the .01 level
★★★significant at the .001 level
[a]For singles, receiving two or three programs is contrasted with receiving one program.

The Ideal Job

Finally, recipients were asked about the type of job they would like to do. Like their dreams (detailed in chapter 6), their job aspirations were varied and far ranging, including developing and owning a business, becoming a nurse, selling real estate, teaching English, and so on.

One example is Karen Roberts. A twenty-four-year-old separated mother of two, Karen was working two part-time jobs. Two nights a week she waitressed at a local bowling alley, while on the weekdays she held a janitorial job cleaning offices for a large utility company from 5:00 until 8:30 P.M. Asked about the type of work that she would like to do, she replied, "Computer programming. It would be a challenge. I'm one of those people that needs a challenge all the time. I don't think it would be the same thing twice."

I asked whether she could see herself doing that at some point. "Oh yeah. You bet. Or see myself sitting behind a desk. That thought . . . that vision often comes to my mind. Sitting in a clean office at Metro Gas and Electric. Especially when you end up cleaning some of the really nice offices that I have, the executive suite ones and stuff. Yeah, I could see myself sitting behind that nice big desk.''

Although some recipients were quite optimistic about the likelihood of one day fulfilling their job aspirations, many also had their doubts. As chapter 6 made plain, although hopes and dreams are important in recipient's lives (among them, the desire for a better job), so too is a good deal of pragmatism. Carol Richardson explains:

> What I wanted to do when I was younger, and I never followed through on it, was getting into secretarial work. I have tried to get the money up to go and take the income tax courses. 'Cause I would like to get into something like that. I've just not been able to get there yet. I was almost planning on going to the technical college this fall to try and take a type-clerk typist course. I know I can do it because this friend of mine was taking it and I was doing her homework for her. So I mean I know I could do it but I just can't lay off of work long enough to go straight onto welfare and just stick with welfare and go out and borrow all that money. For one thing, my age is against me right now. To take a two-year course and then try and get a job after that would be impossible I think. So I kinda . . . tried too late.

Cindy Franklin put it succinctly: "There are only so many good-paying jobs that exist in this society, and there are tons and tons of minimum wage jobs. And as long as we expect people to work them, there are gonna be people who can't make it without help. There's only so many people can rise to the top, and then no more can.''

Although recipients often hope for more than the low-wage work that Cindy Franklin referred to, it is often all they will find. For the people whose stories have been reported in this chapter, the ideal and the reality rarely coincide.

8 ATTITUDES ABOUT WELFARE

> Throughout the course of this interview, I've been wondering, have I had a real need to have been on welfare? And the fact suddenly comes upon me that yeah, I kinda did need welfare. And I feel kind of guilty about that. Not necessarily guilty, but kind of degraded as a human being, that I've had to live off the money that other people stick into a program for the benefit of others.
>
> —*Single male diagnosed as schizophrenic*

M uch has been written about how Americans view welfare, welfare recipients, and the poor in general.[1] Most U.S. citizens believe that people are responsible for their poverty—that is, they fall into poverty and resort to welfare because of insufficient effort, thrift, morality, ability, and so on (see, e.g., Feagin 1975; Kluegel and Smith 1986). Much less has been written about how welfare recipients view their own and other welfare recipients' situations or about how they think the general public views them.[2] This chapter explores these different perceptions in detail, looking at them from the inside out. It also examines how such attitudes influence recipients' behavior with regard to welfare.

Stigma and Welfare Use

Irving Goffman defined *stigma* in the following way:

> While the stranger is present before us, evidence can arise of his possessing an attribute that makes him different from others in

the category of persons available for him to be, and of a less desirable kind—in the extreme, a person who is quite thoroughly bad, or dangerous, or weak. He is thus reduced in our minds from a whole and usual person to a tainted, discounted one. Such an attribute is a stigma, especially when its discrediting effect is very extensive; sometimes it is also called a failing, a shortcoming, a handicap.   (1963:2–3)

The concept of *stigma* has provided a powerful tool for understanding the attitudes and behaviors of people who fall into discredited or unbecoming categories (Pfuhl 1986). Research has shown that considerable social stigma is attached to the use of public assistance programs.[3] As Kerbo notes, "to be a welfare recipient in the United States means degradation; to be stigmatized at the hands of the general society, politicians, and even social workers" (1976:174).

There are several reasons behind such stigma. Use of welfare tends to jar with the independence in which most Americans take pride. Those who rely on government assistance for financial support rather than on their own efforts are perceived as failures. An example of this comes from a 1978 study by Coleman, Rainwater, and McClelland. In interviews conducted in Boston and Kansas City, respondents were asked who they felt constituted the lowest class in society. "The word used most often by our sample members to characterize the life style and income source of people at the bottom was welfare. . . . The principle enunciated . . . was that the welfare class and people at the bottom are nearly synonymous terms, that any American for whom welfare has become a way of life is thereby to be accounted among the nation's lowest-class citizens" (1978:195).

A second reason behind the stigmatization of welfare and welfare recipients is the fear of encouraging dependency on the state. As Goodban notes, "Afraid that handouts will encourage dependency, assistance programs stigmatize those who receive benefits to prevent them from asking for more, and to make it clear to others that there is an emotional price to pay" (1985:404).

As mentioned in chapter 2, this idea dates from the English Poor Laws, which postulated that if public relief were an attractive alternative to employment, people would choose relief over work. This became known as the concept of "less eligibility," which "meant that persons on relief should be kept in a condition necessarily worse than that of the lowest paid worker not on relief, the objective being to make relief undesirable and to provide the recipient with a clear and strong incentive to get off the relief rolls" (Waxman 1983:82). Such undesirable physical conditions would be compounded by a hefty dose of stigma.[4] The question becomes, how do recipients themselves respond to this stigma?

Recipients' Perceptions of Their Situations

What are recipients' general attitudes toward being on welfare? To what extent do they feel responsible for their circumstances? Finally, do they consider that being on welfare has helped or hurt them?

General Attitudes

As described in chapter 3, most individuals applying for public assistance feel anxiety and/or embarrassment during the application process. Furthermore, recipients clearly hope to get out of poverty (chapter 6) and believe in the ethic of work (chapter 7). Thus, it is not surprising that virtually all able-bodied recipients reported disliking being on welfare and expressed a clear desire to get off public assistance (understandably, most incapacitated recipients were thankful for the assistance and planned to remain on the programs unless a viable alternative appeared).

Two specific reasons underlie this. First, many recipients would rather be independent than reliant on taxpayer dollars. As one woman noted, "I'd rather be able to support myself, you know, work, and make the money myself instead of having someone sign a check and send it to me once a month. 'Cause I don't really like to live off other people. I'd rather work and make the money and support myself, in the best way that I could."

A second and closely related reason for recipients wishing to get off the welfare rolls is the lack of privacy and the stigma associated with public assistance programs. As shown in chapter 3, qualification requires extensive documentation, and this demand for documentation continues with update checks, six-month reviews, and so on. Stephanie Coles, a female head of household with two children, was asked if she would like to get off the programs she is on: "I'd love to get off. 'Cause aid makes me sick. They just interfere in your life so much. You gotta do this, and you gotta do it when they say do it. And you gotta go to the doctors they want you to go to. And I don't like that. Unhuh. You don't have any privacy with aid."

While on welfare, Michelle Carson had received AFDC, Food Stamps, and Medicaid for just over a year. Recently off the rolls at the time of our interview, she said, "'Cause when we were on welfare, I didn't really like the feeling. And I always felt like I was bein' watched. I always heard stories that they'll have you investigated or follow you around, see what your living status is like. And I didn't like the feeling of it. So I'm just glad that we're off from it. Really glad (*laugh*)."

The desire to get off welfare expressed by these women is consistent with research findings indicating that most individuals beginning a spell on welfare will exit relatively quickly.[5] This pattern also characterizes the welfare recipients in this study, as shown in the next chapter.

Although wanting to get off the rolls, most welfare recipients were also grateful for the assistance while they needed it. Denise Turner explains.

I would not have been able to even think about these kinds of things, of being successful, or doing any kind of meaningful thing with my life, if it wasn't for the benefits that I've been receiving from Social Services. These are the kinds of things that help people to climb up ladders. And I don't have any of these sources available. I would say that Social Service is a very much needed organization. I think it has made the difference in a lot of people's lives. From just keeling over and dying. Or taking the other extreme, shooting and killing up everybody. I think it's an alternative to poor people. And it's one that I'm grateful that I was able to have access to. Because I would not have been able to live any kind of meaningful existence.

This gratitude became more evident when recipients were asked what they would do if there were no welfare programs at all. As mentioned in chapter 7, Karen Roberts was working two jobs following her separation. She commented, "I probably would have perished a long time ago. I really would have. Starvation, or something. When you've got two kids you do what you have to do. That's really the main reason I went on it too, because of the kids. I had no choice. But if it wasn't for that . . . I would have to say we would have perished a long time ago."

Fifty-five-year-old Joe Hall was asked, "Can you say what you would do now if there weren't any welfare programs?"

I don't know. (*Long pause.*) I'd probably be alongside of the bag lady. I don't know. I really don't know what I'd do. (*Long pause.*) Thank God I got Medical Assistance. It isn't the greatest, you know, but it's something. I can get my blood pressure pills and stuff. That helps. I really . . . I never looked at it that way. I tried to stay off of it as long as I could, till I run completely out of money. The day I went over to see about it, I had fifteen cents in my pocket. So I was gettin' down to the bare minimum.

For Susan Davis, the extensive medical care required by her seizures left her little choice:

Well, in the broadest terms, I suspect that it would've happened like in the days of yore, when you went to the poorhouse. And hopefully there would've been somebody there who could handle a seizure. I know that if I was put in a nursing home, exactly what they'd do, having worked in them. They would put me in a geri-chair, with my helmet on, get me up in the morning, get me in the chair. They would tie that chair to a railing, and then they'd forget about me all day long, except to get me up once or twice to potty myself. How valuable can I be there? How much improvement can I make in that setting? Zip. And how degrading anyway. And so I much prefer the situation I'm in. I think I can give more to the community besides. And have already.

Others mentioned that without welfare they would rely more on family members, and several discussed illegal activities as alternatives. In general, although recipients clearly wanted to get back on their feet as soon as possible, they were nevertheless thankful for the assistance available to them in the meantime.

The Issue of Responsibility

To what extent do welfare recipients feel that being on public assistance is their responsibility? Only 6 percent of the interviewed sample felt that they were solely responsible for being on welfare; 82 percent felt that they were on welfare because of circumstances beyond their control, while 12 percent felt that their being on welfare was due to some combination of the two. The elderly discussed their illnesses. Singles mentioned incapacitation or other traumatic events. Female heads of household mentioned not being able to support their families because of low-paying jobs, no child support, and lack of child care. Married couples mentioned lay-offs or jobs simply not paying enough.

Typical are Colleen Bennett and her husband, Ron, who had been on and off welfare sporadically for several years prior to our interview. Colleen was asked to explain why she felt that their being on welfare was due to outside circumstances: "Loss of jobs, layoffs. Well, when Randy was born we just financially could not pay for a hospital, or a doctor, and stuff like that. It usually was something that just came up out of the blue and happened, and you didn't have any other income."

Quite different was Jody Edwards, who felt mostly responsible for being on welfare. Her case accords with the common American view of welfare mothers. Twenty-three years old when I interviewed her, Jody had been receiving AFDC, Food Stamps, and Medicaid ever since she became pregnant at age eighteen. She had not worked during this time and had no

interest in working. In addition she had experienced drug problems and admitted that living on welfare had made her lazy. I
asked her to elaborate why she felt that being on welfare was
her fault: "Well, I didn't need to get pregnant, you know. . . .
I could have taken birth control. And I could have worked for
these five years instead of not doing anything. I could have just
gone out and put her in day care or done something with her a
long time ago [referring to her daughter]. So I see it as my own
fault. I could be doing something."[6]

This response was unusual, however. For most recipients,
being on welfare is perceived as the result of unfortunate circumstances and situations over which they had little control.

Effect of Being on Welfare

How do welfare recipients perceive the effect(s) of being on
public assistance? That is, to what extent have the programs
helped, hurt, or had little effect?

Several individuals reported that receiving welfare had made
them lazy and continued to do so (4 percent of the sample),
because they saw little point in getting off welfare in order to
work at low-paying jobs with no medical benefits. However,
the following exchange with Karen Roberts was more typical
of those reporting disincentives (14 percent of the sample):

Karen: The programs did make me feel lazy for awhile. And
then . . . I don't know . . . one day I looked in the
mirror and looked at myself and said, "You're not this
way. This isn't the way you were brought up. What
are you doing? Go out and get a job. Be an American,
you know?" (*Laugh.*)

Q: So you decided to get a job, even though you knew
that that would reduce your benefits by as much as
you were getting paid?

Karen: Yeah.

Q: What do you think was the real incentive to get a job?

Karen: Pride. Pride. I looked at myself and I says, "People are
gonna wonder how you get this money, especially when

they know that you're divorced and a final settlement hasn't been run off yet. How are you gonna explain that and yet you don't want anybody to know you're on it? Go out and get a job. It's easier to hide the fact." (*Laugh.*)

For others, being on welfare led not to laziness but to depression and a sense of feeling trapped (8 percent). This was eloquently expressed by Mary Summers.

I wouldn't use the word lazy. I would probably use the word discouraged or depressed. When you take a human being and you take away their money, their livelihood, and you make them live on something that is just the cost of living with no luxuries and no benefits, just the drab cost of living and nothing else, you're going to have depression and you're going to have discouragement. And I think with depression there always comes a form of . . . tiredness. 'Cause you give up and you want to lay down and go to sleep. Not necessarily meaning that you're lazy, and you can't get out there. It's just that they give up hope.

This type of response was more common among those who had been on public assistance for a long time.

On the other hand, a quarter of the recipients interviewed felt that the payments from public assistance were too low to act as much of a disincentive effect. As reported in chapter 4, some households receive relatively little from welfare, and even those receiving the maximum benefits must struggle to get by. When asked if the welfare programs had had a disincentive effect on him, Joe Hall commented, "No. If they were paying me a thousand dollars a month, I could probably get stuck on it. But that two hundred dollars a month I don't get stuck on. No . . . no. . . . that would never happen to me. Maybe at a grand, yeah (*laugh*). But not at two hundred. I can't survive on this. This pays my house payment. That's about all it does, you know. And so (*sigh*) I'm tryin' to get off."

Still others reported that being on welfare made them work harder (16 percent). As noted above, virtually no one enjoys being on welfare, and most want to get off. Consequently, some recipients, such as Marta Green, feel motivated to work even harder.

> It's not makin' me lazy. It's makin' me more ambitious than I was before. Because when I was livin' with my husband, I had my house and food and my part-time job. I had everything I wanted for my life. Now I am here. And I go to school in the morning. Then I come home and do something around the house. And then I look at this place empty and I say, "Welfare, is this what you're going to give me all my life?" And I do not want it. I want to get over this. It's not making me lazy. Because I do not like it. I like to be able to be free (*chooses words very carefully*).

Finally, a number of recipients (46 percent) reported that receiving welfare had had a positive effect on them because the assistance enabled their household to survive or covered medical bills that otherwise would have been impossible for them to pay. Jim Duncan, who was involved in a serious automobile accident, explains: "I'd probably be worse off if I didn't have any assistance. 'Cause with my doctor bills and stuff, I'd get so far behind. Now I can keep my bills paid up. Pay for my wheelchair. 'Cause I woulda never got the bills paid off. It woulda been years."

Ultimately, then, receiving welfare may produce several different effects, both positive and negative. The complexity of the position in which welfare recipients find themselves is implicit in Cindy Franklin's comments below. As related in earlier chapters, she and her husband Jeff had been receiving AFDC for several years, during which time Jeff had worked on finishing his degree at the university.

> We live in a society that really prizes the work ethic. And because of that, I have wondered what it means that we've spent the last three and a half years being provided for, without having to work for it. What kind of long-term effect that's gonna have on us, or how has it affected our personalities? And I don't know the answer to that. Obviously Jeff's been putting in (*sigh*) a heavy schedule. He hasn't been just lazing around. But he hasn't been directly earning money that we can live on. That's the only question that I have. What does that mean for

us to have been dependent? I like to think that in a way it's a positive thing that we've been helped, that we've received it, and have been grateful for it. We have a heightened sensitivity to other people who are in hard times. And we have a real commitment to helping people. . . .

Our culture says that you work for what you get. And part of me wonders would we be better people if we had worked these last three and a half years? Realistically, I think we would have strained ourselves to the breaking point if we had tried to do that. And yet, the question is there. Would it have been the better choice to have worked, rather than to have been dependent? And I don't know the answer.

Recipients' Perceptions of How Others Act and Feel Toward Them

As noted earlier, most Americans hold quite negative attitudes about the welfare system and its recipients. Do those receiving welfare experience such negative attitudes firsthand?

The General Public

Slightly more than two-thirds of the people interviewed reported specific instances of feeling that they were treated differently by the general public when it became known that they were receiving public assistance. These occurrences ranged from blatant antagonism to more subtle forms of disapproval. The most frequently cited cases occurred with the use of Food Stamps.[7]

Several examples are illustrative. Janice Winslow, a thirty-seven-year-old separated mother of three, discussed the difficulties of using Food Stamps.

> You really do have to be a strong person to be able to use Food Stamps and not get intimidated by how people treat you when you use them. And even then it's still hard. You feel people's vibes, you know, in the line. And the checkout people are almost without exception rude, unless you really get to know them. And I always feel like, "God, I'll be glad when I don't have to use these." They never ever leave any change in there.

So every time you check out, they always have to go up to the office to get change, so you got all these people waitin' in line— it's like, you know, "These Food Stamp people."

Once about six weeks ago I turned to the woman behind me and said, "I don't know, I have not once come up here and bought something with Food Stamps where they didn't have to go and get change for, like a five or something, that they had in the drawer." She says, "Well, I guess it's just one of those ways that they're not making it easy for you."

A second example comes from Cindy Franklin.

It's absolutely blatant in the stores. They'll smile and be chatting with you, and then they see you pull out the Food Stamps— they just freeze up. And they scrutinize the food. I mean, I get really hyped. If it's a birthday or something, and I'm buying steak so that we can have a birthday dinner at home—ohh, the looks they get on their faces. Once I had a clerk tell me, "You buy really good food with your Food Stamps" (*laughter*). Jeez. Yeah, there is a difference.

Recipients may develop several strategies for dealing with the stigma of using Food Stamps. Some shop at off times or with checkers whom they know personally. Marta Green explained, "When I go to buy with Food Stamps, I try to go at night so not too many people get behind me. Especially when the employees ask about the I.D. And then they want to see one more I.D. And it's very, very uncomfortable. I guess I cannot be like other people that just carry their Food Stamps in their hands like money. I just . . . can't do that."

Similarly, Jody Edwards noted, "I try really hard to hit a day that nobody's gonna be at the store because I just get all flustered. I have a terrible time using my Food Stamps. Just hate it! Just hate it."

Others may go to stores where the use of Food Stamps is fairly common. For example, Michelle Carson often went into the metropolitan area to shop instead of going to her rural neighborhood grocery store: "Well, when I went grocery shopping, I usually went to Cedar's [a supermarket]. Because I figured a lot of people go in there and use 'em, you know, so I wouldn't feel out of place. Otherwise, it would look bad, and I still felt stupid."

Alternatively, recipients may send someone else to use their Food Stamps or perhaps dress differently. Jill Nelson, an attractive and poised nineteen-year-old, commented, "I feel like I have to be dressed really nice and look nice to use 'em. I don't wanna look all dumpy and look like I fit it [the image of a welfare recipient]."[8]

Recipients felt stigmatized in other ways as well. Cashing their AFDC checks, having to move to the Medicaid section of a nursing home when their savings runs out, telling employers that they have been on public assistance—any of these may make them feel that they are being treated differently from other people. A separated woman with two children discussed one such instance: "When I was looking for apartments, I was living with my mom for a while. And when I was looking, I couldn't prove the fact that I was turned down because of it, but you just know that yourself. The minute you say, 'Well I'm getting aid, or AFDC,' then all of a sudden they sing a different tune. Or the place gets rented out to somebody else."

In discussing the use of her medical card, Cindy Franklin noted, "Some receptionists turn off the friendliness when they see Medical Assistance. Sometimes I catch them looking at me, maybe if I have on a necklace or something. I don't think I look like the stereotypical welfare mother, and I see them scrutinizing me and thinking it over. It's pretty subtle."

Not as subtle were the reactions to Denise Turner's daughter.

My oldest daughter, she graduated from middle school. And she told me last year that she did not want to receive the hot lunch program because the children made a difference. So I had to scrape for the last couple of years while she was in middle school and try to make ends meet so that I could send her with a dollar or two dollars every day. Which is a big chunk out of our budget. The food program at school is a big help. But rather than see her mistreated, or have her friends sit away from her, this is what I had to do. Either have her bring a lunch, or give her money. And I don't think it should be that way. But people are very class conscious about these kinds of programs.

A final example comes from my fieldwork. One of the social service agencies that I visited was located in a very small town. Across the street was a tavern. Locals would often sit and gaze out the window of the tavern in order to observe who was going into the office. They would then gossip and joke about those on welfare, what their situations were, and so on. Potential welfare recipients were generally well aware of this.

These examples illustrate some of the ways in which welfare recipients experience firsthand the negative attitudes held by the general public. Although not all recipients reported such incidents, over two-thirds did, many of them repeatedly.

The response to this animosity is often concealment, a typical strategy among stigmatized groups. According to Goffman, "the issue is not that of managing tension generated during social contacts but rather of managing information about his failing. To display or not to display; to tell or not to tell; to let on or not to let on; to lie or not to lie; and in each case, to whom, how, when and where" (1963:42).

This is why using Food Stamps is particularly hard for many people. Food Stamps are a stigma symbol, identifying the user as a member of a stigmatized group. Subsidized housing, Medicaid cards, and the like similarly function as stigma symbols, causing various degrees of anxiety among recipients.

If concealment is impossible (as in the case of Food Stamps), then an attempt may be made either to minimize contact with the general public (when having to reveal one's welfare status), or to physically dissociate oneself from the image of a "typical" welfare recipient (by dressing according to middle-class standards, watching what one buys in the supermarket, and so on).

Family, Friends, and Acquaintances

How do recipients think their family, friends, and acquaintances react to their being on welfare? As might be expected, close friends and family tend to be more supportive than outsiders. They may dislike the concept of welfare, but many can understand why a relative or friend sought assistance.

Yet there can be animosity as well. Some may strongly disapprove of any member of their family relying on welfare. Such was the case with Kelly McGrath, a divorced mother of four. She was asked about the reactions of her family to her situation: "It varies. The female family members understand. And they never give me any problems or anything. But my brothers always figure I should be out working. I think it's just all the stereotypes that go along with it [receiving welfare]. They just don't want their sister in with that stereotype."

Many recipients let as few people as possible know that they are receiving public assistance. When asked if his friends had any opinions about his being on welfare, David Grey, who was quoted at the beginning of this chapter, responded, "Well, I really don't let 'em know about it. I don't think it's really anything I have to advertise, nor do I want to." Likewise, when Mary Summers was asked if her relatives expressed any feelings about her situation, she replied, "They don't talk about it. In fact, I like to stay away from some of the relatives until I go back to work. I mean, it's just a situation that you don't even wanna get into. Let it blow over, and when you get back [on your feet] and have a little dignity again, well, then you can go back."

Finally, Jennifer Smith was asked about her friends' reactions.

> Well, there's a lot that don't know that I am [on welfare]. There's a lot of 'em I work with. They make some nasty comments about people on ADC, or welfare, as they call it. And I always say ADC, 'cause it sounds better. But I don't really say anything. It doesn't really bother me, 'cause I figure, well, keep my mouth shut. What they don't know don't hurt 'em. It's none of their business. It used to bother me when they'd make their snide remarks, but I figure, well . . . let 'em. Wait till they have to do something like that, and it happens to them. They'll find out.

Recipients' Perceptions of Other Welfare Recipients

To a large extent, those on welfare are critical in their assessments of their fellow recipients. Approximately 90 percent of
the sample felt that those on welfare were either partially or
fully to blame for being on public assistance. While recipients
cited a variety of reasons, most mentioned a lack of ambition
and laziness as important factors in explaining why others are
on welfare. A typical assessment came from Pam Bucholtz, a
married woman who was living with her unemployed husband
on the outskirts of a rural town: "In my point of view I think
they're too lazy to get out and find a job. In our case we're not.
We're out looking. But some of these other people they're the
ones that don't wanna work. They just don't wanna get out
and work. They'd rather sit and collect on the government."

A related notion is that many on welfare are abusing or
cheating the welfare system. An example of this attitude was
from Lisa Hicks, a twenty-two-year-old female head of household: "The money is to take care of your bills and your kids.
Except they don't do that. They take it and party off of it. Or
go out and buy new clothes for themselves. And their kids
don't have anything. They walk around with holes and stuff in
their clothes and hungry all the time because they take and
gamble, or whatever with the money."

Certainly, not every recipient felt that others on welfare
were lazy or abusing the system. Some mentioned circumstances over which individuals had little control. Others mentioned becoming less harsh in their assessments after having
been on welfare themselves. However, as with the general
public, most on welfare are quite critical of their fellow welfare
recipients.

Many recipients also subscribe to the common stereotypes
surrounding welfare: that most recipients are minorities; that
those on welfare are there for long periods of time; that women
have more children to get higher welfare payments; and so on.
Chester Peterson, age sixty-eight, commented,

> I don't know what the percentage is but I would venture to say
> that eighty percent of the people on welfare are black, Hispanic,

or some of the boat people [referring to Cuban refugees]. And they're on there for year after year after year after year. They never get off it. It's just a way of life.

Take these welfare mothers out here. All right, they're getting five sixty, five seventy, seven hundred dollars a month. Now you know, and I know, that they don't spend that much on groceries or rent. All they have to do if they wanna increase their salary is go out and have another kid. And it seems to me, that's what they do. (*Laughter.*)

Another recipient remarked, "I think that's why a lotta these people have children, because they don't wanna work. They wanna have everything handed to 'em. And they figure if they have two, three of 'em [children], they get more money. And a lotta these people, these young women that get that help, they're always in the bars. Out drinkin' and that."

Again, not every welfare recipient resorted to such stereotypes to characterize other welfare recipients. But many did.

If we return to the concept of stigma as a way of understanding their attitudes, however, these responses become less surprising. According to Goffman, "a stigmatized person is first of all like anyone else, trained first of all in others' views of persons like himself . . ." (1963:134). Therefore, "it should come as no surprise that in many cases he who is stigmatized in one regard nicely exhibits all the normal prejudices held toward those who are stigmatized in another regard" (138).

Recipients, however, are careful to distinguish between their own cases and others'. Scott Briar (1966) described this as "a distancing process." This distancing process was clearly evident in the remarks of Dan Wilensky, an out-of-work husband.

Like the people that hang out downtown, the bums. I can't see how they can just be a bum. I mean everybody can find a job one way or another. Like I said we're on General Assistance to survive, okay. And not just to be on it. But once I find a job we'll be off of it. And we probably won't be back on it. 'Cause I can keep a job. But like people that are downtown, the bums and everything, I'm sure they're to the point now where they're so lazy that they won't wanna get a job. So they're just sittin' back and sayin', "Hey, let somebody else pay everything for me." There's both kinds of people. The bums, and then people like us that are having trouble finding the first job.

Similar sentiments were voiced in numerous interviews. As Briar noted, this distancing "reflects the desire of these recipients to dissociate themselves from the image they have of other recipients" (51). Such distancing is a natural response to the stigma attached to welfare recipiency.

To summarize, most recipients view being on public assistance as largely beyond their control and express a strong desire to leave the welfare rolls. Many experience firsthand a variety of negative reactions to their welfare recipiency and often adjust their behavior to minimize their encounters with such attitudes. Finally, recipients tend to share the general view that welfare recipients—excluding themselves—lack ambition and/or are lazy. Like most Americans, recipients attach stigma to the welfare system and its participants. Yet they themselves must face such stigma, including their own. This contradiction and its resolution are at the root of their attitudes and behaviors regarding welfare.

It is often assumed that the poor in general and welfare recipients in particular somehow differ from the general public in their attitudes, perceptions, and beliefs regarding the welfare system (Banfield 1974; Gilder 1981; Mead 1986). For example, many hold that recipients are resigned to living on welfare, are not motivated to leave the welfare system, do not care or feel embarrassed about using public assistance, are sympathetic to other welfare recipients, and so on. The findings reported in this chapter suggest the reverse. In fact, welfare recipients appear to be remarkably similar to the general population in terms of their dislike of welfare and the way they cope with their feelings of disdain.

9 HOW LONG AND HOW OFTEN?

Sure, that's gonna happen [getting a job and off welfare]. I'm gonna make it happen. It's just . . . gonna take some time.

—*Never-married mother of four children*

Since the mid-1970s, a number of longitudinal analyses of the welfare population have been carried out. Several caseload studies in California and New York, as well as data from the Seattle/Denver Income Maintenance Experiments (SIME/DIME), the Panel Study of Income Dynamics (PSID), the National Longitudinal Survey (NLS), and the Survey of Income and Program Participation (SIPP) have followed welfare recipients over time.[1] Although the estimates differ somewhat from study to study, it appears that the majority of households utilizing welfare do so for a fairly short amount of time. For such households, public assistance may serve the purpose of providing temporary relief until economic or domestic conditions improve. A smaller number of welfare recipients remains on the rolls considerably longer. Some of these recipients have undoubtedly become locked in to the welfare system.

This chapter examines whether the households in this study follow such patterns. Using the longitudinal caseload data, the length of time households are on welfare and the likelihood of their returning to public assistance after having left are analyzed. The next chapter explores these issues further by focusing on the specific factors associated with leaving public assistance.

The Length of Welfare Spells

For those currently on welfare, how much longer will they remain on? With regard to households beginning a spell of welfare use, how long will they receive public assistance? Finally, the well-documented rise in the proportion of households headed by females, particularly by black females, has been cause for concern among academics and policymakers alike. What differences exist between black and white female-headed families in terms of their length of time on welfare?

Analysis of Recipients Currently on Welfare

The sample drawn in the initial month of the longitudinal caseload data set comprised a cross-section of welfare users rather than solely new cases. As shown in figure 9.1, these households had been on welfare for varying lengths of time prior to the first sampling month. Approximately half of female and elderly heads of households had been receiving public assistance for more than one year, while 30 percent of married couples and 20 percent of singles had been on welfare more than one year prior to the sampling point.

Consequently, the starting point in figure 9.2 is the initial month of sampling, rather than the beginning of the welfare spell. The question is, therefore, for those currently on public assistance, how long a period of time will elapse before they leave the welfare rolls?[2] Looking first at female heads, 12.6 percent had completed their original welfare spell six months after being sampled. After twelve months, 22.6 percent had exited, and so on. At the end of three years, 51.9 percent, or one out of two female-headed households had completed their original spells of welfare use. Married- and single-headed

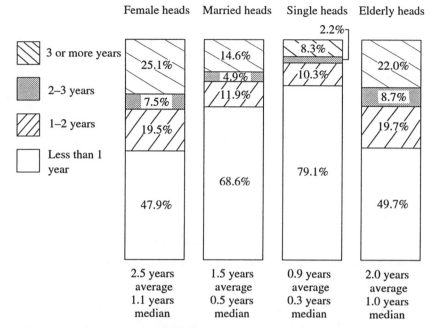

Figure 9.1 Prior Length of Welfare Use

households show higher proportions of cumulative exits. After three years, 74.1 percent of married- and 79.1 percent of single-headed households had completed their original welfare spells. Elderly households, on the other hand, resemble female-headed households in terms of their cumulative spell distribution.

The median exit times (the point at which 50 percent of households had exited) also differed across household categories. Single- and married-headed households tended to exit more quickly than female- and elderly-headed households. While 50 percent of singles had exited after 8.5 months, the median for female heads was 33.6 months (see table B.8 in appendix B).

Figure 9.2 also shows that the four household categories reflect differing exit distributions. A high proportion of single-headed households exited during the first twelve months, after which the distribution begins to level off. For married-headed households, 60 percent exited during the first eighteen months, again with the distribution leveling off afterward. Elderly and female heads of households, on the other hand, had similar

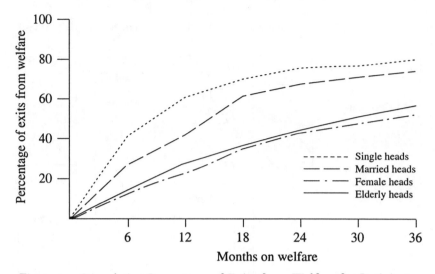

Figure 9.2 Cumulative Percentage of Exits from Welfare for Recipients Currently Receiving Public Assistance

cumulative completed spell distributions, characterized by a slow and steady increase in the proportion who exit over time.[3]

For all household types, the likelihood of exiting welfare diminishes over time. This is especially true for married and single- headed households. The percentage of single-headed households exiting during the first six-month interval was 42.3, while the percentage exiting during the last six-month interval was 8.6 (see table B.8 in appendix B for further detail). This may have been due to a settling-in effect, or those remaining may have been more disadvantaged (e.g., severely undereducated or disabled) and hence less likely to leave (this issue is examined in chapter 10).

Analysis of Recipients Beginning Welfare

To determine the exit probabilities for a beginning cohort of welfare users, I created a synthetic opening cohort.[4] This allowed me to estimate how long a beginning group of welfare recipients would remain on public assistance. A major difference between figures 9.2 and 9.3 is the percentage of cumula-

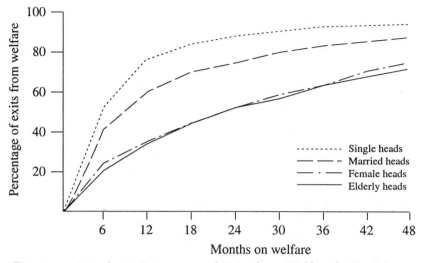

Figure 9.3 Cumulative Percentage of Exits from Welfare for Recipients Currently Beginning Public Assistance

tive exits. A beginning cohort of cases is much more likely to exit during the first year of a welfare spell than is a point-in-time cohort during the first year of observation. I estimated that 35.4 percent of female heads, 60.8 percent of married heads, 76.2 percent of single heads, and 34.7 percent of elderly heads will have left welfare after one year. At the end of three years, 63.8 percent of female heads, 83.2 percent of married couples, 92.3 percent of single heads, and 63.6 percent of the elderly will have exited. For the entire sample, 77.4 percent will have exited after three years.

These findings are consistent with the earlier cited research indicating that most beginning cases are on welfare for a relatively short amount of time. The median exit times for female and elderly heads of household were estimated to be slightly under two years, while for married and single heads the median exit times were 8.6 and 5.7 months, and for the entire sample, 10.3 months (see table B.9 in appendix B). Clearly, most households that use welfare do so for a relatively short period of time. However, if one examines a cross-section of the welfare population at a point in time (as in figure 9.2), the likelihood of exiting is lower, and the length of welfare use is substantially longer. The median exit time for female heads in figure 9.2 was thirty-four months (see table B.8, appendix B). Prior to the initial sampling month, female heads of household had been on welfare a median of thirteen months (see figure 9.1). Thus, their approximate median length of time on welfare was forty-seven months, which is two years longer than the median length of welfare use estimated for a beginning cohort of female-headed households (see table B.9, appendix B).

A hospital analogy helps explain these differences. Most people who enter a hospital remain for a relatively short time; however, the chronically ill tend to stay for much longer. Because the chronically ill accumulate over time in a cross-section, at any given point, a sampling of patients will reveal that the average stay is much longer. Similarly, most households use welfare briefly, yet at any point in time it will appear that the average welfare recipient has been (and will be) on public assistance for a longer time. (Note, however, that the long-term users found in a point-in-time sample will consume a larger proportion of public assistance funds, just as longer-term hospital patients consume a larger proportion of medical care.)

As in figure 9.2, figure 9.3 shows clear differences across household types in the likelihood of exiting. Both female and elderly heads of household are estimated to be less likely to exit from welfare, while single and married heads have a greater probability of exiting. There tends to be a relatively slow but steady increase in the percentage of female and elderly heads who will leave welfare over time, whereas married and single families show a dramatic increase in exits during the first year, which then levels off during the next three years. The majority of single and married heads will use welfare briefly, while elderly- and female-headed households participate for a longer time.

As in figure 9.2, there is a downward trend in the likelihood of exiting over time in all household categories. That is, the longer a household remains on welfare, the less likely it is to leave. This trend is even more pronounced than in figure 9.2.

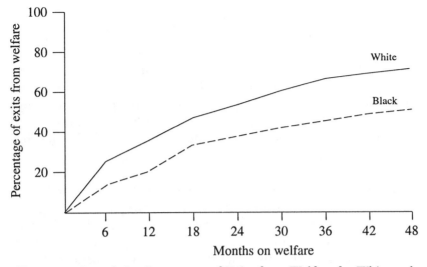

Figure 9.4 Cumulative Percentage of Exits from Welfare for White and Black Female Heads Beginning Public Assistance

Thus, while it is estimated that 37.8 percent of the total sample entering welfare will leave after six months, only 9.4 percent who have been on for forty-two months will exit at the end of forty-eight months (see table B.9, appendix B, for further details).

Analysis of Racial Differences in Length of Welfare Use[5]

Figure 9.4 clearly shows that white female-headed households beginning public assistance are much more likely to exit than their black counterparts. Fifty percent of white female-headed households will have exited from welfare after 21.6 months. For black female heads, the median length is 45.2 months. After four years, almost three out of four white female-headed households will have exited at some point from welfare, as compared to one out of two black female-headed households. (See table B.10, appendix B, for further details.)

The exiting slopes of white and black women are more or less parallel in figure 9.4. Both are characterized by a slow and steady increase in the cumulative percentage of exits over time.

Nevertheless, there is a sizable gap between white and black women (again, see table B.10, appendix B, for further details).

An analysis of socioeconomic and demographic characteristics may explain why black women remain on welfare longer than their white counterparts. Four of the most important variables are education, employment, number of children, and age. An employed, older, high school graduate with one child to care for has substantially greater opportunities for getting off welfare than an unemployed, younger, high school dropout with three children (Wiseman 1977; Coe 1979; Hutchens 1981; Bane and Ellwood 1983; Plotnick 1983; Rank, Cheng, and Cox 1992). Among the welfare recipients in this sample, white women were more likely than black women to have graduated from high school, to be employed, and to have only one child; they also tended to be slightly older (see table B.11, appendix B).

To assess simultaneously the effects of socioeconomic/demographic characteristics and race on the length of welfare utilization, I calculated logistic regression models and, from them, constructed a multivariate life table (found in tables B.12 and B.13 in appendix B). This permits a graphic comparison of the patterns and lengths of welfare use for black and white women with specific backgrounds. Of particular interest is a racial comparison of women with similar socioeconomic and demographic characteristics. Also relevant is a comparison of black and white women with advantageous characteristics (high school educations, employed, fewer than two children) and presumably better opportunities for exiting from welfare, with black and white women with less favorable characteristics (no high school education, not employed, two or more children). In all cases, I assumed that a woman was age twenty-seven at the onset of her welfare spell (this being the median age).

Figure 9.5 illustrates that once one controls for the effects of the above socioeconomic and demographic characteristics, white and black women remain on welfare for virtually identical lengths of time. The racial difference found in figure 9.4 no longer exists in comparisons of women with similar backgrounds. A white, employed, high school graduate with fewer than two children remains on welfare a median of 15.4 months, while her black counterpart is on 15.5 months. At the end of

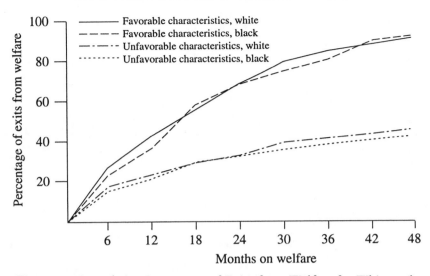

Figure 9.5 Cumulative Percentage of Exits from Welfare for White and Black Female Heads Beginning Public Assistance with Favorable and Unfavorable Characteristics

48 months, 92.2 percent and 92.7 percent of white and black female heads with such characteristics, respectively, will have exited from public assistance. Likewise, white and black women with less favorable characteristics have similar exit probabilities. After 48 months, 46.2 percent of white female heads and 43.6 percent of black female heads will have exited. In other words, black and white women in similar circumstances behaved almost identically.

Returning to Welfare

To establish the likelihood of returning to welfare, I constructed a life table analysis of returns (table B.14, appendix B). The monthly intervals in figure 9.6 refer to the amount of time that has passed since a household has exited from welfare.

As with exiting, there is a strong effect of time on the likelihood of returning to welfare. The longer a family remains off, the less likely it is to return. For female heads, 23.8 percent will reenter the welfare rolls within six months. However, there is a substantial drop in the probability of returning to welfare after six months, and, after twenty-four months, only

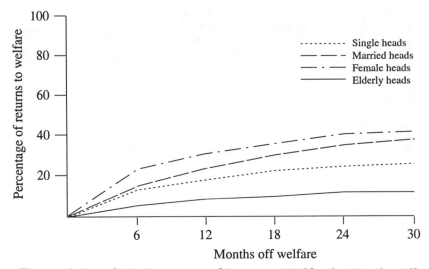

Figure 9.6 Cumulative Percentage of Returns to Welfare by Months Off
Welfare

4 percent of those off welfare will return within the next half
year. This pattern is true for all household groups.

Figure 9.6 suggests that a sizable amount of recidivism occurs within two and a half years of having left a public assistance program(s). While female-headed families are the least
likely to exit, they are also the most likely to return: 41.8
percent will have returned to welfare at some point during the
thirty-month span. Approximately 38 and 26 percent of married and single heads, respectively, will reenter a welfare program within thirty months of having left. Only the elderly are
unlikely to return to welfare. Here, however, the explanation
lies in the manner of exiting. Approximately 70 percent of
elderly heads of household leave welfare because of death (as
discussed in the next chapter), which obviously lowers the rates
of recidivism considerably.

Percentage Remaining Off Welfare

By utilizing the exiting and reentering rates found in tables B.9
and B.14 in appendix B, it is possible to estimate how many
households beginning a spell of welfare will be off three years

TABLE 9.1
Percentage Remaining Off Welfare by Household Type

| Monthly Interval | Household Type | | | | |
	Female Heads	Married Heads	Single Heads	Elderly Heads	Total Sample
0–6	25.3	41.7	52.7	20.8	37.8
6–12	29.4	54.3	69.2	33.5	48.8
12–18	36.1	59.9	74.7	42.3	54.7
18–24	40.7	62.1	79.6	49.7	59.2
24–30	45.1	66.1	82.3	54.2	62.8
30–36	48.2	69.0	84.3	59.4	65.8

later. Table 9.1 presents the percentage of households remaining off welfare over six-month intervals. (Obviously, these percentages will be lower than those found in figure 9.3 since they include households that have reentered welfare, as well as those that have exited for a second or third time.)

After three years, slightly less than half of all female heads will be off public assistance. For married couples, approximately seven out of ten will be off. Eighty-four percent of single heads will no longer be on welfare, while close to 60 percent of the elderly will be off public assistance after a three-year period. For the entire sample, almost half will not be using welfare after one year, and two-thirds will no longer be using public assistance after three years.

As with the exiting and reentering rates, there are clear differences across households in the likelihood of being on welfare after three years. Female and elderly-headed households are more likely to be receiving welfare after several years than are single- or married-headed households. Female heads have lower exiting and higher recidivism rates, resulting in a larger proportion being on welfare. The opposite is true for single heads.

As this table along with the earlier findings suggest, the notion that those who use welfare represent an entrenched class who remain on public assistance for years at a time is simply incorrect. The majority of households using welfare will generally do so for no more than one or two years. On the other hand, many of those exiting will return to the welfare rolls at some point in the future. These families are likely to weave in and out of poverty as their economic conditions improve or worsen. For those who remain on welfare for longer periods, the chances of exiting decrease. These are the individuals who may become locked in to the welfare system. They represent, however, a minority of the households beginning a spell on welfare.

The implication of these findings is that welfare programs generally provide temporary assistance to aid families over periodic times of crisis. The fact that these spells may recur in the future simply indicates the unstable position that many welfare households occupy in the labor force (as seen in chapter 7). In short, these are households attempting to walk a high wire, with little netting below to catch them when they fall.

10 GETTING OFF

You feel different. You feel like you're gonna be able to get everything done, whereas before you just automatically felt bad. It's not even that you realized you felt bad. It's like you had a black cloud hanging over your head, and you didn't know why.
—*Married woman discussing how it felt to get off welfare*

An examination of the administrative reasons for getting off welfare is an appropriate place to begin an in-depth look at the exiting process and the factors that facilitate and constrain it. Although these reasons are at times ambiguous (for example, failure to supply information), they nonetheless are the official justifications for terminating welfare assistance.

As noted earlier, families in this study participated in one or more of three programs—AFDC, Food Stamps, and Medicaid. Each program has its own criteria for terminating eligibility, usually relating to changes within households. The computing system monitors these changes, entering a reason for ineligibility where appropriate. Such reasons can differ depending upon the program. For example, a household may have refused additional support from the Food Stamp program, while at the same time its AFDC eligibility was terminated because of high income or assets. Therefore, it is important to separate the reasons for exiting by program, as shown in table 10.1.

Most of the sampled female-headed families in this study

TABLE 10.1

System-generated Reason Percentages for Exiting Welfare by Household Type

Reasons for Exiting Welfare	Household Type			
	Female Heads	Married Heads	Single Heads	Elderly Heads
Reasons for exiting AFDC				
Income too high	31.4	26.2	—	—
No child under age 18	15.1	17.2	—	—
Ineligible family structure	0.3	0.3	—	—
Head has died	0.3	0.3	—	—
Lack of information	22.3	22.1	—	—
Refused support	10.0	9.4	—	—
Household has moved	13.7	9.4	—	—
Change in laws	6.2	2.9	—	—
Work requirements not met	0.3	10.1	—	—
Other	0.2	1.9	—	—
Reasons for exiting Food Stamps				
Income too high	31.7	45.8	12.8	21.1
Ineligible family structure	6.1	2.3	12.2	26.3
Head has died	0.3	0.3	0.6	8.8
Lack of information	40.2	32.6	62.9	35.1
Refused support	8.6	7.5	4.9	7.0
Household has moved	11.9	8.6	3.3	1.8
Work requirements not met	0.5	0.6	1.5	0.0
Other	0.8	2.3	1.8	0.0
Reasons for exiting Medicaid				
Income too high	35.9	43.4	16.1	16.7
Ineligible family structure	8.9	5.3	27.5	3.2
Head has died	0.3	0.0	4.6	70.0
Lack of information	30.4	29.5	39.0	4.6
Refused support	8.4	9.6	2.3	0.3
Household has moved	14.8	8.8	4.1	0.3
Other	1.2	3.3	6.4	4.9

were participating in the AFDC program (as mentioned in chapter 3). Nearly one-third of these households exited from AFDC because their income and/or assets had risen above the eligibility limits. Another third exited because they either failed to provide sufficient information to determine continued eligibility or simply refused additional support. An additional 15 percent of female-headed families exited AFDC because there was no longer a child under age eighteen in the household, while 14 percent moved and therefore no longer qualified. Finally, 6 percent left because changes in federal and state laws made them ineligible (this occurred primarily when the Reagan budget cuts went into effect). The patterns of exiting from

Food Stamps and Medicaid for female heads are similar. The majority exit because of changes in income/asset level or failure to supply information.

Married couples in this study participated in various combinations of AFDC, Food Stamps, and Medicaid. One-quarter exited AFDC as a result of high income and/or assets. Another 22 percent failed to provide enough information to remain eligible. About 17 percent became ineligible because they no longer had a child under age eighteen in the household. Finally, almost 30 percent of married couples exited from AFDC because they had either refused additional support, moved, or failed to meet the work requirement of the AFDC program. Most of those failing to meet these requirements had worked too many hours during the previous month. A much larger percentage of married couples left Food Stamps as a result of their income/assets being above the program limits (45.8 percent), and a significant percentage left because they failed to provide adequate information (32.6 percent). Married couples exiting the Medicaid program did so primarily because of high income/assets or failure to provide information.

Almost all singles in the study were participating in either the Food Stamp or Medicaid programs. The majority who left Food Stamps had failed to supply the proper information. For Medicaid participants, three reasons for exiting predominated: income/assets above the limits, noneligible family structure, and failure to supply information.

Turning to the elderly, most were Medicaid recipients (83 percent who entered the welfare system received only Medicaid, as shown in figure 3.2). The primary reason for leaving this program (accounting for 70 percent of exits) is death. An additional 16.7 percent exited because their income and/or assets exceeded the program limits.

Exit Routes

Although the percentages differ somewhat across household categories, it is apparent from table 10.1 that there are several major routes for exiting welfare, one of which the majority of households will eventually take.

Increased Income

The most common path out of the welfare system is increased income, generally through gaining employment, increasing current wages, or going from part-time to full-time work.

Ron Bennett, age twenty-seven, had worked on and off in the construction industry for several years. Discussing their reasons for being on assistance, his wife Colleen explained, "Ron gets laid off every winter, 'cause he works in construction. So you figure three to four months out of the year we're usually qualified for some sort of assistance. And it just gets really tiring to go in there and have to fight with them about receiving anything."

At the time of our interview, Ron had recently landed a more stable job as a bricklayer. Colleen described how this would allow them to leave the welfare system:

> Ron just got a job that pays seven dollars an hour. He's working as a bricklayer, and they're gonna train him to become a bricklayer's apprentice. It'll take about two years. If you make under five dollars an hour you're on this line that you can't survive. You don't get any assistance, you don't get medical help, and you're better off not working. That sounds terrible, but that's the way it is. You have to break the five-dollar wage to be able to survive without getting any assistance at all.

Asked if the job would be year-round, Colleen replied, "I'd say probably between nine to ten months a year. And the layoffs he'd have wouldn't be all in a row. It'd be like a thirty-hour week here, maybe twenty-five. So it's not gonna be a permanent layoff for any long periods of time."

Family Structural Change

A second major route out of welfare is through changes in family structure, generally occurring when a female head of household marries or reconciles with her husband or when a child under the age of eighteen no longer lives in the household. Either type of change can disqualify the family from receiving public assistance, particularly AFDC.

Michelle Carson's story is typical. When I interviewed Michelle, she was living temporarily in a motel on the outskirts of a small rural town. She had become pregnant a year earlier at age eighteen. Unable to pay her medical bills, she applied for public assistance. Several months prior to our interview, Michelle had married the child's father. The resulting increase in household income disqualified her from AFDC. I asked how she had gotten off welfare. She replied, "I just told them that I was getting married, and they said, 'Well, how much does he make a month?' And I told them, and they said that they couldn't help me with anything. So, that was the end of that."

Bureaucratic

Bureaucratic decisions represent a third major exit route from the welfare system, stemming from recipients' failure to supply necessary information, changes in welfare regulations (as with the OBRA changes), failure to comply with particular requirements, and so on.

Rosa and Alejandro Martinez are a Hispanic couple in their seventies. They had worked hard throughout their lives, mostly as migrant workers. At the time of our interview, they had recently become the primary caregivers for their granddaughter. The Martinezes could not speak much English, and the entire welfare system was a puzzle to them. They had received Medicaid and SSI in the past but had been dropped for reasons largely unknown to them. Rosa and Alejandro thought that perhaps they had been disqualified because they had failed to report how they had used approximately three thousand dollars they had received from SSI for back payments. In Spanish, Alejandro explained:

> But one is very ignorant and truthfully doesn't know the requirements that the people have. Then they demanded that I report to them why and how I had spent it. But one is very ignorant, and we didn't keep track. They were giving us checks. They were giving us SSI checks, thirty dollars for her and thirty

dollars for me, and the Medical Assistance. Then they cut us off totally, and they sent me a letter telling me to send them the thirty dollars for her and my thirty dollars that they had sent us in July. So I sent it back. From then on we've been totally cut off.

Voluntary

A final exit route is the voluntary decision to cease participating in the system. This type of exit is more typical of those receiving relatively small amounts of assistance. It is also more common for singles (who also are more likely to be receiving smaller amounts of welfare). Voluntary exits often occur when recipients decide that the loss of dignity and/or bureaucratic red tape entailed in public assistance are too high a price to pay for it.

These were the reasons behind Brenda Jackson's decision to discontinue her assistance from welfare. Although seventy-seven years old and in a nursing home, she stressed throughout the interview the importance of being independent and not too reliant on others. She was asked why she had turned down the assistance.

> I told 'em they want to know too much of my business, and to forget it. I don't get nothing but Social Security, that's all. But these other organizations, I said, "What if you want to know this and want to know that, you won't quit" (*laughter*). And I said, "Don't come around here anymore." Because after all, they were going too deep in my affairs, and so I just told 'em forget about it, and don't come back. I don't get no help from no organizations.

Factors Associated with Exiting

The following analysis of the specific factors related to exiting from public assistance is confined to those under age sixty-five. The reasons for this are twofold. First, as shown in table 10.1, most of the elderly exit the welfare system through death, which is obviously a route much different from that taken by

TABLE 10.2
Odds Ratios of Variables Predicting Welfare Exits

Independent Variables	Odds Ratios
Individual characteristics	
High school graduate	1.22★★★
Employed	1.68★★★
White	1.24★★
Not incapacitated	1.24★
Age	1.01
Family structure	
Female head	0.50★★★
Single	2.28★★★
County-level characteristics	
Rural percentage	0.99
Unemployment rate	1.20★★★
Higher poverty	1.04
County caseload increase	1.05★★
Welfare variation	
Lowered benefits	1.23★
Length of welfare use	0.88★

★significant at the .05 level
★★significant at the .01 level
★★★significant at the .001 level

female heads, married couples, or singles. Second, most of the elderly are not in the labor force, while those under age sixty-five are expected to work and support themselves.

Table 10.2 presents the odds ratios for four blocks of variables: individual characteristics, family structure, county level characteristics, and variation in welfare use.[1] It is clear from the model that individual characteristics play a significant role in exiting from welfare. Household heads who are high school graduates, employed, white, and not incapacitated have a significantly greater probability of exiting from welfare. Not surprisingly, employment has the largest effect. Those who are employed have a 68 percent greater probability of exiting public assistance (compared to those not employed) during a six-month interval. These findings are consistent with earlier research and with the human capital theory: that is, individuals who possess more marketable characteristics increase their chances of getting out of poverty or at least off the welfare rolls (e.g., Bane and Ellwood 1983; Blank 1986; Hirschl and Rank 1991).

Family structure is another highly significant factor affecting the likelihood of exiting from welfare. This again is consistent with prior research (Bane and Ellwood 1983; Duncan 1984; Ellwood 1986; Tienda 1990). Female-headed families are less likely to exit from the welfare system than are married couples, while singles are 128 percent more likely to exit than are marrieds.

In the previous chapter, it was apparent that family structure had a sizable impact on the patterns of welfare use in the aggregate. Clearly, it is also a significant factor in a multivariate context. That is, after taking into account a number of pertinent factors, family structure remains significant in affecting the probabilities of exiting. Female-headed families are most constrained in getting off welfare, followed by married couples, and finally by singles. This pattern is understandable. Child care expenses, the earnings gap between men and women, the segmentation of the labor market, and fewer job skills pose serious obstacles to female heads, whereas married couples gain flexibility from the presence of two potential wage earners, and, for obvious reasons, singles not incapacitated face the least constraints of all.

If the family is viewed as an economic unit, it follows that different types of households will vary in their patterns of welfare use. This is important from a policy perspective. It suggests that an individual's flexibility and success in the labor market are mediated partially through family structure. Certainly, factors such as human capital are important as well; nevertheless, the role of the family critically affects the length of time on welfare.

A third block of variables in table 10.2 comprises the overall characteristics of the county where a recipient lives. Wisconsin has seventy-two counties, which vary in terms of unemployment rates, poverty rates, and the changes in the percentage of the population on welfare. Calculating the effects of these variables permits an approximate measure of how well a county is doing economically over time and an estimate of the effect this has on a recipient's likelihood of getting off welfare. Also included in the variables is the county's rural percentage.

Here, the pattern is surprising. The higher a county's unemployment rate, the greater the probability that a welfare recipient will exit the system. In addition, those living in counties with a moderate to high poverty rate are more likely to exit welfare (although the odds ratio is not significant). Finally, as the welfare caseload in a county increases, the chances of exiting also increase.

At first glance, these findings appear startling. How can it be that as the economic conditions in a county worsen, the chances of getting off welfare increase? The key to understanding this relationship is the effect that increased pressure has on finite resources.

There is solid evidence that as economic conditions deteriorate in a county, more households apply and receive welfare. (For example, Hirschl and Rank 1991 have shown that in the United States a county's welfare participation rate is directly related to the unemployment and poverty rates in that county.) However, this increased reliance on public assistance in turn puts greater pressure on the existing system and its resources, both financial and otherwise (e.g., number of staff, physical facilities, available time, and so on). That systems and organizations adapt to such stress by tightening up has been documented in various settings (Lipsky 1980; Elster 1992). For example, Lipsky notes that in human service agencies, "Street-level practice often reduces the demand for services through rationing. The familiar complaints of encountering 'red tape,' 'being given the run-around,' and 'talking to a brick wall' are reminders that clients recognize the extent to which bureaucratic unresponsiveness penalizes them" (1980:100).

Such tightening up may cause a greater number of current welfare recipients to exit for a variety of reasons, including bureaucratic ones (which we saw was an important factor in table 10.1). The most telling variable in this scenario is the strong relationship between the increase in a county's welfare caseload over time and the increased likelihood of exiting. I would argue that as the caseload increases, pressure is exerted in various ways to move current recipients out of the system.[2]

Using the National Longitudinal Survey, O'Neill and her coauthors (1984) also found a positive relationship between depressed economic conditions and welfare exits. In their analysis, state unemployment rates had a significant positive effect on the likelihood of exiting from welfare. In addition, deteriorating economic conditions in the 1980s were associated with a greater rate of exiting among welfare recipients in the state of Washington (Brazzell, Lefbert, and Opitz 1989).[3]

A final block of variables included in table 10.2 deals with variations in welfare use. The lowering of benefits and tightening of eligibility as a consequence of the OBRA changes resulted in higher exiting probabilities. In addition, the longer recipients remained on public assistance, the less likely they were to exit. This finding parallels the exiting probabilities found in the aggregate (as discussed in chapter 9). It may be that these individuals do indeed experience a settling-in effect, which again is consistent with prior research (see Moffitt 1992).

Although some settling in may occur, most welfare recipients eventually leave the system. It should be noted that in some cases families are no better off economically, and in fact may be worse off, than when they were on welfare. Thus, in certain situations, exiting the welfare system is not necessarily a positive economic consequence. This is particularly true when medical benefits are lost.

Nevertheless, for many families, leaving the welfare system does correspond with an increase in a household's standard of living. Perhaps as important as these increases are the positive effects of no longer having to rely on public assistance. As we saw in chapter 8, virtually all recipients dislike having to depend on others for their economic well-being. The loss of that burden is a relief to most.

11 MYTHS AND REALITIES

I think we've covered it pretty well. You know, everything you brought up I've tried to give you an answer and give it to you truthfully.
—Sixty-eight-year-old male, diagnosed with lung cancer

I began this book by stating that one of its purposes was to convey the realities, not the myths, of welfare recipiency. With that goal in mind, I have examined a range of experiences associated with welfare recipiency. These experiences have been revealed through the words of welfare recipients, through longitudinal data, and through my own interactions with the welfare system. I have followed individuals and families from the application process to their eventual exits from the rolls. In between, the text has explored the world of welfare recipients—their problems, their strengths, their lives. This chapter looks at the major themes these experiences reveal, the broader theoretical context within which they should be interpreted, and the implications of such an interpretation.

Major Themes

Surviving on Welfare Is Difficult

Perhaps most apparent from the preceding chapters is the sheer difficulty and pain associated with living on welfare. The notion that public assistance programs provide for a good life, or for even a modest life-style, sharply contrasts with reality.

Severe economic hardship is ever present for those trying to survive on public assistance (as seen in chapter 4). Recipients and their children are often forced to go hungry. All reported forgoing many of the necessities that most of us take for granted. The assistance provided by the government routinely runs out before the end of each month. To be on welfare is by definition to live in poverty. And to live in poverty translates into a day-to-day struggle for survival.

Existing on welfare is also psychologically difficult. Most recipients experience firsthand the stigma associated with receiving welfare (detailed in chapter 8). The general public tends to view people who rely on public assistance as failures and parasites. Recipients encounter such attitudes routinely and, as shown in chapters 3 and 8, often share them.

Finally, there is the social burden that welfare recipients carry. Largely as a result of the economic and psychological strains of living in poverty, relations within and outside the family are under constant pressure (see chapter 5). Relations between spouses, between parents and children, and with outsiders are frequently strained.

Given all this, it seems implausible that anyone would choose such a life. And, in fact, this is precisely what recipients told us. As the fifty-one-year-old divorced mother who was quoted at the beginning of chapter 1 said, "I can't see anybody that would ever settle for something like this just for the mere fact of getting a free ride, because it's not worth it." Living on welfare is a trying experience that virtually all wish to leave far behind.

Frequently Assumed Negative Behavioral Effects Are Negligible

Many assume that the welfare system induces severe negative behavioral changes in its participants, breaking up families, causing women to have more children, encouraging recipients to remain on the rolls for long periods of time, influencing people to drop out of the labor market, and so on.

With an important exception, there is little support for these notions. As shown in chapter 5, women on welfare actually have a lower birthrate than women in the general population. In addition, welfare programs appear to have little effect on the likelihood of marriage or divorce. And as found in chapter 9, those on public assistance tend to remain on the rolls temporarily.

One reason for the lack of an effect on the above types of behavior is that, as noted, no one enjoys living on welfare. The idea that people would desire such a life by having more children, dropping out of the labor market, and becoming female heads of households, is a stretch of the imagination, as most recipients will tell you. Furthermore, a significant number of those on welfare receive fairly small amounts of assistance (as seen in chapters 3 and 4). For example, singles and married couples often receive only modest amounts of in-kind assistance from the Food Stamp program. Such amounts are simply too low to impact behavior in any noticeable way.

Economic hardship, far more than welfare recipiency, influences family interaction and behavior among welfare families (detailed in chapter 5). Public assistance is a by-product of that economic adversity. It alone does little to explain family dynamics.

It should be noted that the setting for this study represents a very conservative test of these findings. Wisconsin is ranked above most states in terms of its ratio of average welfare payments to average earnings and in terms of average and maximum allowed state welfare payments. In view of the strong support for a lack of negative behavioral effects in this setting, it is unlikely that recipients in states with lower welfare benefits would behave substantially differently.

The single negative behavioral effect is the work disincentives embedded in these programs, particularly AFDC and Medicaid. For each dollar a person earns, a dollar is lost from the grant (illustrated in chapter 7)—in effect a 100 percent tax rate. Equally important is that although a job at minimum wage may pay slightly more than welfare, it often lacks medical coverage. Particularly for families with children, this is a very strong disincentive. Yet in spite of it, many on welfare work or eventually will find work.

Situations Differ by Household Type

When we think of welfare recipients, the image that frequently comes to mind is a female-headed family with children. Certainly this group constitutes an important part of the welfare population. Yet other types of families also receive public assistance, among them, married couples, singles, and the elderly. As this book has reported, the situations and circumstances in which welfare recipients find themselves differ widely by these household types. Recipients' reasons for turning to public assistance, their problems and routines, the length of time on welfare, and the paths for exiting from welfare all differ somewhat by household structure (chapters 3, 4, 9, and 10), as do their needs, resources, and constraints.

The issue of diversity in the welfare population is too often neglected. For example, Corbett writes,

> Where issues are complex (e.g., poverty and public dependency), it is easy to engage in perceptual reductionism whereby large amounts of data are summarily reduced to a manageable size and conflicting interpretations are subject to theoretical simplification. For example, it becomes easier to select a portion of the poor to represent, or serve as a proxy for, the entire population, rather than deal with the practical and theoretical consequences of the diversity within the population. A simplified picture makes the policy-making task appear more manageable. (1991:19)

As this book tries to show, the reality is not usually so simple.

Larger Factors Are Important

To understand why people find themselves in the position of needing welfare, one must recognize the important influence of larger factors that lie beyond people's immediate control. This is not to suggest that individual characteristics are irrelevant. They are simply best understood within a wider context.

For female-headed families, divorce or separation, lack of child-support payments, shortage of affordable child care, and the difficulty of finding work with livable wages and benefits combine to make assistance necessary. For married couples, layoffs, low-paying wages, and the lack of benefits are key. For singles, incapacitation and/or recurring health problems are usually behind the need for help. For the elderly, dwindling resources coupled with medical expenses lead to economic insecurity.

Certainly, there are some recipients at whom we could point our finger and say, "It's your fault." Yet for most recipients, this explanation is inadequate. Consider Joe Hall, who worked with the same company for twenty years, was laid off, and has over a hundred job applications out. Can we honestly say that it is his fault? The same is true for Marta Green, Jim Duncan, Susan Davis, and many of the other welfare recipients throughout this book.

Those on Welfare Hold Fundamental Values

The values welfare recipients hold are for the most part fundamental, bedrock American values. What do I mean by this? Simply that what most welfare recipients value, the majority of other Americans value as well. They value their independence, specifically their economic independence. They do not enjoy living off the taxpayers' dollars. They want to get ahead in their lives and to improve their lot. They stress the importance of work. They understand the significance of education. They want to see their sons and daughters successful in their own lives. They believe in persevering and struggling despite the odds against them. They have faith that such efforts will eventually be rewarded.

There is scant evidence that those on welfare somehow believe in a set of values different from those of mainstream America. Rather, what I heard and saw was a reaffirmation of the bedrock values of middle America. This is not to say that welfare recipients are modern-day saints. Far from it. They simply share many of the fundamental principles and values that their fellow Americans cherish. No more, no less.

Recipients Are Not Much Different from the Rest of Us

Perhaps the most salient theme to emerge from this study is that the welfare recipient is fundamentally not much different from you or me. As I stated in chapter 1, there is a tendency to view welfare recipients and the poor as significantly different from the rest of us—they just do not work hard enough; they are not concerned about their future; they lack the right motivation. In short, they get what they deserve.

After spending ten years on this project, I have come to a much different conclusion. These are people who work just as hard as the rest of us, care just as much about their future and their children's future, and hope to get ahead just as much as the next fellow. The difference lies not within them, but primarily within their position in relation to the larger forces found in our society.

Put yourself in the shoes of the welfare recipients described in this book. Suppose that you were raised in a family with very limited economic resources. Perhaps your father was an alcoholic, or your parents had divorced when you were young. You had to start working at an early age. Although you completed high school, you could not devote extensive time to your studies. Education beyond high school was simply out of the question. As a result, the only jobs you could get paid fairly little, had no benefits, and did not allow you to build marketable skills.

Now suppose that a crisis occurs in your life: you experience a severe injury; you suffer a divorce and receive no support; you are laid off of work; you simply grow old and ill. What do you do? Like the welfare recipients in the previous pages, you would probably search as long as possible for viable alternatives, hunting for a new job, relying on relatives, drawing on your unemployment insurance or savings accounts, and so on. With your searches coming up empty and your resources gone, where do you turn? Your options would in fact be few. With great reluctance, you would probably turn to the welfare system for temporary help until you could get back on your feet.

My guess, then, is that many of us would behave like the welfare recipients in this book if we found ourselves in similar positions. We would be frustrated by having to rely on welfare, hope to become economically self-sufficient, overwhelmed by the struggle of living in poverty, and continue to work hard despite the odds. Some of us might eventually resign ourselves to such a life, but most would struggle and eventually meet with some success.

My aim here is not to portray welfare recipients as heroes or martyrs. But neither are they villains. Rather, they are simply no better or worse than the rest of us. Given a similar set of circumstances, would you or I feel and act much differently? Perhaps, but I think not.

Finally, Michael Katz has written,

> We can think about poor people as "them" or as "us." For the most part, Americans have talked about "them." Even in the language of social science, as well as in ordinary conversation and political rhetoric, poor people usually remain outsiders, strangers to be pitied or despised, helped or punished, ignored or studied, but rarely full citizens, members of a larger community on the same terms as the rest of us.   (1989:236)

For the people in this book, it would indeed be more appropriate to use the word "us" rather than "them."

The Broader Context

Chapter 2 reviewed various theories and explanations people have used to understand the circumstances surrounding poverty and welfare utilization. These were divided into individ-ual, cultural, and structural perspectives.

How do the results from this study accord with these overall explanations? Let me begin by discussing those perspectives that do not sit well with the facts.

Explanations Lacking Support

The general public favors the attitudinal/motivational explana-tion for people being poor and on welfare. This explanation argues that people on welfare do not have the right attitudes, drive, or motivation. Were they to exert themselves, they would rise from the ranks of poverty and welfare dependency. It is appealing because it is simple, makes intuitive sense, and does not question the status quo of the society we live in. It assumes that there is a sense of justice or fairness at play. People are by and large accountable and hence deserving of their fate of im-poverishment.

Unfortunately, there is little support for such an explanation. As I mentioned earlier, the research findings in this study indi-cate that welfare recipients are just as motivated as the next fellow, if not more so. If motivation were all that mattered, 95 percent of the families in this book would no longer be poor and on welfare.

A similar type of explanation, but of a more structural na-ture, is what Schiller (1989) has referred to as the "Big Brother argument." The thesis here is that the current welfare system creates dramatic behavioral changes in people who are exposed to it. Such changes then foster welfare dependency and long-term poverty (see, e.g., Murray 1984; Mead 1986).

Again, I find little support for such an explanation. Welfare payments are just too meager to motivate most people to alter their behavior radically. This is not to say that welfare recipi-ents do not divorce, have children, and so on, just that public assistance has little to do with these behavioral vicissitudes.

It is important to note than when I say there is little support for a motivational or a Big Brother argument, this is not to imply that there is absolutely no support. Stereotypes endure because they accrete some grain of truth. I have indeed encountered people who were obviously lazy or perhaps corrupted by the welfare system. But they represent a very small minority of the total welfare population. Moreover, they certainly have not cornered the market on laziness or corruption. One can find such people throughout society—rich and poor. My earlier point bears repeating: welfare recipients are our fellow Americans—no better, no worse.

Cultural explanations of poverty and welfare use focus on the counterproductive cultural traits and values that welfare recipients reputedly possess. Welfare dependency is viewed as part of a cultural process in which children learn from their parents and from their surrounding environment that relying on welfare, bearing children out of wedlock, dropping out of school, and so on, are acceptable behaviors.

Once again, this study furnishes little support for this theory. The values and beliefs of welfare recipients mirror those of mainstream America. Parents desperately want their children to succeed and thrive in their own careers. Of the recipients studied, most had parents who never received any public assistance, and many were on the rolls for the first time themselves. Certainly, they express their share of frustrations, as evidenced in chapters 4, 5, and 6. But these frustrations arise not from a deviant culture but rather from being unable to achieve their mainstream goals and desires. The notion that a counterproductive, self-perpetuating culture reigns in these households is unsupported.

Those who posit cultural reasons for welfare dependency, however, are generally referring to severely depressed inner-city areas. This study is considerably broader and more representative in its geographic scope, although inner-city residents are found in the sample. Had I focused exclusively upon the inner city, it is certainly possible that I might have found more evidence of the importance of cultural factors. Regardless, as I stated in chapter 1, those living in major metropolitan inner-city areas constitute a very small percentage of the overall poverty population. They are simply not representative of most people who are poor and on welfare.

Clarifying the Focus: A Structural
Vulnerability Explanation

Having dealt with those theories that appear inadequate to explain why individuals and families find themselves on welfare and in poverty, I now turn to an explanation that I believe succeeds where they fail. Sheldon Danziger has written,

> Most analysts and policy-makers now avoid the simple statements that characterized the antipoverty policy debates of the late 1960s and early 1970s. Those debates typically viewed the poor either as, on the one hand, victims of their own inadequacies, often mired in a culture of poverty, or, on the other, as victims of societal deficiencies such as inadequate schooling, lack of labor market opportunities, and discrimination.
>
> (1989:42)

The point is a good one. The answer to why individuals are poor and on welfare is generally not black or white but rather occupies a shade along a spectrum. Equally important, one must focus on how the various pieces of the puzzle fit together. What are the mechanisms by which different levels of explanations interlock? Finally, one must also keep in mind that welfare recipients come from many different kinds of households. How do these differences relate to the predicaments in which recipients find themselves? A view that generalizes to all the poor, or to all the welfare population, will be achieved only with great caution.

Nevertheless, I do believe that we can come to a broad understanding of why a large proportion of welfare recipients find themselves in the position of relying on public assistance. It is an explanation that combines aspects of human capital theory with the more structural components of our society. Three major intersections of these perspectives are discussed below. I call this "a structural vulnerability explanation."

The issue of vulnerability. Human capital characteristics are important to understanding the lives of welfare recipients. Household heads on welfare are to varying degrees lacking in marketable skills and training. Education is often limited. So too are family resources and assets. In addition, factors such as race and gender can be understood as components of human capital, in that employers may use such characteristics to screen and/or limit potential employees. In short, the basket of goods and resources necessary to compete effectively within our economic system often comes up short.

Such characteristics do have a bearing on employment and on the likelihood of entering and exiting from public assistance. Recipients with greater human capital are more likely to become employed and are more likely to leave the welfare rolls. In short, personal characteristics do affect several important dimensions of welfare recipiency.

Yet do these characteristics in and of themselves cause dire poverty and welfare recipiency? The answer is largely no. If they were solely responsible, how might we explain the fluid movements of people in and out of welfare recipiency (as we saw in chapter 9). For many people, personal characteristics remain constant, yet welfare status and poverty status have not. An explanation that focuses on human capital alone cannot in and of itself account for such transitions.

What I argue is that while these characteristics alone do not cause welfare use, they place the individual in an economically vulnerable position when faced with a crisis such as loss of employment, changes in family status, illness and incapacitation, and so on (as detailed in chapter 3). Individuals and households lacking personal resources, human capital, and economic assets will have a more difficult time weathering such storms. As a result, they are more likely to turn to public assistance as a stopgap solution until they are able to get back on their feet. For some people that period of time is short, while for others it may be longer.

Many of the welfare recipients introduced in the preceding pages typify these patterns. For example, Colleen Bennett and her husband Ron weaved in and out of the welfare system as their economic situation improved or deteriorated. They are a household straddling the borderline between self-sufficiency and dependence. One wrong step, and they are likely to land back on welfare. They simply do not have the resources and assets necessary to tide them over for more than several weeks.

When Ron was laid off from his construction job, the Bennetts were able to survive only briefly without assistance. Furthermore, because of limited training and skills, Ron is likely to have more trouble finding another job than would an individual with greater human capital.

This pattern is in contrast with middle- and upper-class families experiencing crises. These families can draw on a larger pool of resources and assets to tide them over and so can remain afloat much longer. Furthermore, because of greater education and skills, jobs are easier and faster to come by. As a result, few middle- or upper-class families will reach the point of needing low-income government welfare programs for economic assistance.[1]

The events precipitating the economic crises leading to welfare use often result from broader economic, social, and political forces that lie beyond the direct control of the individual. A complete discussion of the nature and scope of these forces would constitute a book in and of itself. Let me simply mention several of the more pertinent that earlier chapters have shown to be particularly relevant to individual recipients.

Changes in the economy have a clear connection with the financial doldrums affecting many households (e.g., Schiller 1989). For example, much has been written about the shift from a manufacturing to a service economy. This shift has led to layoffs and cutbacks that have disrupted many lives. Michael Harrington (1984), among others, has written extensively about these effects.

Likewise, the stagnation of wages, coupled with the creation of an increasing number of low-paying jobs without benefits, has adversely affected many. During the past fifteen years the economy has produced a significant percentage of such jobs (Bluestone and Harrison 1982; Thurow 1987; Burtless 1990). Similarly, since 1973, per capita income (adjusted for inflation) has remained flat (U.S. Bureau of the Census 1992b). For younger families with children, median income (adjusted for inflation) declined by one-third between 1973 and 1990 (Edelman 1992).

As the economy moves in and out of recessionary periods

(with unemployment rates rising and falling), particular groups of people are hard hit. Traditionally, blue-collar workers suffer most during these periods, although recently white-collar workers have been hurt as well.

To what extent these changes reflect a dual economy, the growing importance of a global economic system, a by-product of capitalism, or some other macro explanation is difficult to say. What is certain is that they are real and that they have had, and continue to have, a negative impact on particular segments of the population.

Broad social forces have also placed particular individuals and households at economic risk. For example, the increase in family disruption coupled with the lack of child-support payments and affordable child care have done serious harm to women and specifically female-headed households. Weitzman (1985) has written extensively about the negative impact of no-fault divorce on women and their children.

Other social and demographic forces also affect people's economic well-being. These include the occupational segregation of the labor market by gender and race (Bergmann 1986), the aging of our society and the resulting economic burden placed on working-age adults (Soldo and Agree 1988), and the increasing isolation of economically depressed areas such as inner cities and rural regions (C. Duncan 1992; Jencks 1992).

Political forces also play a role. Decisions dealing with macroeconomic policy, low-income assistance, job-training programs, child-support payments, birth control clinics, health care, and enforcement of antidiscriminatory policies, to name a few of countless programs and policy directives, can reduce or intensify the impact of detrimental events on people's lives. In general, the 1980s and 1990s have seen a reduction in federal programs and policies directly and indirectly affecting the poor and the near-poor (Levitan 1990).

Certainly, the events precipitating an economic crisis in a household also involve individual judgments and decisions (such as the decision to divorce, the decision to leave or remain at a job, the decision to have children, and so on). Perhaps if people had made different decisions, they would not have found themselves in such dire economic straits. However, in many of the cases described in the preceding pages, the events leading to an economic crisis lay largely beyond the control of the sole individual. Not totally, but to a large extent.

To summarize, one key to understanding why people are on public assistance is to recognize the vulnerability created by a lack of human capital, which, when coupled with a severe crisis, can push people into economic tailspins. The events precipitating these crises are often a result of, or at least exacerbated by, structural changes and forces in our society. Thus, the economic tailspin leading to welfare utilization results from both individual and structural factors.

Structural impact upon human capital deficiencies. Within my structural vulnerability argument there is a second major intersection of human capital characteristics and the structural forces in society. Given that human capital bears on poverty and welfare use (by causing varying degrees of vulnerability), why do some people lack human capital to begin with? Here again a broader structural outlook is helpful.

Analyses of the American system of stratification have shown that while some amount of social mobility does occur (Blau and Duncan 1967; Featherman and Hauser 1978; Duncan 1984), social class as a whole tends to reproduce itself (Beeghley 1989). Those whose parents are from a working or lower class are likely to remain working or lower class themselves. Similarly, those whose parents fall into the upper class are likely to remain upper class. To a great extent, differences in human capital are the result of familial social class differences.

Why does this pattern exist? A number of explanations address the reproduction of social class (e.g., Bowles and Gintis 1976; Bourdieu and Passeron 1977; Giroux 1983; Clignet 1992). Most agree that variations in economic and social class result in significant differences in resources and opportunities for children. These difference in turn affect children's future life chances and outcomes, including the accumulation of human capital.

A game analogy illustrates the process of class reproduction (see Beeghley 1989). Imagine three players beginning a game of Monopoly. Normally, each player would be given $1,500 at the start of the game. The playing field is in effect level, with the individual players' outcomes determined by the roll of the dice as well as their own skills and judgments.

Now imagine a modified game of Monopoly, in which the players start out with quite different advantages and disadvantages, much as they would in life. Player 1 begins with $5,000 and several Monopoly properties on which houses have already been built. Player 2 starts out with the standard $1,500 and no properties. Finally, player 3 begins the game with only $250. Who will be the winners and losers in this modified game of Monopoly? Both luck and skill are still involved, but given the differing sets of resources and assets that each player begins with, they are much less important in predicting the game's outcome. Certainly, it is possible for player 1 to lose and for player 3 to win, but that is unlikely given the unequal allocation of resources at the start of the game. Moreover, while player 3 may win any individual game, over the course of hundreds of games, the odds are that player 1 will win considerably more often, even if player 3 is much luckier and more skilled.

In similar fashion, children from lower- or working-class backgrounds simply do not have the range and depth of opportunities as children from middle- or upper-class backgrounds. One has only to look at the vast differences in educational quality by residence and income to begin to grasp the magnitude of these opportunity differences (e.g., Kozol 1991).

The connection between social class and future career and life outcomes has been demonstrated repeatedly. Beeghley states,

> The fact is that the vast majority of the sons of blue-collar workers end up as blue-collar workers. And when their daughters are employed, most of them end up as either administrative support or blue-collar workers. The result is that they are always economically insecure, always prone to impoverishment, regardless of how hard they work. Similarly, the vast majority of the sons of white-collar workers end up as white-collar workers. And when their daughters are employed, they too end up as white-collar workers, typically in jobs above the level of administrative support. (1989:69)

Likewise, in an analysis of the levels of socioeconomic achievement for children from welfare families, Schiller writes, "Thus it is concluded that a substantial portion of the AFDC sons' underachievement can only be explained in terms of a relative constriction in opportunities, with that constriction itself based on the economic status of the origin family" (1970:439).

Or as Harrington wrote some thirty years ago in *The Other America,* "The real explanation of why the poor are where they are is that they made the mistake of being born to the wrong parents, in the wrong section of the country, in the wrong industry, or in the wrong racial or ethnic group. Once that mistake has been made, they could have been paragons of will and morality, but most of them would never even have had a chance to get out of the other America" (1963:23)

In an analysis using data from the Panel Study of Income Dynamics to estimate the effects of family and community background on children's economic status, Corcoran and coauthors concluded, "Our own studies . . . have estimated sizable background effects on earnings, hourly wages, family income, and welfare program participation. We have found parental income (especially poverty), race, and parental and community welfare use to be especially strongly associated with children's economic outcomes" (1990:366).

Finally, Wachtel (1971) describes the process cogently:

If you are black, female, have parents with low socioeconomic status, and [are] dependent upon labor income, there is a high probability that you will have relatively low levels of human capital which will slot you into low-paying jobs, in low wage industries, in low wage markets. With this initial placement, the individual is placed in a high risk category, destined to end up poor sometime during her working and nonworking years. She may earn her poverty by working fulltime. Or she may suffer either sporadic or long periods of unemployment. Or she may become disabled, thereby reducing her earning power even further. Or when she retires, social security payments will place her in poverty even if she escaped this fate throughout her working years. With little savings, wealth, or private pension income, the retiree will be poor.   (6)

It follows that many of the families in this study lacked human capital not because they failed to work hard or were unmotivated but because of the structural constraints imposed by the reproduction of social class. As I wrote in chapter 5, the childhoods of the sampled recipients were characterized by substantially reduced life chances and options. Although some children in such positions can conceivably become bankers or lawyers, most will not. The decks are simply stacked against them, and this increases the likelihood that their accumulation of human capital will be limited.[2]

Two levels of understanding economic vulnerability. There is a third point of intersection between individual human capital and structural factors that is key to my structural vulnerability argument—specifically, that there are two levels at which we can understand the underlying mechanisms producing economic vulnerability. An analogy to another game—musical chairs—illustrates these two levels. The key is whether one chooses to analyze the losers of the game or the game itself.

Imagine eight chairs and ten players. The players begin to circle around the chairs until the music suddenly stops. Who fails to find a chair? If the focus is on the winners and losers of the game, some combination of luck and skill will be involved. In all likelihood, the losers will be those who are in an unfavorable position when the music stops, somewhat slower, perhaps not as strong, somewhat less agile, and so on. In one sense, these are appropriately cited as the reasons for losing the game.

However, if the focus is on the game itself, it is quite clear that, given only eight chairs, two players are bound to lose. Even if all players were suddenly to double their speed and agility, there would still be two losers. From this broader context, it really does not matter what the loser's characteristics are.

I would argue that this analogy can be applied to our economic and social systems. Given that there is unemployment, given that there are periods of recession, given that there are low-paying jobs lacking benefits, given that there is occupational segregation in the labor market, given that there is a lack of affordable child care, given that there are no provisions to care for those who can no longer participate in the economy because of illness or incapacitation, someone is going to lose at this game. The losers will generally be those who lack human capital and thus cannot compete as effectively as those who have acquired greater human capital. Yet, as Wright and Lam note, "Given a game that some are destined to lose, it is appropriate to do research on who the losers turn out to be. But we should not mistake an analysis of the losers for an analysis of the game itself" (1987:53).

Certainly, the impact and nature of the structural factors affecting the game may vary over time. In musical chairs, one of the ten chairs may be removed—or three or four; likewise, the rules of the economic game can and do change, which in turn affects the number of overall losers.[3] Such changes result from a variety of factors, including social policy. Consequently, the numbers of losers produced by the economic, social, and political systems in this country are not written in stone. However, while the numbers can and do fluctuate, I would argue that a significant number of losers are generally being produced at any point in time by the overall game. From this perspective, simply increasing individual human capital will shuffle persons up or down in terms of their positions in the competitive queue, but it will do little to change the overall rates of unemployment, low-paying jobs, and so on.[4]

The earlier example of Colleen and Ron Bennett can be seen in this light. On the one hand, their economic vulnerability is a result of their lack of human capital, which in turn hinders their ability to compete effectively in the labor market. On the other, the seasonal and unstable nature of the construction industry contributes to their economic vulnerability. The same is true for many of those whose stories this book has told. Depending on whether one chooses to analyze the losers of the game or the game itself, the causes of economic vulnerability will differ. They are in a real sense, both correct interpretations.

To summarize, the structural vulnerability perspective helps explain why a large proportion of those receiving welfare find themselves in the position of relying on public assistance. The explanation combines aspects of human capital theory with the more detrimental outcomes of various structural forces in our society. It argues that people lacking human capital are more economically vulnerable if a crisis occurs. Such crises are often the result of broader economic, social, and political forces in our society. In addition, the lack of human capital is largely a result of the reproduction of social class. Children from lower-class backgrounds begin with fewer resources and opportunities, which in turn limits their future life chances and outcomes, including the accumulation of human capital. Finally, although lack of human capital and the vulnerability this leads to explain who the losers of the economic game are, the more structural components of our economic, social, and political systems explain why there are losers in the first place.

Implications

Several implications follow from this analysis. Perhaps the most important is that our traditional approaches of dealing with poverty and welfare recipiency on an individual level will be largely ineffective. Given the root causes of poverty and welfare use suggested in this and other studies,[5] we are only misleading ourselves by focusing on the attitudes, motivation, work ethic, or alleged dependency of those on public assistance. Likewise, if social policy focuses on human capital alone as the determinant of poverty and welfare use, this again will miss the underlying dynamic. Only an understanding that welfare use is a result of structural factors impacting on the lack of human capital will serve. Human capital influences who the winners and losers of the economic game will be but does little to explain the game's tendency to produce economic losers in the first place. Social policy would be more effective if it focused on reducing the number of losers that the overall game produces.

For several reasons, however, we are unlikely to break with our individualistic interpretations of poverty and welfare use. First, as the next chapter discusses, this approach is consistent with several of our most important values. These include individualism, self-reliance, and the belief that ample opportunities exist for all who are willing to work for them. The idea of social class reproducing itself appears almost un-American in light of such values.[6] As I stated at the beginning of this book, the realities found in this study are in many respects more troubling than the myths.

Second, it is much more difficult to deal with a problem that results from deeply embedded economic and social structural processes rather than from individual failings. It is easier to argue that the government simply needs to cut back its role in helping the poor in order to provide individual incentives for hard work, particularly in tight economic times. Such a solution provides a handy justification for doing less, not more. Likewise, it is easier to suggest that our problems in education can be solved by allowing people more flexibility in the selection of schools than to look at the vast economic problems that school systems are facing.

Third, such approaches are politically appealing. To use the poor and welfare recipients as scapegoats, or at best as subjects of neglect, is often politically expedient. Conversely, the message of deeper structural problems generally is not well received. Structural class differences have never been a powerful political issue in the United States; the concepts of individual opportunities and their availability have proved far more important.

For these reasons and more, we are unlikely to address the issue of poverty and welfare use much differently in the future. As Dunbar writes,

> In short, no one seems to believe that poverty is caused by the malfunctioning of the economy. Poverty is blamed on the inadequacies of the poor, perhaps abetted by marginal education, insufficient upbringing, and ill-designed government programs. Never on the economy, except as it may now and again be sluggish, never on governmental allocations of national resources, never on the investment decisions of private businesses, which along with federal priorities, determine whom this economy serves and for what purposes.   (1988:15)

Only when large-scale economic failures occur do we occasionally reevaluate our individualistic assumptions. For example, most Americans understood that the widespread poverty during the Great Depression was not the result of individual failings but rather of structural economic problems. As a result, the federal government became actively involved in the issue of public welfare. Likewise, the welfare states of most modern capitalist industrial societies are thought to temper the effects of the free market system. For example, Schottland refers to a welfare state as "a modern, democratic Western state in which the power of the state is deliberately used to modify the free play of economic and political forces in order to effect a redistribution of income" (1967:10).

What has occurred in the political debate in the United States over the past twenty-five years (led particularly by the conservative wing) is that the cause and effect of the welfare state and poverty have been reversed. Rather than viewing the free market system as generating a degree of poverty and therefore necessitating that government play a role in tempering that poverty, the argument has become one in which the government is viewed as creating poverty by interfering with the free market system, which in turn creates disincentives and dependency. The argument has been turned on its head.[7]

Yet as this book shows, there is little support for such an argument. Defining the issue of poverty and welfare use as a problem of government interference is wishful thinking at best. In fact, given the root causes of poverty and welfare use suggested in this analysis, there are limited means available to address the issue. Unless there is a major restructuring, I believe various groups in our society will continue to need both temporary and longer-term government assistance. We are deluding ourselves if we think that we can get rid of poverty using one or another simple approach. We cannot. Unfortunately, this is a highly disturbing implication of my analysis.

The reader might ask whether I am simply reiterating the Biblical axiom, "You have the poor among you always." The answer is yes, but a highly qualified yes. While the poor have been and will continue to be with us in the foreseeable future, the extent and magnitude of poverty can and does change over time. I do not wish to suggest that there is nothing we can do to address the issue of why people are in need of public assistance. There are ways that I believe can temper the magnitude and likelihood of poverty. They are relatively cost-efficient, particularly in the sense that they are likely to reap long-term economic and social benefits. In addition, many of them are politically feasible, appealing across a wide political spectrum.[8] Finally, to use an earlier analogy, these ideas offer a means to reduce the number of losers produced by the overall game, as opposed to shuffling people up or down in the competitive queue. The focus is not on the welfare system per se, but rather on various strategies designed to alleviate some of the need for public assistance.

Employment Policies

Perhaps most important are those policies intended to produce low levels of unemployment, creating jobs with livable wages and benefits, and to prepare people to fill such jobs. As Schiller notes, "Jobs—in abundance and of good quality—are the most needed and most permanent solution to the poverty problem" (1989:210). Of course, it is one thing to suggest this policy and quite another to accomplish it. Our ability to create and sustain such an economy is open to debate. Nevertheless, if we wish to address the issue of poverty and welfare use, this is a key policy approach.

As shown in the preceding pages, many of those receiving public assistance were either looking for work or working at low-wage jobs. If they were able to land jobs paying a livable wage and providing reasonable benefits, it would represent a major economic improvement in their lives. How might this be accomplished?

Schiller (1989) argues for the importance of having a multi-dimensional and coordinated approach to producing an effective employment policy. This includes putting in place aggregate demand policies, training policies, and public service employment policies.

Aggregate demand policies are designed to stimulate the creation of more jobs in the economy. This can be done in a variety of ways, including increased government expenditures, consumer tax cuts, greater investment and depreciation allowances, and easier and cheaper access to credit.

Assuming that aggregate demand policies make more jobs available, training policies are a second important component of an overall effective employment policy. Job training programs that focus on improving human capital to make people more attractive to potential employers can be quite valuable for both the individual and the employer. In addition, as the United States competes increasingly in a global economy, it becomes essential to invest in the training and skills of its workers.

The effectiveness of job training programs in the past has been modest. In summarizing the research, Bassi and Ashenfelter write,

> These findings suggest that employment and training programs have been neither an overwhelming success nor a complete failure in terms of their ability to increase the long-term employment and earnings of disadvantaged workers. Our ability to improve the lot of any given participant and the collective economic well-being of the disadvantaged has been modest— as has been the level of resources devoted to this endeavor (1986:149).

Programs that have provided more comprehensive services and facilities to their participants have been more successful in placing people in the labor market and increasing their earnings potential.

A third component of an overall effective employment policy is public service employment. This involves the government becoming a more active player in creating jobs directly. Despite the considerable debate over the merits of public service employment, the advantages are threefold. First, it directly expands employment opportunities. Second, it can target such opportunities to those areas and for those groups most in need.

And third, well-designed public service employment can provide much needed improvements and services for communities and society.

Taken together, the policies of aggregate demand, job training, and public service employment have considerable potential for improving the lives of the poor. As Schiller writes,

> The end product of a coordinated employment policy should be an abundance of jobs that provide decent wages and advancement opportunity. The benefits of such jobs are as obvious as is the necessity for them. They will provide the incomes necessary to lift families out of poverty, to keep them together, and to give them promise of a secure future. Their benefits will reach to the children of the poor, who will have the means and incentive for staying in school. Employment policy has the potential, then, of minimizing both present and future poverty.
>
> (1989:209)

Individual Assets

Developing and building assets among low-income families, as discussed by Michael Sherraden (1991), represents another step toward tempering the effects of poverty and the need for public assistance. As this study relates, families lack the resources and assets necessary to tide them over during rough times. Yet given the problems they face daily, these households have trouble accumulating such assets and human capital.

Sherraden argues that government policy should provide incentives and resources that would allow low-income families to build their economic assets, much as it does for middle- and upper-class families (e.g., home mortgage tax deductions, lowered capital gains tax, etc.). His basic assertion is that "asset accumulation and investment, rather than income and consumption, are the keys to leaving poverty. Therefore, welfare policy should promote asset accumulation—stakeholding—by the poor. An asset-based welfare policy would seek to combine welfare assistance with economic development" (1991:294). Current welfare programs do not foster asset accumulation because households can only qualify when asset and income levels are desperately low.

One specific policy tool for fostering asset accumulation is to establish what Sherraden calls "Individual Development Accounts,"

> earnings-bearing, tax-benefited accounts in the name of each individual, initiated as early as birth, and restricted to designated purposes. Regardless of the category of welfare policy (housing, education, self-employment, retirement, or other), assets would be accumulated in these long-term restricted accounts. The federal government would match or otherwise subsidize deposits for the poor, and there would be potential for creative financing from the private sector and account holders themselves. IDAs would be designed to promote long-range planning, savings and investment, and achievement of life goals.   (1991:297).

Such a policy would allow low-income households to grow less vulnerable to the types of crises described in chapter 3. In addition, it would begin to mitigate in a modest way the vast differences in resources across social class and their effects on the accumulation of human capital.

Tax Benefits for Low-Income Workers

A third method to temper poverty and welfare use would be to create tax benefits to assist low-income workers. The current Earned Income Tax Credit (EITC) is an example of such an approach. The EITC gives low-income workers with children a modest refundable tax credit.

Sheldon Danziger (1990) argues for the importance of expanding the concept of a refundable tax benefit to other areas in order to assist low-income workers. For example, he suggests that such an approach be used to make the current child-care tax credit refundable for poor families. In addition, Danziger proposes replacing the flat personal exemption with a per capita refundable credit. Because of their refundability, such credits would do considerably more to aid the poor and near-poor taxpayers than does the current system. These tax policies would also have the advantage of being relatively easy to implement because the credits are already in place.

Policies to Buffer the Economic Consequences
of Family Change

This study has described the severe economic consequences of family change, particularly for female-headed families with children. Such families are usually created through separation and divorce or through having a child out of wedlock. Policies addressing these changes and their economic consequences could be quite beneficial in tempering the effects of poverty and subsequent need for public assistance.

The child support policies suggested by Irvin Garfinkel (1992), and partially enacted in the Family Support Act of 1988, are a politically feasible strategy for addressing the economic consequences of family change. A common problem for female-headed families is that mothers often fail to receive court-ordered child support payments. The ability to enforce absent parents' responsibility to fulfill their court-ordered financial obligations represents a useful way to reduce the likelihood of poverty and welfare use among such families. Garfinkel argues that a child support assurance system should contain three key elements. First, whichever parent is not living with the child would pay a set percentage of his or her income for child support. Second, the support payments would be automatically withheld from the nonresident parent's paycheck in the same manner as Social Security payments. Third, a minimum benefit would be assured. If nonresident parents were not making enough income to meet this benefit level, the government would make up the difference.

A second strategy to addressing the economic consequences of family change would be to enact policies intended to reduce the number of unwanted teenage pregnancies and therefore the number of families headed by never-married females. Marian Wright Edelman (1987) has written extensively on what such policies might look like. According to Edelman, two components are critical to reducing unwanted teenage pregnancy. First, education concerning sexuality, parenthood, and contraception must be made available, along with access to contraception. Research indicates that such knowledge does not necessarily lead to greater sexual activity but rather encourages those teens who are sexually active to behave more responsibly.

However, simply providing the means to avoid pregnancy does not ensure that teenagers will do so. The second critical component to reducing teen pregnancy is motivation. The typical motivating factor is the loss of potential opportunities in the future—education, career, income, and so on. Policies that begin to provide better opportunities to lower-income teenagers (such as employment opportunities, educational opportunities, or building assets and resources) will likely increase the motivation to avoid pregnancy. This is succinctly expressed in a report from the Children's Defense Fund, which states, "In many ways, the best contraceptive is a real future" (1985:3).

A third approach to dealing with the economic consequences of family change is to make child care accessible and affordable to lower-income families. Summarizing the state of child care services in America, the National Research Council stated, "Existing child care services in the United States are inadequate to meet current and likely future needs of children, parents, and society as a whole. For some families, child care services are simply unavailable; for many others, care may be available, but it is unaffordable or fails to meet basic standards of quality" (1990:xii). Given that we expect female heads of household to participate in the labor force, and given that both spouses in a married-couple household often work out of economic necessity, child care is an imperative. Policies that increase the access to and affordability of good-quality child care will go a long way toward helping many female-headed families and married-couple households.

Universal Health Care

A fifth policy initiative that would help virtually every low-income family would be decent-quality universal health care. Too often, the elderly and those suffering from serious health problems are forced to reduce their assets and income in order to qualify for Medicaid. Providing universal health care would eliminate the need to destitute oneself in order to get medical coverage. In addition, such a system would eliminate one of the major disincentives for welfare recipients to take jobs—that is, loss of health insurance. And for the working poor without medical coverage, universal health care would provide substantial relief.

David Ellwood has written in detail about the types of strategies needed to reduce the poverty among American families. At the top of his list is providing every citizen with medical protection. He writes:

> Helping the poor sometimes involves difficult trade-offs among competing values. Not so for medical protection. Medical coverage primarily involves money—money that we generally are providing already. Medical protection outside a welfare system reinforces autonomy, work, and family and helps integrate people into at least one part of the mainstream. Failing to provide care or providing it only to nonworking and single-parent families puts us at odds with our values.   (1988:108)

Community Resources and Opportunities

Finally, just as promoting the accumulation of individual assets, resources, and human capital is important, so too is investing in the lower-income communities where welfare recipients often live. Community development and community organization are useful ways to achieve this.

Strengthening the major institutions found within lower-income communities is vital, because they have the power to improve the quality of life, foster the accumulation of human capital, and increase the overall opportunities for community residents. Among such institutions are schools, businesses and industries, lending establishments, community centers, and so on. A wide range of strategies can be used to strengthen these institutions to meet the needs of the community.[9] Creating greater equity in funding across school districts, attracting businesses into lower-income communities, opening up the lending practices of banks and savings and loans to people in economically depressed areas—all would provide substantial benefits.

In some cases, basic services and institutions are absent. For example, community organizer Ernie Cortes has worked extensively in Texas with Communities Organized for Public Services (COPS). They were able to mobilize the Hispanic community to exert pressure on the Texas legislature. That pressure resulted in state funds allocated for providing basic sewer and water services in poor unincorporated areas along the Mexican border. Many other examples can be found of grassroots organizations working for and strengthening the basic foundations in communities (e.g., ACORN, Habitat for Humanity, Industrial Areas Foundation). Grassroots organizational techniques have the potential to push for the redistribution of resources to particularly needy communities.

Community development and community organizational techniques also build on the strengths of those within the community. For example, chapter 5 told how a number of welfare recipients developed networks of family and friends to provide occasional support. These networks can also exist community-wide. One such has been developed at Grace Hill Neighborhood Services in St. Louis. Called the Member Organized Resource Exchange (MORE), the system draws on the resources of people in the community to provide exchanges of needed goods and services. Howard Husock explains:

> In St. Louis, in a poor black neighborhood of housing projects, brick rowhouses, and vacant lots north of downtown and aside the Mississippi, residents have access to a network of help that money can't buy. Money, in fact, is not accepted. To obtain assistance—someone to fix a car, watch a baby, move furniture, or stay with an infirm parent—residents must themselves contribute a service of their own to the "resource exchange." Residents who aren't well enough to make "deposits," but who may well need to make withdrawals, can gain credits when volunteers from suburban churches and synagogues contribute labor in their name. It is a system that involves more than 4,000 people, 70 percent with annual incomes below $10,000. They keep track of their "balance" through a computer network with its own ATM-style cards, good at terminals at local stores, designed with the help of volunteer computer industry consultants.   (1992:53)

Systems like this provide support and resources to community members while simultaneously empowering them.[10]

The concept of people organizing together to address problems and accomplish specific goals dates to the beginning of human history. It is at our country's roots as well. Community organizer Si Kahn elaborates:

> Most of the rights and benefits we have now weren't just given to us. People organized to get them. Many of the things we now take for granted had to be fought for. Today most of us who work have pension plans, paid vacations, paid holidays, sick leave, and overtime benefits. We didn't get these benefits because the companies suddenly decided to give them to us. We have them because millions of people in the 1930s and at other times organized unions to force their companies to give them these benefits, which were then adopted by the society as a whole. The fact that women have the vote or that people of color have some of their civil rights protected came about not because of the good-heartedness of the government, but because these groups organized to demand those rights. Even public schools and public education came about because people in this country organized to insist that their children, as well as the children of the rich, had a right to education.   (1991:10)

The six approaches just described have the potential to temper and reduce the likelihood of poverty and the need for public assistance. As such, they are useful and productive. They include establishing a coordinated employment policy, building individual assets, providing tax benefits to assist low-income workers, addressing the economic consequences of family change, providing universal health care, and developing and building community resources and opportunities.[11] All focus on reducing the number of losers that the overall game produces. In addition, they are mutually reinforcing and can be seen as an overall multifaceted strategy for dealing with poverty. However, it must also be emphasized that none of them will "solve" the problem of poverty. As long as the current economic, social, and political systems exist in this country, some people will be economically vulnerable. While there are a number of positive aspects about our free market capitalist system, there is also a price—a price that has been exacted in the lives of the people throughout this book. The point is to begin to temper and reduce this price.

Conclusion

Without doubt, there will continue to be a need for public assistance programs in the future. Politicians will continue to debate over the amounts to be spent on them, the degree of necessary incentives, various programmatic changes, and so on. They may debate the merits of universal programs such as a children's allowance system compared to the more targeted programs we currently have. Regardless, a sizable number of Americans will remain in dire circumstances. We can choose to address their need through constructive assistance; we can choose to ignore it; we can choose to punish those who seek help. Regardless, the need will continue.

One final thought: For policies to effectively temper the extent of poverty, they should be based on the assumption that the poor and welfare recipients hold much in common with the rest of the population. As shown throughout this book, those on welfare share the attitudes and values of mainstream America. This fact is too often missing from the policy and academic debate. As Dunbar states, social science "treats the poor like a foreign nation or refashions them into objects unlike us. . . . [It is] a discipline that speaks mainly for the approval of other social scientists and of legislators, and seldom consults the poor themselves" (1988:18). Effective as well as humane policies will be based on the assumption of commonalities between the poor and the nonpoor. All of the above policy ideas implicitly assume such commonality. This, I believe, is a key to their potential success.

The findings from this study provide a backdrop against which to view the myths and realities of welfare recipiency. As I reiterated earlier, the realities are in many respects more troubling than the myths. There is something oddly comforting in the idea that people get what they deserve, that if they are poor and on public assistance, they must be at fault. As I discuss in the final chapter, such beliefs are deeply embedded in our American culture and are thus particularly hard to overcome. Nevertheless, such beliefs reflect the myths rather than the realities of welfare recipiency.

12 CONCLUDING THOUGHTS

You get the looks and the feels. You can more or less feel it. . . . People feel that their good, hard-earned money is being spent on you guys. That you're not doing anything to help better yourself. And I mean you can't come right out and say, "Hey, I'm doing everything I can." "Quit looking at me like that." So . . . they just go on thinking. It gets to you after awhile, but you learn to live with it.
—Forty-five-year-old long-term welfare recipient

Throughout this book, I have tried to report clearly the many facets of welfare recipients' lives. Although I am left with a number of thoughts about these lives, two memories in particular stand out. The first is of Carol Richardson, whom I described at the beginning of chapter 6. It was quite obvious when we talked on that hot summer afternoon that Carol had experienced considerable hardship throughout her life. Yet it was equally obvious that this was a woman who would not give up; who felt that with enough time and effort she would be able to rise out of poverty. During the interview, she spoke of both the adversity and the determination in her life. Her convictions and hopes in the face of her hardships were startling.

The second memory is equally startling. It is that of the local townspeople looking through a tavern window in order to see who was entering the social service office across the street to apply for welfare. Jokes, laughter, and derogatory comments filled the air. "What a good-for-nothing lazy bum," "Why don't they get a job." "Seems like she's been on for years." "They're what's wrong with this country!" The comments were unflattering and unceasing.

Perhaps these two images best capture the essence of the welfare experience described in this book. My concluding thoughts are largely about their juxtaposition.

Throughout our history, Americans have enthusiastically embraced individualism. For example, Herbert Gans begins his book, *Middle American Individualism,* "America has often been seen—and has seen itself—as constantly in flux. Still, as anyone who has ever read de Tocqueville's *Democracy in America* knows after just a few pages, there are many ways in which the United States has changed only slightly in over 150 years, and one of the stable elements is the continued pursuit of individualism by virtually all sectors of the population" (1988:1). Closely associated with such individualism is the concept of self-reliance. Perhaps as a result of our frontier history, self-reliance has always been viewed as an important component of the American character.

Yet a third related aspect of our value system is the widely shared belief that the United States is a land where opportunities exist for all who are willing to work for them and that individual virtue and talent can overshadow the constraints of class, race, or ethnicity. Such is the message engraved at the foot of the Statue of Liberty and viewed by millions of immigrants as they sailed past her beacon. Some ninety years after Liberty's torch was lit, President Bush, as every president has, echoed this belief: "For over 200 years, the most exceptional aspect of American society has been the belief, the hope, that this is a land where people can make a better life for themselves and their children. It's this spirit, the commitment to the American Dream, that has made our country and our society the most dynamic in the world" (1992:22).

Largely as a result of these beliefs, we enthusiastically celebrate those who have risen from rags to riches—the Horatio Algers, the Abraham Lincolns, or the Clarence Thomases of this country. Their success stories are vivid proof that those who work hard can overcome humble beginnings. That it is possible in this country to go from poverty and hard knocks to the Supreme Court bench.[1] That with enough individual effort, literally anything is possible. In short, that the American dream is alive and well in this land of opportunity.

In pointed contrast stand those who do not support themselves economically. Those who depend upon the government for their survival. Those who are no longer self-reliant. In short, those whom we call welfare recipients. Because their predicaments are in sharp contradiction with the American dream, we often look at them with disdain, blaming the individual for the problem. Such a response presumes that life is guided by a sense of fairness or justice—those who do well must deserve to win, and those who fail must deserve to lose.

Consequently, welfare recipients serve as ever-present scapegoats. Their mistake is threefold. First, they are poor and thus particularly vulnerable to attack. Second, they are disproportionately composed of traditionally disenfranchised groups in our society, such as racial minorities, women, children, the incapacitated, and so on. And third, they rely on public tax dollars for support.

When economic times are hard, welfare recipients become an even more convenient target for attack. A recent example was the 1991 governor's race in Louisiana. During a campaign stop, David Duke, the Republican candidate, characterized welfare as a subsidy for criminals to a cheering crowd of retirees (*St. Louis Post-Dispatch,* October 31, 1991). In a forum held at the American Association of Retired Persons' state convention, Duke noted that, "The elderly who have contributed all their lives have been forgotten by a welfare system that encourages laziness" (*St. Louis Post-Dispatch,* October 31, 1991). Throughout his campaign, Duke placed the responsibility for many of the economic and social problems experienced by Louisianians on the shoulders of welfare recipients. The message was greeted by enthusiastic crowds along the way.

Of course, these types of attacks on welfare recipients are nothing new. As discussed in chapter 2, they go back centuries. The local townspeople looking disparagingly out of a rural

Wisconsin tavern window and the cheering crowds in Louisiana have a long history behind them.

The fact that empirical research on the poor and welfare recipients offers little justification for such attacks does not seem to matter much. As Michael Katz has written,

> Still, as even a casual reading of the popular press, occasional attention to political rhetoric, or informal conversations about poverty reveal, empirical evidence has remarkably little effect on what people think. Part of the reason is that conventional classifications of poor people serve such useful purposes. They offer a familiar and easy target for displacing rage, frustrations, and fear. They demonstrate the link between virtue and success that legitimates capitalist political economy. And by dividing poor people, they prevent their coalescing into a powerful, unified, and threatening political force. Stigmatized conditions and punitive treatment are powerful incentives to work, whatever the wages and conditions. (1989:10)

This, then, is one side of the welfare experience. It is epitomized by a denigration of those relying on public assistance. It is represented by ignorance, self-righteousness, and bigoted stereotypes. And it is deeply troubling but not surprising, given our society's emphasis on individualism, self-reliance, and the belief in opportunities.

Yet there is another side to the welfare experience. It is reflected in Carol Richardson's hope and resolution. Ironically, it too is part of the American character. It is found in the words and actions of many of those appearing throughout this book. This side is characterized by faith, resilience, and determination. It is revealed in the caring of Susan Davis, in the hopes of Marta Green, in the drive of Denise Turner, and in the courage of Jim Duncan. This is the untold story of the welfare experience. These are the realities that are rarely discussed, perhaps because they put a human face on suffering and misery.

Given the degrading and humiliating conditions that welfare recipients live in, it is quite remarkable that they are not totally demoralized. That most are not speaks highly of the human condition, and of the American spirit. I have come away from this project filled not with pity for these families, but with respect. The courage necessary to face the daily obstacles and hardships that these households encounter commands such respect.

It is this side of the welfare experience that is rarely reported. The political rhetoric, the academic writings, the gossip among neighbors are all to varying degrees guilty of not attempting to walk in the shoes of those whom they so quickly characterize. Were they to do so, I believe their characterizations would be much different.

I hope that this book has allowed you to walk in those shoes. My purpose has been to neither glorify nor demean but rather to provide a real sense of who these people are. Rather than the cutout, cardboard caricatures that populate so much political rhetoric and neighborhood gossip, these are real people, dealing with real problems. They have their share of good and bad qualities, like most of us. They are, after all, our fellow citizens.

The question for us to ask ourselves is, Do we continue down the path we have taken—that of castigating the poor and the recipients of public assistance, without a careful reading of the evidence? Or do we begin to explore an alternative path, one that involves a conscientious reexamination of the issue of poverty and those in need of assistance, as well as a serious look at our own beliefs about the manner in which our society operates? To use an earlier analogy, perhaps we should begin to analyze the game itself, rather than simply those who lose at it.

Such a reexamination may prove quite painful. But the fact that over thirty million Americans each year fall below the poverty line, many relying on some form of government assistance, demands such a reexamination. The fact that another twenty million Americans are near poverty, one paycheck away from public assistance, demands that reexamination. The fact that there are American children and their parents suffering from hunger each month, demands a reexamination. And the fact that there are people in this country sleeping on heating grates demands that reexamination. We simply do not have the luxury to continue with our cardboard characterizations of 20 percent of our population.

There is also a moral question to be asked: Specifically, what is our collective responsibility for the bottom 20 percent of our population, and what ethical obligations do we as individuals and as a society have to attempt to alleviate such economic suffering and misery? Some of the answers to this question lie in our reexamination of the causes and consequences of poverty.

However, the answers also lie beyond such a reexamination. They lie in the kind of society we wish to live in. As many have noted before, the mark of a noble society is to be found, not in the manner in which it helps the rich, but in how it helps the poor. Not in its virtues during good times, but in its character during hard times. Not in how it protects the powerful, but in how it defends the vulnerable. These are the attributes by which a great society should be judged. Having seen in these pages the poor and vulnerable, their faces and hard times, we must each make that judgment.

APPENDIX A
METHODOLOGY

The methodological specifics of this study include the historical background, the geographical setting, the types of data collected, the units of analysis, the time period during which the data was gathered, the methodological limitations, and finally the analytical techniques used.

Study Design

Background of the Study

This research began in 1981 with a research grant written by Dr. Doris Slesinger and Dr. Alice Robbins at the University of Wisconsin. The project involved following Wisconsin welfare recipients over time. That spring, Dr. Slesinger asked if I would like to join the project as a research assistant. Since I had been interested in the areas of social stratification and the family, my answer was a quick yes. The project was subsequently headed by Dr. Paul Voss of the Department of Rural Sociology. I remained at the position of research assistant until 1984, when I completed my dissertation on the dynamics of welfare utilization.

The following year, I received a fellowship at the Frank Porter Graham Child Development Center within the University of North Carolina and continued to explore the original data set. It was obvious that many questions remained to be analyzed. Something else was equally obvious—only half the story of welfare recipiency was being told. That is, while the statistical data were quite valuable, there was no information regarding welfare recipients' feelings, experiences, beliefs, and so on. Without such information, one was left with a half-finished sketch of the welfare picture.

Wanting to fill in the rest of the picture and aided by a faculty research grant at Washington University, during the summer of 1986, I conducted in-depth interviews with fifty families on welfare. I asked them to describe their experiences and attitudes. This information complemented the statistical analysis obtained from the original data set. It is one thing to report that a family of four has three hundred dollars a month to live on; it is quite another to hear each member describe that experience. The interviews were tape-recorded and later transcribed, which took an additional year.

Finally, from 1986 to 1988, I engaged periodically in fieldwork—going to welfare offices, attending job training programs, visiting low income neighborhoods, and so on. This allowed me to gain firsthand knowledge about various aspects of the welfare system and its impact on the welfare recipient.

The Setting

The setting for this study was the state of Wisconsin. In many respects, it is preferable to focus on a state rather than on the nation as a whole. The welfare system in the United States varies widely from state to state. For example, both AFDC and General Assistance payments vary, as does the extent of Medicaid coverage. Job training programs and requirements also differ across states. As a result, looking at a single state makes for a more cohesive analysis, and Wisconsin is a particularly good state to study. In many respects, welfare reform nationwide has been aiming toward what already exists in this state. Many of the reforms in the welfare system contained in the Family Support Act have existed in Wisconsin for many years. The AFDC–Unemployed Parent program has operated there since its inception, strong job training programs are offered, enforcement of child support payments first began in Wisconsin, health maintenance organizations have been used widely to provide medical care for those on welfare, and so on. The state has been on the forefront of developing and operating its system of public assistance.

Historically, Wisconsin has also been one of the most generous states in determining and allocating welfare benefits. During the 1980s, the state ranked near the top in terms of average and maximum allowed payments for AFDC. Ratios of average AFDC payments to average earnings also place the state near the top. Yet the overall demographic and socioeconomic backgrounds of Wisconsin recipients are fairly similar to national welfare samples (see Rank and Voss 1984b).

The Data

I used three separate yet complementary sources of data throughout this book. All deal with a similar population, but the emphasis in each data set clearly differs. The quantitative sample is longitudinal and designed for statistical modeling of various events, while the qualitative sample and the fieldwork provide greater insight into those events. As Bryman (1988), Denzin (1989), and Rank (1992) have discussed, blending quantitative and qualitative data permits a more complete understanding of social reality.

Longitudinal caseload sample. Since the early 1970s, Wisconsin has recognized that there were a number of problems in its administration of the AFDC, Food Stamp, and Medicaid programs (Guy 1982). In 1971, the Wisconsin Department of Health and Social Services initiated a project designed to produce a computer-based information system in order to handle these problems more efficiently. This system became known as the Computer Reporting Network (CRN). By late 1978, a decision was made to implement the CRN system statewide, with distributed data processing in the counties and a data base system located in Madison. As of September 1980, more than 99 percent of all cases in the state's seventy-two counties had been loaded into the CRN system.

Applicants for AFDC, Food Stamps, and/or Medicaid are required to fill out a combined application form. County caseworkers review the forms for accuracy and completeness. The information is then keyed directly into the CRN system at a terminal in the county office. Within minutes, a case determination sheet is printed out in the county office indicating the case eligibility and benefits. In addition to processing new applications, workers at the county level may also make changes to case records already active in the data base. For example, complete reviews of each case are required at set intervals, and items that have changed are reentered into the data base. Likewise, any changes that have been reported prior to a case review will also be entered into the system.

A 2 percent random sample was drawn of all cases participating as of September 30, 1980, in one or more of the three programs. The sample was built by combining two simple random samples of 1 percent each, generated by randomly selecting two two-digit numbers and using these to select cases based on the last two digits of the case head's Social Security number. The total number of eligible cases on the CRN system in September 1980 was approximately 140,000, resulting in a sample size of 2,796 case heads (or households). These households had been on welfare for varying amounts of time. Some were new, others had been on for six months, and so on.

The cases were then followed at six-month intervals (from September 1980 through September 1983) by matching the case head's Social Security number against the entire end-of-month CRN file for each succeeding interval. All analytical files were stripped of personal identification information (e.g., names, addresses, telephone numbers, etc.) and the original Social Security numbers were replaced with a unique identification number to permit cases or individuals to be matched across months. The sample includes September 1980, March 1981, September 1981, March 1982, September 1982, March 1983, and September 1983. There is no refusal rate, since case records rather than actual individuals were sampled.

The period from September 1980 to September 1983 was marked by a major administrative policy change that affected welfare recipients. From November 1981 to January 1982, the Reagan administration's budget cuts went into effect in Wisconsin (incorporated in the Omnibus Budget Reconciliation Act of 1981). The regulations reduced benefit levels for various welfare programs and tightened eligibility requirements. The OBRA changes had an impact on the AFDC, Food Stamp, and Medicaid programs. These changes were accomplished largely through reducing the amount of allowable deductions for earnings and work-related expenses. Thus, the incentives for working while on welfare were reduced. This became apparent in the fourth period of observation—March 1982.

In-depth qualitative interviews. During the summer of 1986, I gathered qualitative data through in-depth interviews. A random sample of welfare recipients was generated based on access to the entire universe of recipients in one county during May 1986. The sample was stratified by household type, as well as welfare eligibility status. Of interest were different types of families both on and recently off the welfare rolls. These included female-headed families, married couples, singles, and the elderly. Because the interviews were face-to-face, it was impractical to randomly sample the entire state, given the cost and time constraints involved. Thus I chose a representative county that reflected the overall state population in terms of urban and rural areas, occupational diversity, and so on.

The response rate was 76 percent. This rate represents the number of interviews conducted, divided by all households I attempted to locate (whether contact was made or not). For those contacted successfully, the refusal rate was 5 percent.

The criteria for inclusion in the sample were current residence in the county and the ability to communicate. Seven sampled households left the county before they could be interviewed. In addition, five elderly individuals could not communicate because of serious disabilities. Finally, one case involved an individual of Asian background who was unable to speak English and for whom no translator could be found. Because these cases did not meet the sampling criteria, they were not included in the calculation of the response rate.

Individuals without telephones were tracked down, several interviews were conducted in Spanish with the aid of an interpreter; in short, all avenues were used to contact sampled recipients. Participating respondents were paid fifteen dollars.

Fifty families were interviewed (in addition, five households were interviewed in the pretest). The composition of the sample approximately mirrored that of the longitudinal caseload data set.[1] The interviews were conducted in respondent's homes and averaged between one and a half to three hours long. All interviews were tape-recorded.

For female-headed families, the elderly, and single welfare recipients, the head of household was interviewed. For married couples, I attempted to interview both husband and wife together. However, in several cases only the wife was available to interview.[2]

At the onset of each interview, respondents were informed that there were no right or wrong answers to the questions being asked but that I was simply interested in understanding their honest appraisals of their feelings, experiences, and behavior. In addition, it was stated clearly to all recipients that the interviews had nothing to do with the welfare administration and that the project was sponsored by the university. My assistant and I also stated orally and in writing that all responses would be confidential.

Most respondents appeared to be open and frank about their feelings and behaviors. For example, individuals would often volunteer sensitive information (e.g., about incest, violence in the family, painful childhoods, etc.), and would frequently express genuine emotion during the interviews. Overall, rapport between interviewer and interviewee was excellent. This was assessed in two ways. Following each interview the overall perceived rapport during the interview was noted on the field notes. Rapport was also assessed by listening to each interview several times.

The interviews were open-ended and semistructured around several major topics such as attitudes regarding welfare, family dynamics (marriage, divorce, pregnancies, raising children, etc.), employment, the experience of getting on and off public assistance, and so on. Based on my prior research and knowledge of the field, the interview schedule was constructed to cover what I felt were the areas most critical to understanding a household's experience of being on public assistance. As a reliability check on the answers given during the interviews, information from respondents' caseload records (which had been made available from the state) was compared to information given during the interviews. The match was high, lending credibility to the interview data.

In addition to the actual interviews, field notes were taken that described the setting in which each interview took place, the recipient's dwelling, the surrounding neighborhood, the physical appearance of the recipient, and any other relevant information that could provide greater insight into the recipient's situation. Photographs were also taken of recipients who gave their consent.

The interviews were then transcribed from the recording tape and entered as files into a mainframe computing system. The transcriptions reflected the exact wording and manner in which responses were given. Each transcription was then triple-checked with the original tape for accuracy.

Names of individuals have been changed to protect the confidentiality of the respondents. In addition, the names of many of the places mentioned during the interviews have been changed. The major urban area in the county is referred to as "Ridgeton." The interviews have been slightly edited for this book—unnecessary phrases such as *you know* have been largely removed in order to make the comments more readable. However, none of the original wording has been altered.

Fieldwork. A third source of data was obtained through fieldwork. The underlying idea was to explore observable aspects of the welfare system, as well as other commonalities that touch upon the lives of welfare recipients. The fieldwork took place between 1986 and 1988 and occurred almost entirely in the same county as the in-depth qualitative interviews.

Several aspects of the welfare system were observed. I began by visiting various social service offices in order to sit in on the process of applying for public assistance. Offices were located in both urban and rural locations and served a wide range of individuals and families.

I then attended several job training programs that were mandatory for welfare recipients. Visits to low-income housing projects and neighborhoods were also a part of the fieldwork. Similarly, I visited a number of food pantries. In addition to making extensive fieldnotes, I took photographs to provide a visual record of various aspects of the welfare system.

Throughout the fieldwork I had the opportunity to speak with dozens of individuals associated with the welfare system. These included not only welfare recipients but also those dealing directly with welfare recipients, such as case workers, state employees, volunteers, social workers, and so on.

Units of Analysis

In both the longitudinal and qualitative samples, the sampling unit was the person listed as the applicant for one or more of the three major welfare programs—AFDC, Food Stamps, and/ or Medicaid. The applicant, as well as those residing in the household, form the household unit.

The welfare population contains several dominant types of households. Because they are eligible for different programs, these households do not participate in the welfare system in the same manner. Furthermore, the situations each type of household finds itself in differ widely. Both theoretically and methodologically, it is important to differentiate in the analysis among several broad categories of households.

This analysis concentrates on four major household categories: (1) female heads of household with children (no spouse present);[3] (2) married couples (with or without children); (3) single heads of household (no children or spouse present); and (4) elderly household heads (sixty-five and over). Approximately 40 percent of both the quantitatively and qualitatively sampled households were female-headed with children, while married heads, single heads, and the elderly each constituted roughly 20 percent of the total. Male-headed households with children made up less than 1 percent of the quantitative sample, and therefore this category is excluded from the analysis.

The Time Period

This study took place during the 1980s. As noted, a major administrative change in the welfare system occurred with the Omnibus Reconciliation Act in 1981. In addition, the economy experienced a recession in 1981 and 1982, with unemployment rates topping off at 9.5 percent nationally and 10.7 percent in Wisconsin. From 1983 onward during the study period, unemployment and inflation rates dropped as the economy recovered from the 1981–82 recession. The national poverty rate was at 13 percent in 1980, climbed to 15.2 percent in 1983, and then dropped to 13.5 percent in 1988. The Wisconsin poverty rates followed the same pattern.

Limitations

While there are unique advantages to this study, there are also several important limitations. These include the generalizability of the results, the methodological and time differences across data sets, and the validity of the findings from the in-depth interviews. It is especially important to keep these drawbacks in mind when generalizing the results to a larger context.

As noted, this study focuses on welfare recipients from one state—Wisconsin. The advantages of this focus have been mentioned as well. However a significant limitation of this approach is the difficulty of generalizing results to the national welfare population. For example, would welfare recipients in North Carolina, Missouri, or California behave in a similar fashion? Ultimately, it is impossible to know. Thus, generalizing the findings to welfare recipients across the United States should be done only with caution.

Also related to the issue of generalizability is the fact that households receiving AFDC, Food Stamps, and/or Medicaid were sampled. Although these represent the three major public assistance programs in the United States, other welfare programs exist as well (e.g., General Assistance, Supplemental Security Income, etc.). Our sample, therefore, is not a random sample of all welfare recipients.[4]

Another limitation is that the three data sets were gathered at three different times. The longitudinal caseload sample was followed from 1980 to 1983, the in-depth interviews were gathered in 1986, and the fieldwork occurred from 1986 to 1988. Yet the three data sets are used in conjunction with one another, meaning that I assumed that the behavior, attitudes, and circumstances of welfare recipients were consistent from 1980 to 1988. Although one can make a number of arguments for why this is a safe assumption, there is no definitive proof.[5] Recipient behavior may have changed as a result of period differences.

A final limitation of this study concerns the validity of the findings from the in-depth interviews. This limitation holds any time individuals are interviewed on sensitive subjects. As noted earlier, I tried to address this concern by comparing answers given during the interviews with the data in their caseload record (e.g., regarding education, length of time on welfare, etc.). There was a high degree of consistency across responses.[6] In addition, I stressed at the beginning of each interview that there were no right or wrong answers to the questions but rather that honesty and accuracy were my primary concern. Yet in spite of these precautions, no absolute assurance can be given that interviewees did not modify, conceal, or distort the truth.[7]

Analysis

Quantitative Techniques

Throughout the book, several statistical techniques have been used to analyze the quantitative data. They both describe and predict various events, and they fall under the general category of event history analysis (see Allison 1982, 1984; Blossfeld,

Hamerle, and Mayer 1989). My intent is to present a direct and understandable display of the data, which event history analysis can provide.

Event history analysis focuses on the occurrence and determinants of various events. Getting a job, becoming pregnant, or exiting from welfare are all specific events that can be analyzed through this approach. Typically, the data used are longitudinal and contain a record of when particular events occur. The quantitative data set is ideally suited for such an analysis.

In order to describe the occurrence of particular events, I rely upon the life table. The life table is a technique often used by demographers and medical researchers. Although primarily found in mortality analysis, it can be applied to other areas of research as well. Where starting and terminal events can be defined and where the interval of time between these events is of interest, the life table is often useful in describing the patterns of the event under examination (e.g., death, birth, marriage). I use the life table to describe the patterns of employment, marriage, births, welfare exits, and other events critical to welfare recipients.

The life table examines whether specific events occur across intervals of time. In this analysis, the intervals of time comprise six-month periods. During each six-month interval, one can calculate the probability of an event occurring. Furthermore, based on these probabilities, the cumulative probability of an event occurring across the entire study period can be calculated. These cumulative probabilities are the basis of many of the figures in chapters 3 through 10.

In addition, the standard life table can be expanded to describe more complicated patterns. One such approach is known as the logistic regression multivariate life table (see Guilkey and Rindfuss 1987; Rank 1988a). This allows us to examine the occurrence of events for particular individuals while taking into account a variety of background characteristics (used in chapter 9).

For the prediction and modeling of specific events, an event history analysis incorporating logistic regression techniques was used. The distinction between continuous and discrete time is important with such an approach. Methods that assume "that the time of event occurrence is measured exactly are known as continuous time methods" (Allison 1984:14). Those that treat events as occurring during specific periods are known as discrete-time methods. This analysis relies on a discrete-time methodology. Events are observed at six-month intervals, rather than at the exact time of occurrence, and hence a discrete-time methodology is the more appropriate. While there are pros and cons to both approaches, the method used here solves two major problems of event histories—censoring and time-varying independent variables.

In event history data, censoring typically occurs when a case has reached the end of the study without experiencing the event. Thus, the time of event occurrence is known only to be greater than some value. This represents censoring on the right. Left-censoring is much less common, although more troublesome, and occurs when the time of event occurrence is known only to be less than some value. In the present analysis, the problem of right-censoring exists. That is, a number of households passed through the three-year study period without the particular event(s) of interest having occurred. To deal with this problem, one could exclude the censored cases, assign the maximum length of time observed to the censored cases, or create a dichotomous dependent dummy variable representing "event not occurred/event occurred" for the entire time interval. None of these approaches is desirable, however, because each introduces serious biases into the coefficient estimates (see Allison 1982).

A second problem with event history data is the existence of time-varying independent variables. The variables used to explain the occurrence of an event often change over time (e.g., income, number of children, etc.). These changes may be critical in predicting the occurrence or nonoccurrence of an event. As Allison notes, "There is simply no satisfactory way of incorporating time-varying explanatory variables in a multiple regression predicting time of an event" (1984:11).

The approach taken in this analysis handles both the problems of censoring and time-varying independent variables. A separate observational record was created for each interval of time that a case was at risk of a particular event occurring. For example, consider the issue of exiting from welfare. During the first six-month interval, approximately twenty-seven hundred cases were at risk of exiting from welfare. At the second six-month interval, roughly two thousand cases were at risk, and so on. The total sample constructed includes approximately ten thousand records. Thus a case that was on welfare through all six intervals contributed six records, while a case that exited during the third interval contributed three records.

For each record, a dichotomous dependent variable was created in which "1" represents having exited from welfare and "0" represents remaining on welfare. The independent variables were assigned the values they took on at each interval. Finally, the ten thousand records were pooled into a single sample. The dependent variable was analyzed by logistic regression through the method of maximum likelihood. The probability of exiting from welfare during a six-month interval was therefore modeled.

Both censoring and time-varying explanatory variables are appropriately handled by this procedure (see Allison 1984). Households that did not exit and were therefore censored contributed all the information that is available—namely, that they did not exit during any of the six intervals in which they were known to be at risk. On the other hand, time-varying independent variables were easily incorporated into the model because each interval at risk was treated as a separate observation. Changes in an explanatory variable were accounted for within the variable itself. In addition, it was easy to control for differences in the occurrence of events over time by including either a set of independent dummy variables for each time period or a continuous variable for length of exposure.

The coefficients derived from these models are transformed throughout the book into easily interpretable odds ratios. By taking the antilogs of the coefficients, I was able to obtain odds ratios that provide a straightforward interpretation as to the magnitude of an explanatory variable's effect upon the dependent variable. For example, an odds ratio of 1.68 of employment on exiting from welfare would indicate that those who are employed have a 68 percent greater probability of exiting from welfare than those who are not employed.

Qualitative Techniques

For the qualitative data, the in-depth interviews were coded and categorized by various topics. All transcriptions were entered as files into a mainframe computing system that allowed for the selecting and sorting of interview data. As Schatzman and Strauss (1973), Charmaz (1983), Lofland and Lofland (1984), Babbie (1989), and Strauss and Corbin (1990) suggest, attention was paid to both the similarities and differences across responses. Field notes were also organized by specific topics.

The interviews and field notes furnish a wealth of information not available from the longitudinal data set. They were designed to provide insight and understanding into the mechanisms underlying the events modeled in the quantitative analysis. They were also designed to furnish information about attitudes and behaviors that were not studied in the longitudinal sample. As mentioned earlier, because the verbatim transcriptions were in computer files, they could be scanned for specific subject matter using a computer editor, allowing me to focus on general tendencies, differences, and variation across interviews. In addition, entire interviews could be analyzed to establish the overall context in which events occurred.

In chapters 3 through 10, I preferred to quote from the interview transcriptions without lengthy reinterpretations of their meaning. Most recipients did an excellent job of expressing themselves. I believe that the reader gains considerably more insight into the issues of welfare recipiency by being able to gauge recipients' experiences firsthand.

In qualitative data analysis, there is always the issue of how well the quotes chosen represent the overall sample. Transcriptions from interviews generate substantial quantities of written data, and therefore a range of quotes can be chosen or not. I selected quotes based on whether they were representative and characteristic of major themes, generalities, or categories found within the sample. In addition, I attempted to use quotes across a broad range of the respondents. And third, I chose quotes that were particularly revealing of overall categories and generalities. As Wolcott noted in regard to writing up qualitative research, "The trick is to discover essences and then to reveal those essences with sufficient context, yet not become mired trying to include everything that might possibly be described" (1990:35). In my selection of quoted material, I have done my best to reveal essences without getting bogged down in unnecessary specifics.

As discussed earlier, the transcriptions were slightly edited for this book. Within the interview material, ellipsis points represent a slight pause during or between sentences. In addition, emotions that came through strongly on the tapes are noted in italics in parentheses, while explanatory notes are found in brackets. The phrase "Voice over" indicates that two people were speaking at the same time.

Several chapters rely solely on the quantitative or qualitative data. Other chapters however, draw from both types of data. The data sets were designed to complement one another. As I have argued elsewhere (Rank 1988b), quantitative analysis tends to answer the questions of what, where, and when, while qualitative data best address issues of how and why. Clearly, our interest lies in both.

APPENDIX B

TABLES USED TO GENERATE FIGURES AND ODD RATIOS IN TEXT AND SUPPLEMENTARY TABLES

TABLE B.1

Life Table Analysis of Births Among Women Aged 18 to 44 on Welfare

Monthly Interval	Number at Risk	Number of Births	Percentage of Births	Cumulative Percentage of Births
0–6	795	15	1.89	1.89
6–12	950	26	2.74	4.58
12–18	910	22	2.42	6.89
18–24	717	12	1.67	8.44
24–30	624	13	2.08	10.35
30–36	553	7	1.27	11.49

TABLE B.2

Logistic Regression Model Predicting Childbearing Among Women Aged 18 to 44 on Welfare (N = 4,196)

Independent Variables	Coefficients	Odds Ratios
Demographic		
Not high school graduate	0.497★★★	1.64
Employed	0.137	1.15
Nonwhite	0.749★★	2.11
Age	0.402★★★	1.49

TABLE B.2 *(Continued)*

Independent Variables	Coefficients	Odds Ratios
Household		
Number of children	−0.698	0.50
Child under age 4	1.230★★	3.42
Married	0.267	1.31
Welfare variation		
Receiving all three programs	0.030	1.03
Lowered benefits	0.008	1.01
Length of welfare use	−0.475★	0.62
Constant	−11.065★★★	

★significant at the .05 level
★★significant at the .01 level
★★★significant at the .001 level

TABLE B.3
Life Table Analysis of Marriage for Female Heads of Households on Welfare

Monthly Interval	Number at Risk	Number of Marriages	Percentage of Marriages	Cumulative Percentage of Marriages
0–6	1.052	24	2.28	2.28
6–12	914	30	3.28	5.49
12–18	772	17	2.20	7.56
18–24	655	11	1.68	9.12
24–30	588	14	2.38	11.28
30–36	532	11	2.07	13.12

TABLE B.4
Life Table Analysis of Dissolutions for Married Couples on Welfare

Monthly Interval	Number at Risk	Number of Dissolutions	Percentage of Dissolutions	Cumulative Percentage of Dissolutions
0–6	457	17	3.72	3.72
6–12	332	18	5.42	8.94
12–18	227	7	3.08	11.74
18–24	163	9	5.52	16.61
24–30	136	4	2.94	19.07
30–36	116	3	2.59	21.16

Logistic Regression Model Predicting Marriage for Unmarried Female Heads of Households on Welfare (N = 4,491)

Independent Variables	Coefficients	Odds Ratios
Demographic		
Employment	−0.249	0.78
White	0.469**	1.60
Age	0.050	1.05
Children		
Number of children	0.153	1.17
Child under age 4	0.266	1.30
Welfare variation		
Receiving all three programs	−0.217	0.80
Lowered benefits	−0.026	0.97
Length of welfare use	−0.059	0.94
Constant	−5.412***	

*significant at the .05 level
**significant at the .01 level
***significant at the .001 level

Logistic Regression Model Predicting Dissolutions for Married Couples on Welfare (N = 1,392)

Independent Variables	Coefficients	Odds Ratios
Demographic		
Husband employed	−0.145	0.87
Wife employed	0.635**	1.89
White	−0.009	0.99
Wife's age	0.064	1.07
Children		
Number of children	0.378	1.46
Child under age 4	0.625*	1.87
Welfare variation		
Receiving all three programs	0.331	1.39
Lowered benefits	−0.357	0.70
Length of welfare use	0.423	1.53
Constant	−6.680***	

*significant at the .05 level
**significant at the .01 level
***significant at the .001 level

TABLE B.7
Logistic Regression Models Predicting Employment for Female Heads, Married Males, and Single Heads on Welfare[a]

Independent Variables	Female Heads	Married Males	Single Heads
Demographic			
Age	0.024 (1.02)	0.050 (1.05) *	0.062 (1.06) *
High school graduate	0.390 (1.48) ***	0.173 (1.19) *	0.217 (1.24) *
White	0.182 (1.20)	0.322 (1.38) ***	0.062 (1.06)
Male	—	—	0.008 (1.10)
Children			
Number of children	−0.501 (0.61) *	0.497 (1.64) **	—
Child under age 4	−0.430 (0.65) ***	0.132 (1.14)	—
Welfare variation			
Receiving all three programs[b]	−0.678 (0.51) ***	−0.491 (0.61) ***	0.267 (1.31)
Lowered work incentives	−0.415 (0.66) ***	−0.009 (0.99)	−0.626 (0.53)
Length of welfare use	0.156 (1.17)	0.073 (1.08)	0.077 (1.08)
Constant	−1.694 **	−3.999 ***	−3.276 ***
N	4,870	1,493	616

* significant at the .05 level
** significant at the .01 level
*** significant at the .001 level
*Odds ratios are in parentheses.
[b]For singles, receiving two or three programs is contrasted with receiving one program.

TABLE B.8
Life Table Analysis of Exits from Welfare for a Point-in-Time Cohort

Monthly Interval	Number at Risk	Number of Exits	Percentage of Exits	Cumulative Percentage of Exits
		Female Heads		
		(median exit time, 33.6 months)		
0–6	1,142	144	12.61	12.61
6–12	998	114	11.42	22.59
12–18	884	147	16.63	35.46
18–24	737	85	11.53	42.91
24–30	652	47	7.21	47.02
30–36	605	56	9.26	51.93
		Married Heads		
		(median exit time, 14.3 months)		
0–6	525	138	26.29	26.29
6–12	387	88	22.74	43.05
12–18	299	97	32.44	61.52
18–24	202	27	13.37	66.67
24–30	175	21	12.00	70.67
30–36	154	18	11.69	74.10
		Single Heads		
		(median exit time, 8.5 months)		
0–6	506	214	42.29	42.29
6–12	292	93	31.85	60.67
12–18	199	49	24.62	70.36
18–24	150	26	17.33	75.49
24–30	124	8	6.45	77.08
30–36	116	10	8.62	79.05
		Elderly Heads		
		(median exit time, 28.8 months)		
0–6	601	86	14.31	14.31
6–12	515	78	15.15	27.29
12–18	437	60	13.73	37.27
18–24	377	46	12.20	44.93
24–30	331	38	11.48	51.25
30–36	293	33	11.26	56.74
		Total Sample		
		(median exit time, 20.6 months)		
0–6	2,774	582	20.98	20.98
6–12	2,192	373	17.02	34.43
12–18	1,819	353	19.41	47.15
18–24	1,466	184	12.55	53.79
24–30	1,282	114	8.89	57.89
30–36	1,168	117	10.02	62.11

Life Table Analysis of Exits from Welfare for a Synthetic Opening Cohort

Monthly Interval	Number at Risk	Number of Exits	Percentage of Exits	Cumulative Percentage of Exits
Female Heads (median exit time, 22.1 months)				
0–6	194	49	25.26	25.26
6–12	380	52	13.68	35.48
12–18	530	77	14.53	44.86
18–24	562	77	13.70	52.41
24–30	536	74	13.81	58.98
30–36	512	60	11.72	63.79
36–42	401	38	9.48	67.22
42–48	288	25	8.68	70.07
Married Heads (median exit time, 8.6 months)				
0–6	151	63	41.72	41.72
6–12	251	82	32.67	60.76
12–18	238	56	23.53	69.99
18–24	300	46	15.33	74.59
24–30	185	37	20.00	79.67
30–36	155	27	17.42	83.22
36–42	133	13	9.77	84.86
42–48	65	9	13.85	86.95
Single Heads (median exit time, 5.7 months)				
0–6	207	109	52.66	52.66
6–12	261	130	49.81	76.24
12–18	187	59	31.55	83.74
18–24	149	46	30.87	88.76
24–30	109	22	20.18	91.03
30–36	93	13	13.98	92.28
36–42	72	3	4.17	92.60
42–48	58	3	5.17	92.98
Elderly Heads (median exit time, 22.1 months)				
0–6	72	15	20.83	20.83
6–12	229	40	17.47	34.66
12–18	296	45	15.20	44.59
18–24	304	44	14.47	52.61
24–30	287	32	11.15	57.89
30–36	283	38	13.43	63.55
36–42	235	29	12.34	68.05
42–48	154	16	10.39	71.37
Total Sample (median exit time, 10.3 months)				
0–6	624	236	37.82	37.82
6–12	1,121	304	27.12	54.68
12–18	1,251	237	18.94	63.27
18–24	1,315	213	16.20	69.22
24–30	1,117	165	14.77	73.76
30–36	1,043	138	13.23	77.23
36–42	841	83	9.87	79.48
42–48	565	53	9.38	81.41

TABLE B.10

Life Table Analysis of Exits from Welfare by Race for a Synthetic Opening Cohort

Length on Welfare	Number at Risk	Number of Exits	Percentage of Exits	Cumulative Percentage of Exits
White Female Heads				
(median exit time, 21.6 months)				
0–6	132	34	25.76	25.76
6–12	265	37	13.96	36.12
12–18	356	48	13.48	44.73
18–24	368	58	15.76	53.44
24–30	334	56	16.77	61.25
30–36	297	38	12.79	66.21
36–42	224	20	8.93	69.23
42–48	153	13	8.50	71.84
Black Female Heads				
(median length, 45.2 months)				
0–6	42	6	14.29	14.29
6–12	85	6	7.06	20.34
12–18	132	22	16.67	33.62
18–24	143	9	6.29	37.80
24–30	147	11	7.48	42.45
30–36	158	8	5.06	45.36
36–42	133	8	6.02	48.65
42–48	101	5	4.95	51.19
Total Sample				
(median length, 24.2 months)				
0–6	174	40	22.99	22.99
6–12	350	43	12.29	32.45
12–18	488	70	14.34	42.14
18–24	511	67	13.11	49.73
24–30	481	67	13.93	56.73
30–36	455	46	10.11	61.10
36–42	357	28	7.84	64.15
42–48	254	18	7.09	66.69

TABLE B.11
Recipient Characteristic Percentages by Race

Recipient Characteristics	White Female Heads	Black Female Heads
Education		
Less than twelve years	35.4	57.7
Twelve years or more	64.6	42.3
Employment		
Not employed	71.3	82.8
Employed	28.7	17.2
Number of children		
0–1	51.6	44.4
2 or more	48.4	55.6
Age		
Less than 20	8.5	11.7
20–24	29.3	36.7
25–29	23.1	24.4
30–34	17.3	11.7
35–39	12.2	7.2
40 or more	9.6	8.3

TABLE B.12
Logistic Regression Models Used in Constructing the Multivariate Life Table

Recipient Characteristics	Months on Welfare							
	6	12	18	24	30	36	42	48
Employed	-0.013	0.269	0.235	0.339*	0.654***	0.946***	1.041***	0.630*
High school graduate	-0.178	0.012	0.234	0.145	0.206	0.029	-0.088	0.264
Less than 2 children	0.464*	0.256	0.234	0.569	-0.117	0.093	0.513	0.230
White	0.100	0.103	-0.315	0.154	0.384	0.047	-0.437	0.039
Age	0.096	0.089	0.065	0.149	-0.044	0.107	0.246	0.105
Constant	-3.944*	-4.429*	-3.479**	-6.326*	-0.506	-5.202*	-0.423***	-5.482**
N	162	334	465	491	462	435	343	243

*significant at the .05 level
**significant at the .01 level
***significant at the .001 level

TABLE B.13

Multivariate Life Table Analysis of Exits from Welfare by Race for a Synthetic Opening Cohort

Length on Welfare	White Female Head		Black Female Head	
	Percentage of Exits	Cumulative Percentage of Exits	Percentage of Exits	Cumulative Percentage of Exits
	Employed/High School Graduate/Less Than Two Children			
0–6	27.31	27.31	23.52	23.52
6–12	21.47	42.92	18.20	37.44
12–18	21.91	55.43	34.50	59.02
18–24	31.04	69.26	24.86	69.21
24–30	34.18	79.77	19.42	75.19
30–36	29.38	85.71	27.42	82.00
36–42	26.62	89.52	46.51	90.37
42–48	25.66	92.21	24.20	92.70
Median length		15.4 months		15.5 months
	Not Employed/High School Dropout/Two or More Children			
0–6	17.87	17.87	15.12	15.12
6–12	8.54	24.88	7.06	21.11
12–18	6.44	29.72	11.43	30.13
18–24	5.20	33.38	3.87	32.83
24–30	10.51	40.38	5.17	36.31
30–36	4.68	43.17	4.28	39.03
36–42	1.89	44.24	4.43	41.73
42–48	3.51	46.20	3.26	43.63
Median length		57.5 months		69.7 months

TABLE B.14
Life Table Analysis of Returning to Welfare

Length Off Welfare	Number Entering Interval	Number of Returns	Percentage of Returns	Cumulative Percentage of Returns
		Female Heads		
0–6	488	116	23.77	23.77
6–12	340	32	9.41	31.15
12–18	255	20	7.84	36.36
18–24	146	7	4.79	39.41
24–30	76	3	3.95	41.80
		Married Heads		
0–6	398	62	15.58	15.58
6–12	320	30	9.38	23.50
12–18	265	24	9.06	30.43
18–24	163	11	6.75	35.13
24–30	94	4	4.26	37.89
		Single Heads		
0–6	397	53	13.35	13.35
6–12	338	19	5.62	18.22
12–18	300	15	5.00	22.31
18–24	247	7	2.83	24.51
24–30	167	4	2.40	26.32
		Elderly Heads		
0–6	312	17	5.45	5.45
6–12	257	9	3.50	8.76
12–18	206	3	1.46	10.09
18–24	145	3	2.07	11.95
24–30	78	0	0.00	11.95
		Total Sample		
0–6	1,595	248	15.55	15.55
6–12	1,255	90	7.17	21.61
12–18	1,026	62	6.04	26.34
18–24	701	28	3.99	29.28
24–30	415	11	2.65	31.15

TABLE B.15
Logistic Regression Model Predicting Welfare Exits ($N = 6,997$)

Independent Variables	Coefficients	Odds Ratios
Individual characteristics		
High school graduate	0.201 ***	1.22
Employed	0.517 ***	1.68
White	0.214 **	1.24
Not incapacitated	0.215 *	1.24
Age	0.011	1.01

TABLE B.15 *(Continued)*

Independent Variables	Coefficients	Odds Ratios
Family structure		
Female head	−0.696★★★	0.50
Single	0.825★★★	2.28
County level characteristics		
Rural percentage	−0.009	0.99
Unemployment rate	0.186★★★	1.20
High poverty	0.042	1.04
County caseload increase	0.050★★	1.05
Welfare variation		
Lowered benefits	0.208★	1.23
Length of welfare use	−0.128★	0.88
Constant	−3.087★★★	

★significant at the .05 level
★★significant at the .01 level
★★★significant at the .001 level

NOTES

1. Introduction

1. Of course, some politicians, such as Mario Cuomo, the governor of New York, defend those who are poor and on welfare, although these are far less common. Cuomo has criticized politicians from both parties for "welfare scapegoating"—blaming the country's economic problems on welfare spending and the poor. As he stated in a recent speech, "The poor people don't have any power. That's why welfare's such a terrific issue. Who's going to march against you, a 15-year-old girl with a baby? She doesn't even get to the polls" (*New York Times,* March 15, 1992).

2. For instance, President Reagan noted during one of his weekly radio addresses, "In 1964, the famous War on Poverty was declared. And a funny thing happened. Poverty, as measured by dependency, stopped shrinking and then actually began to grow worse. I guess you could say, 'poverty won the war.' Poverty won, in part, because instead of helping the poor, government programs ruptured the bonds holding poor families together" (February 15, 1986; quoted in Danziger 1989).

3. As an example, J. Anthony Lukas in his review of Mickey Kaus's book, *The End of Equality,* writes "Finally, for a book about the social condition of the American people, there are very few American people in these pages. Not a single poor person or welfare client lends specificity to all

these abstractions. But that would be another book" (*New York Times,* July 12, 1992).

4. While the size of the poor population classified as "the underclass" is relatively small, it does appear that their numbers are growing. For example, Ricketts and Mincy (1988) note that although the overall poverty population grew by 8 percent between 1970 and 1980, the number of poor individuals living in concentrated poverty areas grew by 36 percent. In addition, see Jencks (1992).

2. The Welfare Debate

1. In addition, see Domestic Policy Council (1986) and Working Group on the Family (1986).

2. As chairman of the Governors Association in 1988, then-Governor Clinton strongly supported passage of the Family Support Act.

3. I have not included Social Security in the discussion because it is a nonmeans-tested program.

4. For the exact number of recipients and expenditures on various welfare programs during any specific year, consult the *Green Book: Overview of Entitlement Programs,* prepared yearly for the Committee on Ways and Means and published by the U.S. Government Printing Office.

5. "The official poverty line" came into being in 1964. It was developed by the Social Security Administration under the direction of Mollie Orshansky and has remained largely intact since then. It is calculated by estimating what it would cost a family (ranging from one member to nine or more members) to purchase a minimally adequate diet for a year. This amount is then multiplied by three, which represents the poverty line for that family. Each year the levels are tied to changes in the Consumer Price Index to account for changing prices. In 1991, the poverty line for a family of four was $13,924. For an extended discussion of the measurement of poverty, see Ruggles (1990).

6. And here the reason is the extremely high cost of living in Alaska. Taking that into account, families receiving the maximum AFDC and Food Stamp payments in Alaska will still be in a dire economic situation.

7. For a sampling of survey results, see Free and Cantril (1967), Huber and Form (1973), Feagin (1975), Nilson (1981), Kluegel and Smith (1986), and Smith and Stone (1989).

8. Unfortunately, both supporters and attackers have often overlooked two important aspects of Lewis's thinking. Lewis felt that perhaps only 20 percent of the U.S. poverty population lived in a culture of poverty (Lewis 1966b). Furthermore, he often stressed the importance of providing opportunities for those living in a culture of poverty; in his view, eradicating the culture without providing real opportunities would be counterproductive.

9. However, Marx viewed class conflict as part of an ongoing dialectical process. Ancient society was characterized by the conflict between master

and slave, feudalism by the lord/serf conflict, and so on. The class conflict between the haves and have-nots eventually leads to the destruction of any particular historical epoch. Thus, history is a continuing dialectical process of thesis and antithesis, leading to successive syntheses (or new historical epochs). This concept forms the basis of what Marx termed "historical materialism."

10. In addition, these administrations have blamed welfare programs for a variety of social ills. For example, the Bush administration (through Marlin Fitzwater, the White House press secretary, and Vice President Dan Quayle) attributed the May 1992 riot in Los Angeles to liberal welfare programs and policies. As Fitzwater put it:

> We believe that many of the root problems that have resulted in inner-city difficulties were started in the '60s and '70s and that they have failed. We believe there's a very direct relationship between people's pride in their community and having a job, first of all, having the hope of income and improving their lives . . . and being able to own their own property or homes to give them a stake in the community. We think the social welfare programs of the '60s and '70s ignored that, and we're now paying a price.
>
> (*St. Louis Post Dispatch*, May 5, 1992)

In a lecture at Keio University in Japan two weeks after the riot, Quayle argued that the welfare system was responsible for the plight of cities in the United States because the programs "basically practiced and preached the idea of dependence, and dependency has created inertia, lack of drive, lack of self-help" (*St. Louis Post-Dispatch*, May 14, 1992).

3. Getting On

1. For example, see Jacobs (1966), Schwartz (1975), Edelman (1977), Morgan (1979), Prottas (1979), Lipsky (1980), Goodsell (1984), and Susser and Kreniske (1987).

2. Obviously, however, in-take workers were aware of my presence and may have adjusted their behavior accordingly.

3. Several sizable differences attributable to race exist among female heads entering the welfare system. As noted earlier, black female heads tend never to have been married rather than to have been separated/divorced. In our sample, 68.6 percent of black female heads entering the welfare system were never married, compared to 25.8 percent of white female heads. In addition, black female heads are more likely to have a child under the age of four (66.2 percent), have fewer than 12 years of education (53 percent) and to reside in a major metropolitan county (87.3 percent) than their white counterparts entering the welfare system. See table B.11 for several racial differences in the cross-section.

4. The major metropolitan county in this study contains approximately one and a half million residents. Other metropolitan and nonmetropolitan counties are defined according to the criteria used by the U.S. Census Bu-

reau. They correspond roughly to the more general conception of urban versus rural counties.

4. Day-to-Day Living

1. Several studies attempting to document the extent of hunger in America (e.g., Brown and Pizer 1987, the Food Research and Action Center 1991, and Cohen, Burt, and Schulte 1993) have found that those on public assistance routinely run out of food at the end of the month. In addition, the Food Research and Action Center report estimated that 4.7 million children under the age of twelve in the United States go hungry at some point during the month, typically near the end.

2. Or, as William Cobbett the English journalist, essayist, and politician of the late eighteenth and early nineteenth centuries wrote, "To be poor and independent is very nearly an impossibility."

5. Family Dynamics

1. Social scientists know that people's recollections of past events and attitudes are liable to be distorted (see Sudman and Bradburn 1982). This is particularly true for experiences in the distant past, such as childhood. And yet without retrospective questions, multidecade longitudinal studies would be the only source of information about these experiences. Even taking into account the potential inaccuracies, I believe the interviews yielded several generalities that are both valid and revealing.

2. Of course, this is the type of information that can become distorted with time or may simply be kept from children. It should therefore be interpreted cautiously. However, it does correspond roughly with percentages in other data sets. For example, the National Survey of Households and Families is a national random sample of approximately thirteen thousand households interviewed in 1987 and 1988. In an analysis of intergenerational welfare use, I found that 76 percent of respondents who had received welfare during the previous year reported that their parents had never used welfare when they were growing up, 15 percent reported that their parents used welfare sometimes, and 9 percent said their parents used welfare frequently. For those who reported some amount of welfare use during one or more of the six years prior to the interview, the percentages were identical (Rank, Cheng, and Cox 1992).

3. Certainly, this process is not common to all families. Indeed, Greg Duncan (1984) has demonstrated that a fair amount of income mobility occurred among households during the ten-year period he studied. However, most of these fluctuations were from one income quintile to an adjacent one.

4. The data for this table are taken from the first month of the longitudinal sample and can be seen as a representative cross-section of the welfare population at a given time.

5. This argument goes back hundreds of years. For example, England's Poor Law Report of 1834 argued that allowing every man with a family the amount necessary to purchase bread at the price of "five quarten loaves per week, with two quarten loaves added for each number of his family" was leading to an increase in family size (Galper 1970).

6. The two standard age brackets used for estimating fertility rates are fifteen to forty-four and eighteen to forty-four. The analysis is confined to the second bracket, since very few women aged fifteen to seventeen head households on welfare. However, using either age bracket would allow a comparison of welfare fertility rates with the overall national and state rates.

The analysis pools married and unmarried women together. This is standard procedure for calculating and reporting overall fertility rates of women. However, marital status is also taken into account in the aggregate comparisons, as well as in the multivariate analysis.

The event being modeled in the life table and logistic regression analyses found in appendix B is the first observed spell of childbearing. Once a birth has occurred, women are no longer included in later time intervals. The numbers of women experiencing a birth are extremely small, which prevents a detailed analysis of the occurrence and determinants of a second observed birth. In addition, when analyzing repeatable events, a number of statistical questions are raised (see Allison 1984). I did, however, include such women in the total sample in a separate analysis. No significant differences from the results presented here were found.

Once women exit from the welfare rolls, they are no longer included in the analysis even if they subsequently reenter the welfare system, because this would distort the representativeness of the sample. However, I did conduct separate analyses including such women and found no significant differences from the results presented here.

Finally, I include in the analysis all women who have been on welfare for at least nine months, since some women enter the welfare system because of an upcoming birth. In these cases, cause and effect is reversed—a forthcoming birth leading to welfare use, rather than welfare use leading to birth. Including only women who have been receiving welfare for at least nine months eliminates this bias.

7. The average fertility rate over the three-year period was 38.3. However, the one-year rate of 45.8 was used for comparison purposes because using the three-year average would distort the representativeness of the sampled welfare population (e.g., longer-term cases would be overrepresented).

8. These characteristics were categorized as follows: age (eighteen through twenty-four, twenty-five through twenty-nine, thirty through thirty-four, thirty-five through thirty-nine, forty through forty-four; children (no children, one or more children); marital status (married with spouse present, not married); race (white, black); and education (less than twelve years, twelve or more years). The fertility rates for each of these categories were calculated for women on welfare. The rates were then multiplied by the proportion of

women in each category in the Wisconsin and national populations. This technique results in a direct standardization using the general population as the standard (see Shryock and Siegel 1976). The population proportions for the nation were based on information from the U.S. Bureau of the Census (1981), while the Wisconsin proportions were derived from the Wisconsin Department of Health and Human Services (1981) and the U.S. Bureau of the Census (1981).

9. The variable definitions and contrasts are as follows: education (less than twelve years, twelve or more years); employment (employed, not employed); race (white, nonwhite); current age of recipient; number of children present in recipient's household; age of youngest child (child under age four in the household, no child under age four in the household); marital status (married with spouse present; never married; separated, divorced, widowed); number of programs received (all three programs—AFDC, Food Stamps, Medicaid—received, one or two programs received); changes in regulations (before OBRA, after OBRA); length of time on welfare, in exact years and months, since the beginning of the current spell, a date that could precede the beginning of the study. Employment status, number of children, age of youngest child, and number of welfare programs received were lagged to avoid causality problems with fertility status.

10. Caution is warranted in the interpretation of the length of welfare variable on fertility. Without a control group of poor women not receiving public assistance, it is difficult to determine whether the welfare programs themselves or some other factor(s) were lowering the fertility rate over time.

11. Of course, this compares two slightly different events—the divorce/separation rate for welfare recipients and the divorce rate only for the overall population. State and national data for a combined divorce/separation rate (which would undoubtedly be somewhat higher) were not available.

12. The variable definitions and contrasts are as follows: employment (employed, not employed); race (white, nonwhite); current age of recipient; number of children present in recipient's household; age of youngest child (child under age four in the household, no child under age four in the household); number of programs received (all three programs—AFDC, Food Stamps, Medicaid—received, one or two programs received); changes in regulations (before OBRA, after OBRA); length of time on welfare, in exact years and months, since the beginning of the current spell, a date that could precede the beginning of the study.

13. It should be noted that in this study, as is true for the country as a whole (by 1994), married couples are able to qualify for AFDC. As a result, the possibility of married couples splitting up to qualify for cash assistance is not particularly germane.

14. The tendency to use welfare as a causal factor in explaining family dynamics is a classic example of misinterpreting a correlational relationship as a causal relationship. As Arthur Okun has noted, a naive person seeing an automobile with a flat tire will assume that the hole in the tire must be at the

bottom, since that is where the tire is flat (see Solow 1990, for further examples of such logic with regard to the poor). A similar type of logic is often used regarding welfare recipients; that is, if a family is receiving welfare and experiences high family disruption, welfare must be causing the family disruption. Such causal reasoning is simply spurious.

15. An interesting parallel is found in many Western European countries, where low birthrates and the fear of labor shortages have led to relatively generous financial policies designed to increase fertility rates. Overall these policies have appeared to have had little effect on raising birthrates.

6. Beliefs and Hopes

1. The beliefs and hopes of the poverty-stricken have been explored occasionally in the past; those of welfare recipients have been less commonly addressed. Studies looking at the beliefs of the poverty-stricken include Whyte (1943), Liebow (1967), Anderson (1978), Auletta (1983), Williams and Kornblum (1985), MacLeod (1987), and Duncan (1992). Those focusing on the beliefs and hopes of welfare recipients include Stack (1974), Sheehan (1975), Dunbar (1988), Simpson (1990), Edin (1991), and Sidel (1992).

7. Working

1. It is important to keep in mind (as chapter 10 will demonstrate) that a number of individuals leave the welfare system as a result of becoming employed. These individuals do not show up in the employed percentages in table 7.1.

2. For an extended discussion of this issue, see Edin (1991) and Edin and Jencks (1992). Their analyses of mothers on AFDC in Chicago indicated that virtually all had sources of unreported income. This cash came from various kinds of work or from friends and relatives.

3. The variable definitions and contrasts are as follows: current age of recipient; education (less than twelve years, twelve or more years); race (white, nonwhite); sex (male, female); number of children present in recipient's household; age of youngest child (child under age four in the household, no child under age four in the household); number of programs received (all three programs—AFDC, Food Stamps, Medicaid—received, one or two program received); lowered work incentives (before OBRA, after OBRA); length of time on welfare, in exact years and months, since the beginning of the current spell, a date that could precede the beginning of the study.

8. Attitudes About Welfare

1. For example, see Nilson (1981), Hendrickson and Axelson (1985), and Smith and Stone (1989).

2. Studies that have looked at this include Briar (1966), Handler and

Hollingsworth (1971), Cole and Lejune (1972), Kerbo (1976), Goodban (1985), and Popkin (1990).

3. For example, see Horan and Austin (1974), Williamson (1974a, 1974b), Keith (1980), Moffitt (1983), Waxman (1983), Camasso and Moore (1985), and Kluegel and Smith (1986).

4. In addition, it is often posited that the stigma surrounding welfare programs plays a functional role in the rationing of scarce resources, recruiting and maintaining a labor force, and preventing deviant behavior (Loewenberg 1981).

5. For example, see Bane and Ellwood (1983), Duncan (1984), and Coder and Ruggles (1988).

6. It should be noted, however, that Jody's daughter has suffered from a severe disability since birth, increasing her need for adequate medical coverage (i.e., Medicaid).

7. And, of course, one of the latent functions of Food Stamps is indeed to stigmatize the recipient, thereby increasing their motivation to remain on the program only briefly.

8. Some of this stigma may be reduced as states begin having recipients use plastic debit cards instead of Food Stamp coupons.

9. How Long and How Often?

1. Some of these studies include Rydell et al. (1974), Boskin and Nold (1975), Saks (1975), Wiseman (1977), Rein and Rainwater (1978), Mott (1983), Plotnick (1983), Bane and Ellwood (1983), Duncan (1984), O'Neill et al. (1984), Plant (1984), Blank (1986), Coder and Ruggles (1988), Coder, Burkhead, and Feldman-Harkins (1988), Ruggles (1989), and Fitzgerald (1991).

2. For a detailed methodological and analytical discussion of the issues in this and the next section, see Rank (1985).

3. While it is helpful to compare graphically the cumulative exit distributions of various family structures, it is also important to determine whether these distributions differ from each other statistically. To do so, survival scores were calculated for each observation by comparing its survival time to that of all other observations. To make subgroup comparisons, a statistic D was calculated from the survival scores using the algorithm of Lee and Desu (1972). Using the Lee-Desu coefficients, all comparison groups did in fact differ significantly beyond the .001 level in their patterns of exiting—the exception being female and elderly heads. As was seen in figure 9.2, both these groups had a slow but steadily upward progression of cumulative exits. When all four household types are compared, the exiting distributions differ statistically from each other.

4. In order to do so, prior length of welfare use was first calculated for the entire sample. Next, if a case had been on welfare for six months, as an example, it was not included in the zero-to-six-month intervals. Rather, cases were only included in intervals in which they are observed at the beginning

and ending point of the interval. The above case would be included in the six-to-twelve-month interval. If such a household had not exited during this interval, it would then be included in the twelve-to-eighteen-month interval, and so on. If it had exited during the six-to-twelve-month interval, it would be eliminated from entering later intervals. In this manner, a set of exit probabilities for a beginning or synthetic opening cohort was constructed (figure 9.4 is similarly constructed).

5. For a detailed methodological and analytical discussion of the issues in this section, see Rank (1988a).

10. Getting Off

1. The variable definitions and contrasts are as follows: education (less than twelve years, twelve or more years); employment (employed, not employed); race (white, nonwhite); incapacitation status (not incapacitated, incapacitated); current age of recipient; family structure (female-headed family, single, married couple); county percentage classified as rural; monthly unemployment rate of the county; poverty status (higher poverty—defined as over 10 percent of the county population below the poverty line—lower poverty—defined as at or below 10 percent of the county population below the poverty line); the half-year percentage increase in a county's caseload population on welfare; lowered benefits (before OBRA, after OBRA); length of time on welfare, in exact years and months, since the beginning of the current spell, a date that could precede the beginning of the study.

2. A similar process can be seen in some states experiencing hard economic times and lean budgets. In several of these states, the response is to tighten eligibility requirements to make it harder to qualify for and to remain on public assistance.

3. Of course, there are other explanations for these findings. For example, as economic conditions worsen, families on welfare may seek opportunities elsewhere.

11. Myths and Realities

1. Nevertheless, middle- and upper-class families do receive considerable government benefits from programs and tax policies other than public assistance (e.g., the ability to deduct interest on home mortgages, college loan programs, etc.).

2. A hypothetical example illustrates both the concept of vulnerability and the impact of social class on future life chances, particularly the accumulation of human capital. It is a situation that occurs across socioeconomic class—an adolescent who experiences a serious drug problem. How might the outcome of this crisis differ according to class lines?

For the middle- or upper-class adolescent, arrest is unlikely. Families in these socioeconomic groups have the resources to provide for private rehabilitation. While the drug problem may recur, high-quality treatment increases the likelihood that it will be addressed, thus minimizing its potential to damage. As a result, our hypothetical adolescent's ability to accumulate human capital will not be dramatically impaired.

For the lower-class adolescent, arrest is much more likely. This would almost certainly cause severe harm to the adolescent's future, particularly because it would seriously constrain the accumulation of human capital. If an arrest does not follow, the probability of getting immediate high-quality professional treatment is slim, given the family's limited economic resources. As a result, the problem may remain, continuing to stand between the adolescent and the accumulation of human capital. Put simply, middle- and upper-class families, have more slack in the rope to work with; lower-class families have far less leeway.

3. I am indebted to Michael Sherraden for pointing this out to me.

4. For example, Blau (1992) notes that most introductory economics textbooks discuss the "natural unemployment rate" in the American economy—that is, the rate of unemployment inherent or systemic in a free market economy. In other words, it is generally accepted that a certain degree of unemployment will exist regardless of the individual characteristics of those participating in the labor market.

5. In a review of the literature, Morris and Williamson write, "On both theoretical and empirical grounds, then, we believe the following conclusions are warranted: The greater the changes in individual characteristics required by an antipoverty strategy, the less likely that the strategy will have a major impact on a participant's economic status" (1986:4).

6. For example, President Bush noted that class is for "European democracies or something else—it isn't for the United States of America. We are not going to be divided by class" (DeMott 1992:9–10). For an extended discussion of why Americans often have difficulty thinking in terms of social class, see the work just cited.

7. One leading proponent of this argument is Tommy Thompson. In a speech before the Heritage Foundation, Thompson discussed his views.

> As governor of Wisconsin, I have been waging my own anti-socialist revolution against a welfare system that has devastated once strong and vibrant urban communities. The citizens who live in those communities—casualties of the War on Poverty—deserve to be freed from welfare's downward spiral. . . . Our revolution is built upon the proven foundations of American greatness—free enterprise, family values and self-sufficiency—that flourished in the years before the bureaucratic welfare state grew so tangled and constricting.
>
> (*St. Louis Post-Dispatch,* December 14, 1992)

8. It should be noted that one can often get political consensus on very broad goals, such as reducing the extent of poverty. The consensus breaks down when discussion turns to the actual specifics of how to accomplish those goals. Thus, there is wide disagreement in the political arena as to the most effective strategies for reducing poverty.

9. Many of the current strategies being discussed (e.g., microenterprises, community development banks, enterprise zones) have been practiced extensively in developing countries. This transfer of ideas from developing countries back to developed countries is known as "reverse technology transfer." For example, the Grameen Bank in Bangladesh has provided a model that has helped to shape the lending practices of community development banks in the United States. Gerald Sherman writes,

> The Grameen Bank of Bangladesh uses a method of lending that takes the bank to the villages and requires the formation of peer groups to make loans. This method relies upon peer pressure and a rigorous and rigid process to deliver loans to the poor without the need for collateral. The process requires involvement of the poor borrowers in the loan approval process and also requires them to save money. It uses money as the tool to bring about other needed social changes. This method of lending is being adopted by many other countries throughout the world and is being used in Chicago, rural Arkansas, and on three Indian Reserves in Canada.   (1989:64–65)

For a detailed description of the Grameen Bank, see Hossain (1988).

10. See Vosler, Haywood, and Graber (1992), for an extended discussion of the concepts behind the community approach to supporting low-income neighborhoods in general and the ideas behind Grace Hill Neighborhood Services in particular.

11. And, certainly, there are other approaches as well. However, it is my belief that the six I have discussed are among the most important.

12. Concluding Thoughts

1. What is interesting about Supreme Court Justice Clarence Thomas and his story of rags to riches is his use of the welfare stereotype to distance himself from other members of his family. According to columnist Clarence Page (*St. Louis Post-Dispatch,* July 26, 1991), in a speech by Thomas to a conference of black conservatives in 1980, he referred to his sister on welfare in the following way, "She gets mad when the mailman is late with her welfare check. That's how dependent she is. What's worse is that now her kids feel entitled to the check, too. They have no motivation for doing better or getting out of that situation." Perhaps the most interesting aspect regarding Thomas's story is its distorted nature. Page writes,

> When reporters recently tracked down Thomas' sister, Emma Mae Martin, living in a beat-up frame house with a hole in the roof in Pin Point, GA., a few steps from where she and her two younger brothers were born, they didn't find a story of welfare dependency. Instead, they found a story of hard work by three generations of a family struggling like most other families do, just to make ends meet. Martin was deserted by her husband in 1973, just as her father had disappeared 25 years earlier. She worked two minimum-wage jobs while her brother attended law school, but stopped working to take care of an elderly aunt who had suffered a stroke. That led to four or five years on welfare, trying to make it on $169 a month. That's over. She now works as a cook at the same

hospital where her mother is a nurse's assistant, and she sometimes has to report to work at 3 a.m.

Page concluded, "On the heels of his stunning speech, the Reagan administration, scouting black conservatives at the time, offered him the chairmanship of the Equal Employment Opportunity Commission, which led to his federal judgeship and eventually his nomination to the Supreme Court. There's a lesson in this, I suppose. A little scapegoating can take you a long way in politics, even when you use your own sister."

Appendix A: Methodology

1. The demographic characteristics of the qualitative sample include household structure (44 percent female headed, 20 percent married, 18 percent singles, 18 percent elderly), residence (86 percent urban, 14 percent rural), race of household head (64 percent white, 28 percent black, 8 percent other), education of household head (52 percent twelve or more years of education, 48 percent less than twelve years of education), employment status of household head under age sixty-five (40 percent employed, 60 percent not employed), average length on welfare (female heads, 4.2 years; marrieds, 1.6 years; singles, 0.9 years; elderly, 3.1 years), and median length on welfare (female heads, 1.8 years; marrieds, 0.8 years; singles, 0.2 years; elderly, 2 years).

2. Six of the ten interviews with married couples were conducted with both the husband and wife. The remaining four were conducted with the wife only.

3. This category also includes a small number of women without children but pregnant.

4. On the other hand, some of the sampled households were indeed receiving other public assistance programs as well. The point, however, is that these programs were not used to determine the sample selection. The AFDC, Food Stamp, and Medicaid programs were selected because they were on-line in the CRN data base.

5. A good case can be made that recipient attitudes and behavior should not have varied much during this time as a result of period effects. With the exception of the OBRA changes, which are controlled for in the quantitative analysis, there were no major changes in the welfare system. Furthermore, the unemployment rate and other economic indicators were similar in 1980 and 1986 when both samples were drawn. In addition, it is unlikely that the attitudes and perceptions of welfare recipients would have changed during this period: that is, being on welfare remained highly stigmatized, benefits remained at low levels, the minimum wage remained the same, and so on.

6. Of course this relates much more to the issue of reliability than to validity. That is, someone might simply be a consistent liar across time. On the other hand, as Mark Twain once wrote, "If you tell the truth you don't have to remember anything."

7. My gut feeling is that the interviewees were for the most part straightforward and open in their responses. As Auletta noted in his discussions with members of the underclass, "Ultimately like any reporter, I relied on my sniffer. Mine told me these people generally were pretty straight, certainly a lot straighter than many politicians I interview" (1983:xv). My sniffer concurs with Auletta's—that is, I believe the respondents were for the most part honest and open.

REFERENCES

Adams, Bert. 1986. *The Family: A Sociological Interpretation*. San Diego, Calif.: Harcourt Brace Jovanovich.

Allison, Paul A. 1982. "Discrete-Time Methods for the Analysis of Event Histories." In Samuel Leinhardt, ed., *Sociological Methodology*, pp. 61–98. San Francisco: Jossey-Bass.

———. 1984. *Event History Analysis*. Beverly Hills, Calif.: Sage Publications.

Anderson, Elijah. 1978. *A Place on the Corner*. Chicago: University of Chicago Press.

———. 1990. *Streetwise: Race, Class, and Change in an Urban Community*. Chicago: University of Chicago Press.

Anderson, Martin. 1978. *Welfare: The Political Economy of Welfare Reform in the United States*. Palo Alto, Calif.: Hoover Institution.

Auletta, Ken. 1983. *The Underclass*. New York: Vintage Books.

Babbie, Earl. 1989. *The Practice of Social Research*. Belmont, Calif.: Wadsworth.

Bahr, Stephen J. 1979. "The Effects of Welfare on Marital Stability and Remarriage." *Journal of Marriage and the Family* 41: 553–560.

Bane, Mary Jo and David T. Ellwood. 1983. "The Dynamics of Dependence: The Routes to Self-Sufficiency." Unpublished manuscript prepared for the Department of Health and Human Services, Washington, D.C.

————. 1986. "Slipping into and out of Poverty: The Dynamics of Spells." *Journal of Human Resources* 21: 1–23.

————. 1989. "One Fifth of the Nation's Children: Why Are They Poor?" *Science* 245: 1047–1053.

Bane, Mary Joe and Paul A. Jargowsky. 1988. "The Links Between Government Policy and Family Structure: What Matters and What Doesn't." In Andrew J. Cherlin, ed., *The Changing American Family and Public Policy*, pp. 219–261. Washington, D.C.: The Urban Institute Press.

Banfield, Edward C. 1974. *The Unheavenly City Revisited*. Boston: Little, Brown.

Bassi, Laurie J. and Orley Ashenfelter. 1986. "The Effect of Direct Job Creation and Training Programs on Low-Skilled Workers." In Sheldon H. Danziger and Daniel H. Weinberg, eds., *Fighting Poverty: What Works and What Doesn't*, pp. 133–151. Cambridge: Harvard University Press.

Beck, E. M., Patrick Horan, and Charles Tolbert. 1978. "Stratification in a Dual Economy: A Structural Model of Earnings Determination." *American Sociological Review* 43: 704–720.

Becker, Gary S. 1964. *Human Capital*. New York: Columbia University Press.

Becker, Howard S. 1986. *Writing for Social Scientists: How to Start and Finish Your Thesis, Book, or Article*. Chicago: University of Chicago Press.

Beeghley, Leonard. 1989. *The Structure of Social Stratification in the United States*. Boston: Allyn and Bacon.

Bergmann, Barbara R. 1986. *The Economic Emergence of Women*. New York: Basic Books.

Blank, Rebecca M. 1986 (September). "How Important is Welfare Dependence?" Working Paper Series. National Bureau of Economic Research, Cambridge, Massachusetts.

Blau, Joel. 1992. *The Visible Poor: Homelessness in the United States*. New York: Oxford University Press.

Blau, Peter and Otis Dudley Duncan. 1967. *The American Occupational Structure*. New York: John Wiley and Sons.

Block, Fred. 1987. "Rethinking the Political Economy of the Welfare State." In Fred Block, Richard A. Cloward, Barbara Ehrenreich, and Frances Fox Piven, eds., *The Mean Season: The Attack on the Welfare State*, pp. 109–160. New York: Pantheon.

Block, Fred, Richard A. Cloward, Barbara Ehrenreich, and Frances Fox Piven. 1987. *The Mean Season: The Attack on the Welfare State*. New York: Pantheon.

Blossfeld, Hans-Peter, Alfred Hamerle, and Karl Ulrich Mayer. 1989. *Event History Analysis: Statistical Theory and Application in the Social Sciences*. Hillsdale, N.J.: Lawrence Erlbaum Associates.

Bluestone, Barry. 1970. "The Tripartite Economy: Labor Markets and the Working Poor." *Poverty and Human Resources* 5: 15–35.

Bluestone, Barry and Bennett Harrison. 1982. *The Deindustrialization of America:*

Plant Closings, Community Abandonment, and the Dismantling of Basic Industries. New York: Basic Books.

Boskin, Michael J. and Frederick C. Nold. 1975. "A Markov Model of Turnover in Aid to Families with Dependent Children." *Journal of Human Resources* 10: 467–481.

Bourdieu, Pierre and Jean-Claude Passeron. 1977. *Reproduction in Education, Society and Culture*. London: Sage.

Bowles, Samuel and Herbert Gintis. 1976. *Schooling in Capitalist America: Educational Reform and the Contradictions of Economic Life*. New York: Basic Books.

Brauer, Carl M. 1982. "Kennedy, Johnson, and the War on Poverty." *The Journal of American History* 69: 98–119.

Brazzell, Jan F., Irving Lefbert, and Wolfgang Opitz. 1989. "The Impact of Population Size and the Economy on Welfare Caseloads: The Special Case of Welfare Reform." *Applied Demography* 4: 1–7.

Briar, Scott. 1966. "Welfare from Below: Recipients' Views of the Public Welfare System." In Jacobus tenBroek, ed., *The Law of the Poor*, pp. 46–61. San Francisco: Chandler.

Brown, J. Larry and H. F. Pizer. 1987. *Living Hungry in America*. New York: New American Library.

Bryman, Alan. 1988. *Quantity and Quality in Social Research*. London: Unwin Hyman.

Burtless, Gary. 1990. *A Future of Lousy Jobs? The Changing Structure of U.S. Wages*. Washington, D.C.: Brookings Institution.

Bush, George. 1992. "Agenda for American Renewal." Washington, D.C.: Bush-Quayle '92 General Committee.

Cain, Glen G. 1976. "The Challenge of Segmented Labor Market Theories to Orthodox Theory." *Journal of Economic Literature*, 14:1215–1257.

Camasso, Michael J. and Dan E. Moore. 1985. "Rurality and the Residualist Social Welfare Response." *Rural Sociology* 50: 397–408.

Caplovitz, David. 1963. *The Poor Pay More: Consumer Practices of Low-Income Families*. New York: The Free Press.

Charmaz, Kathy. 1983. "The Grounded Theory Method: An Explication and Interpretation." In Robert M. Emerson, ed., *Contemporary Field Research*, pp. 109–126. Boston: Little, Brown.

Cherlin, Andrew J. 1992. *Marriage, Divorce, Remarriage*. Cambridge: Harvard University Press.

Children's Defense Fund. 1985. "Preventing Children Having Children." A Special Conference Report, Clearinghouse Paper No. 1. Washington, D.C.: Children's Defense Fund.

Clignet, Remi. 1992. *Death, Deeds, and Descendants: Inheritance in Modern America*. New York: Aldine de Gruyter.

Clinton, Bill and Al Gore. 1992. *Putting People First: How We Can All Change America*. New York: Times Books.

Coder, John, Dan Burkhead, and Angela Feldman-Harkins. 1988. "A Look at Welfare Dependency Using the 1984 SIPP Panel File." Survey of Income and Program Participation Working Paper No. 8828. Washington, D.C.: U.S. Department of Commerce, Bureau of the Census.

Coder, John and Patricia Ruggles. 1988. "Welfare Recipiency as Observed in the SIPP." Survey of Income and Program Participation Working Paper No. 8818. Washington, D.C.: U.S. Department of Commerce, Bureau of the Census.

Coe, Richard D. 1979. "An Examination of the Dynamics of Food Stamp Use." In Greg J. Duncan and James N. Morgan, eds., *Five Thousand American Families—Patterns of Economic Growth,* vol. 7, pp. 183–226. Ann Arbor: Institute for Social Research, University of Michigan.

Cohen, Barbara E., Martha R. Burt, and Margaret M. Schulte. 1993. "Hunger and Food Insecurity among the Elderly." Project Report. Washington, D.C.: The Urban Institute.

Cole, Stephen and Robert Lejeune. 1972. "Illness and the Legitimation of Failure." *American Sociological Review* 37: 347–356.

Coleman, Richard, Lee Rainwater, and K. McClelland. 1978. *Social Standing in America: New Dimensions of Class.* New York: Basic Books.

Corbett, Thomas. 1991. "The Wisconsin Welfare Magnet Debate: What Is an Ordinary Member of the Tribe to Do When the Witch Doctors Disagree?" *Focus* 13 (Fall and Winter): 19–28.

Corcoran, Mary, Roger Gordon, Deborah Laren, and Gary Solon. 1990. "Effects of Family and Community Background on Economic Status." *American Economic Review* 80: 362–366.

Curtis, Lynn A. 1975. *Violence, Race, and Culture.* Lexington, Mass.: Lexington Books.

Danziger, Sheldon. 1989. "Fighting Poverty and Reducing Welfare Dependency." In Phoebe H. Cottingham and David T. Ellwood, eds., *Welfare Policy for the 1990s,* pp. 41–69. Cambridge: Harvard University Press.

———. 1990. "Antipoverty Policies and Child Poverty." *Social Work Research and Abstracts* 26: 17–24.

Darity, William A., Jr., and Samuel L. Meyers, Jr. 1984. "Does Welfare Dependency Cause Female Headship? The Case of the Black Family." *Journal of Marriage and the Family* 46: 765–779.

Dash, Leon. 1989. *When Children Want Children: An Inside Look at the Crisis of Teenage Parenthood.* New York: Penguin.

DeMott, Benjamin. 1992. *The Imperial Middle: Why Americans Can't Think Straight About Class.* New Haven: Yale University Press.

Denzin, Norman K. 1989. *The Research Act: A Theoretical Introduction to Sociological Methods.* Englewood Cliffs, N.J.: Prentice-Hall.

Doeringer, Peter B. and Michael J. Piore. 1975. "Unemployment and the 'Dual Labor Market.' " *The Public Interest* 38: 67–79.

Domestic Policy Council. 1986 (December). "Up from Dependency: A New National Public Assistance Strategy." Report to the president by the Domestic Policy Council Low Income Opportunity Working Group. Washington, D.C.: U.S. Government Printing Office.

Draper, Thomas W. 1981. "On the Relationship Between Welfare and Marital Stability: A Research Note." *Journal of Marriage and the Family* 43: 293–299.

Dunbar, Leslie. 1988. *The Common Interest: How Our Social-Welfare Policies Don't Work, and What We Can Do About Them.* New York: Pantheon.

Duncan, Cynthia M. 1992. "Persistent Poverty in Appalachia: Scarce Work and Rigid Stratification." In Cynthia M. Duncan, ed., *Rural Poverty in America*, pp. 111–133. New York: Auburn House.

Duncan, Greg J. 1984. *Years of Poverty, Years of Plenty.* Ann Arbor: Institute of Social Research, University of Michigan.

Duncan, Greg J., Martha S. Hill, and Saul D. Hoffman. 1988. "Welfare Dependence Within and Across Generations." *Science* 239: 467–471.

Duncan, Greg J. and Saul D. Hoffman. 1988. "The Use and Effects of Welfare: A Survey of Recent Evidence." *Social Service Review* 62: 238–257.

Edelman, Marian Wright. 1987. *Families in Peril: An Agenda for Social Change.* Cambridge: Harvard University Press.

———. 1992. "Vanishing Dreams of America's Young Families." *Challenge* 35: 13–19.

Edelman, Murray J. 1977. *Political Language.* New York: Academic Press.

Edin, Kathryn. 1991. "Surviving the Welfare System: How AFDC Recipients Make Ends Meet in Chicago." *Social Problems* 38: 475–491.

Edin, Kathryn and Christopher Jencks. 1992. "Reforming Welfare." In Christopher Jencks, *Rethinking Social Policy: Race, Poverty, and the Underclass*, pp. 204–235. Cambridge: Harvard University Press.

Ellwood, David T. 1986 (January). *Targeting "Would-Be" Long-Term Recipients of AFDC.* Princeton, N.J.: Mathematica Policy Research.

———. 1987. "Understanding Dependency: Choices, Confidence, or Culture?" Paper prepared for the U.S. Department of Health and Human Services, Washington, D.C.

———. 1988. *Poor Support: Poverty in the American Family.* New York: Basic Books.

Elster, Jon. 1992. *Local Justice: How Institutions Allocate Scarce Goods and Necessary Burdens.* New York: Russell Sage Foundation.

Feagin, Joe R. 1975. *Subordinating the Poor: Welfare and American Beliefs.* Englewood Cliffs, N.J.: Prentice-Hall.

Featherman, David and Robert Hauser. 1978. *Opportunity and Change.* New York: Academic Press.

Fienberg, Stephen E. 1980. *The Analysis of Cross-Classified Categorical Data.* Cambridge: MIT Press.

Fitzgerald, John. 1991. "Welfare Durations and the Marriage Market: Evidence from the Survey of Income and Program Participation." *Journal of Human Resources* 26: 545–561.

Food Research and Action Center. 1991. *Community Childhood Hunger Identification Project: A Survey of Childhood Hunger in the United States.* Washington, D.C.: Food Research and Action Center.

Free, Lloyd and Hadley Cantril. 1967. *The Political Beliefs of Americans: A Study of Public Opinion*. New Brunswick, N.J.: Rutgers University Press.

Galbraith, John Kenneth. 1992. *The Culture of Contentment*. Boston: Houghton Mifflin.

Galper, Jeffrey. 1970. "The Speenhamland Scales: Political, Social, or Economic Disaster?" *Social Service Review* 44: 54–62.

Gans, Herbert. 1972. "Positive Functions of Poverty." *American Journal of Sociology* 78: 275–289.

———. 1988. *Middle American Individualism: The Future of Liberal Democracy*. New York: The Free Press.

———. 1991. *People, Plans, and Policies: Essays on Poverty, Racism, and Other National Urban Problems*. New York: Columbia University Press.

Garfinkel, Irwin. 1992. *Assuring Child Support: An Extension of Social Security*. New York: Russell Sage Foundation.

Gilder, George. 1981. *Wealth and Poverty*. New York: Basic Books.

Giroux, Henry A. 1983. *Theory and Resistance in Education*. London: Heinemann Educational Books.

Glazer, Nathan. 1984. "The Social Policy of the Reagan Administration: A Review." *The Public Interest* 75: 76–98.

———. 1988. *The Limits of Social Policy*. Cambridge: Harvard University Press.

Glazer, Nathan and Daniel P. Moynihan. 1970. *Beyond the Melting Pot: The Negroes, Puerto Ricans, Jews, Italians, and Irish of New York City*. Cambridge: MIT Press.

Goffman, Erving. 1963. *Stigma: Notes on the Management of Spoiled Identity*. Englewood Cliffs, N.J.: Prentice-Hall.

Goodban, Nancy. 1985. "The Psychological Impact of Being on Welfare." *Social Service Review* 56: 403–422.

Goodsell, Charles B. 1984. "Welfare Waiting Rooms." *Urban Life* 12: 467–477.

Goodwin, Leonard. 1972. *Do the Poor Want to Work? A Social-Psychological Study of Work Orientations*. Washington, D.C.: Brookings Institution.

———. 1983. *Causes and Cures of Welfare: New Evidence on the Social Psychology of the Poor*. Lexington, Mass.: Lexington Books.

Gordon, David M. 1972. *Theories of Poverty and Underemployment: Orthodox, Radical, and Dual Labor Market Perspectives*. Lexington, Mass.: Heath.

Guilkey, David and Ronald R. Rindfuss. 1987. "Logistic Regression Multivariate Life Tables: A Communicable Approach." *Sociological Methods and Research* 16: 276–300.

Guttentag, Marcia and Paul F. Secord. 1983. *Too Many Women? The Sex Ratio Question*. Beverly Hills: Sage.

Guy, Laura. 1982. "Computer Reporting Network Public Use Sample for Wisconsin Economic Assistance Recipients, July 1981." Madison: University of Wisconsin.

Hacker, Andrew. 1992. *Two Nations: Black and White, Separate, Hostile, Unequal*. New York: Scribner's.

Halle, David. 1984. *America's Working Man: Work, Home, and Politics among Blue-Collar Property Owners*. Chicago: University of Chicago Press.

Handel, Gerald. 1982. *Social Welfare in Western Society*. New York: Random House.

Handler, Joel F. and Ellen Jane Hollingsworth. 1971. *The "Deserving Poor": A Study of Welfare Administration*. Chicago: Markham.

Harrington, Michael. 1963. *The Other America: Poverty in the United States*. Baltimore, Md.: Penguin.

———. 1984. *The New American Poverty*. New York: Holt, Rinehart and Winston.

Hartwell, R. M. 1986. "The Long Debate on Poverty." Paper presented at the Political Economy Seminar Series, Washington University, St. Louis, Missouri.

Hendrickson, Robert M. and Leland J. Axelson. 1985. "Middle-Class Attitudes Toward the Poor: Are They Changing?" *Social Service Review* 59: 295–304.

Hirschl, Thomas A. and Mark R. Rank. 1991. "The Effect of Population Density on Welfare Participation." *Social Forces* 70: 225–235.

Hodson, Randy and Robert L. Kaufman. 1982. "Economic Dualism: A Critical Review." *American Sociological Review* 47: 727–739.

Horan, Patrick and Patricia Austin. 1974. "The Social Bases of Welfare Stigma." *Social Problems* 21: 648–657.

Hossain, Mahabub. 1988. *Credit for Alleviation of Rural Poverty: The Grameen Bank in Bangladesh*. Washington, D.C.: International Food Policy Research Institute.

Howell, Joseph T. 1972. *Hard Living on Clay Street: Portraits of Blue Collar Families*. Garden City, N.Y.: Anchor Press.

Huber, Joan and William H. Form. 1973. *Income and Ideology: An Analysis of the American Political Formula*. New York: The Free Press.

Husock, Howard. 1992. "Bring Back the Settlement House." *The Public Interest* 109: 53–72.

Hutchens, Robert M. 1981. "Entry and Exit Transitions in a Government Transfer Program: The Case of Aid to Families with Dependent Children." *Journal of Human Resources* 16: 217–237.

Jacobs, Paul. 1966. "Keeping the Poor Poor." In Leonard H. Goodman, ed., *Economic Progress and Social Welfare*, pp. 159–184. New York: Columbia University Press.

———. 1968. *Prelude to Riot: A View of Urban America from the Bottom*. New York: Random House.

Jaynes, Gerald David and Robin M. Williams, Jr. 1989. *A Common Destiny: Blacks and American Society*. Washington, D.C.: National Academy Press.

Jencks, Christopher. 1992. *Rethinking Social Policy: Race, Poverty, and the Underclass*. Cambridge: Harvard University Press.

Jencks, Christopher and Paul E. Peterson. 1991. *The Urban Underclass.* Washington, D.C.: Brookings Institution.

Kahn, Si. 1991. *Organizing: A Guide for Grassroots Leaders.* Silver Spring, Md.: NASW Press.

Katz, Michael B. 1986. *In the Shadow of the Poorhouse: A Social History of Welfare in America.* New York: Basic Books.

——. 1989. *The Undeserving Poor: From the War on Poverty to the War on Welfare.* New York: Pantheon Books.

Kaus, Mickey. 1992. *The End of Equality.* New York: Basic Books.

Keith, Pat M. 1980. "Demographic and Attitudinal Factors Associated with Perceptions of Social Welfare." *Sociology and Social Welfare* 7: 561–570.

Kerbo, Harold R. 1976. "The Stigma of Welfare and a Passive Poor." *Sociology and Social Research* 60: 173–187.

——. 1983. *Social Stratification and Inequality: Class Conflict in the United States.* New York: McGraw-Hill.

Kluegel, James R. and Eliot R. Smith. 1986. *Beliefs about Inequality: Americans' Views of What Is and What Ought to Be.* New York: Aldine de Gruyter.

Komarovsky, Mirra. 1962. *Blue-Collar Marriage.* New York: Random House.

Kozol, Jonathan. 1991. *Savage Inequalities: Children in America's Schools.* New York: Crown.

Lee, E. and M. Desu. 1972. "A Computer Program for Comparing *K* Samples with Right-Censored Data." *Computer Programs in Biomedicine* 2: 315–321.

Lemann, Nicholas. 1989. "The Unfinished War." *The Atlantic* (January): 53–68.

LeMasters, E. E. 1975. *Blue-Collar Aristocrats: Life-Styles at a Working-Class Tavern.* Madison: University of Wisconsin Press.

Levitan, Sar A. 1990. *Programs in Aid of the Poor.* Baltimore, Md.: Johns Hopkins University Press.

Lewis, I. A. and William Schneider. 1985. "Hard Times: The Public on Poverty." *Public Opinion* 8: 2–7, 59–60.

Lewis, Oscar. 1959. *Five Families: Mexican Case Studies in the Culture of Poverty.* New York: Basic Books.

——. 1966a. *La Vida: A Puerto Rican Family in the Culture of Poverty.* New York: Random House.

——. 1966b. "The Culture of Poverty." *Scientific American* 215: 19–25.

——. 1969. "The Culture of Poverty." In Daniel P. Moynihan, ed., *On Understanding Poverty: Perspectives from the Social Sciences,* pp. 187–200. New York: Basic Books.

Lichter, Daniel T., Felicia B. LeClere. and Diane K. McLaughlin. 1991. "Local Marriage Markets and the Marital Behavior of Black and White Women." *American Journal of Sociology* 96: 843–867.

Liebow, Elliot. 1967. *Tally's Corner: A Study of Negro Streetcorner Men.* Boston: Little, Brown.

Lipsky, Michael. 1980. *Street-Level Bureaucracy: Dilemmas of the Individual in Public Services*. New York: Russell Sage Foundation.

Loewenberg, Frank M. 1981. "The Destigmatization of Public Dependency." *Social Service Review* 55: 434–452.

Lofland, John and Lyn H. Lofland. 1984. *Analyzing Social Settings: A Guide to Qualitative Observation and Analysis*. Belmont, Calif.: Wadsworth.

MacLeod, Jay. 1987. *Ain't No Makin' It: Leveled Aspirations in a Low-Income Neighborhood*. Boulder, Colo.: Westview Press.

McLanahan, Sara and Karen Booth. 1989. "Mother-Only Families: Problems, Prospects, and Politics." *Journal of Marriage and the Family* 51: 557–580.

Maital, Shlomo and Kim I. Morgan. 1992. "Hungry Children Are a Bad Business." *Challenge* 35: 54–59.

Marx, Karl and Friedrich Engels. 1968. *Selected Works*. New York: International Publishers.

Mead, Lawrence. 1986. *Beyond Entitlement: The Social Obligations of Citizenship*. New York: The Free Press.

———. 1992. *The New Politics of Poverty: The Nonworking Poor in America*. New York: Basic Books.

Merton, Robert K. 1949. *Social Theory and Social Structure*. Glencoe, Ill.: The Free Press.

Mincer, Jacob. 1958. "Investment in Human Capital and Personal Income Distribution." *Journal of Political Economy* 66: 281–302.

Moffitt, Robert. 1983. "An Economic Model of Welfare Stigma." *American Economic Review* 73: 1023–1035.

———. 1992. "Incentive Effects of the U.S. Welfare System: A Review." *Journal of Economic Literature* 30: 1–61.

Morgan, Betty. 1979. "Four Pennies to My Name: What It's Like on Welfare." *Public Welfare* 37: 13–22.

Morris, Michael and John B. Williamson. 1986. *Poverty and Public Policy: An Analysis of Federal Intervention Efforts*. New York: Greenwood Press.

Mott, Frank L. 1983 (February). "Welfare Incidence and Welfare Dependency Among American Women: A Longitudinal Examination." Columbus: Center for Human Resource Research, Ohio State University.

Moynihan, Daniel P. 1965. *The Negro Family: The Case for National Action*. Washington, D.C.: U.S. Department of Labor.

———. 1970. *Maximum Feasible Misunderstanding: Community Action in the War on Poverty*. New York: The Free Press.

Murray, Charles. 1984. *Losing Ground: American Social Policy 1950–1980*. New York: Basic Books.

———. 1988. *In Pursuit: Of Happiness and Good Government*. New York: Simon and Schuster.

National Research Council. 1990. *Who Cares for America's Children? Child Care Policy for the 1990s*. Washington, D.C.: National Academy Press.

Neckerman, Kathryn M. and Joleen Kirschenman. 1991. "Hiring Strategies, Racial Bias, and Inner-City Workers." *Social Problems* 38: 433–447.

Nilson, Linda Burzotta. 1981. "Reconsidering Ideological Lines: Beliefs About Poverty in America." *Sociological Quarterly* 22: 531–548.

O'Connor, James. 1973. *The Fiscal Crisis of the State*. New York: St. Martin's Press.

O'Hare, William P. 1987. "America's Welfare Population: Who Gets What?" *Population Trends and Public Policy*, no. 13 (September): 1–16.

O'Neill, June A., Douglas A. Wolf, Laurie J. Bassi, and Michael T. Hannan. 1984 (June). *An Analysis of Time on Welfare*. Final report to the U.S. Department of Health and Human Services. Washington, D.C.: The Urban Institute.

Parsons, Paul. 1989. *Getting Published: The Acquisition Process at University Presses*. Knoxville, Tenn.: University of Tennessee Press.

Patterson, James T. 1986. *America's Struggle Against Poverty: 1900–1985*. Cambridge: Harvard University Press.

Pfuhl, Jr., Erdwin H. 1986. *The Deviance Process*. New York: Van Nostrand.

Piven, Frances Fox and Richard A. Cloward. 1971. *Regulating the Poor: The Functions of Public Welfare*. New York: Pantheon.

Plant, Mark W. 1984. "An Empirical Analysis of Welfare Dependence." *American Economic Review* 74: 673–684.

Plotnick, Robert D. 1983. "Turnover in the AFDC Population: An Event History Analysis." *Journal of Human Resources* 18: 65–81.

Popkin, Susan J. 1990. "Welfare: Views from the Bottom." *Social Problems* 37: 64–79.

Pratt, William F., William D. Mosher, Christine A. Bachrach, and Marjorie C. Houn. 1984. "Understanding U.S. Fertility: Findings from the National Survey of Family Growth, Cycle III." *Population Bulletin* 39: 1–43.

Prottas, Jeffrey Manditch. 1979. *People-Processing: The Street-Level Bureaucrat in Public Service Bureaucracies*. Lexington, Mass.: Lexington Books.

Rainwater, Lee. 1987 (October). "Class, Culture, Poverty and Welfare." Paper prepared for the U.S. Department of Health and Human Services.

Rank, Mark R. 1985. "Exiting from Welfare: A Life-Table Analysis." *Social Service Review* 59: 358–376.

———. 1988a. "Racial Differences in Length of Welfare Use." *Social Forces* 66: 1080–1101.

———. 1988b. "The Blending of Quantitative and Qualitative Data in Family Research." Paper presented at the National Council on Family Relations Pre-Conference Workshop on Theory Construction and Research Methodology, Philadelphia, Pennsylvania, November 11–13.

———. 1992. "The Blending of Qualitative and Quantitative Methods in Understanding Childbearing among Welfare Recipients." In Jane F. Gilgun, Kerry Daly, and Gerald Handel, eds., *Qualitative Methods in Family Research*, pp. 281–300. Newbury Park, Calif.: Sage.

Rank, Mark R., Li Chen Cheng, and Donald Cox. 1992. "The Dynamics and Determinants of Intergenerational Welfare Use." Paper presented at the Faculty Research Forum, George Warren Brown School of Social Work, Washington University, St. Louis, Missouri, December 2.

Rank, Mark R. and Thomas A. Hirschl. 1992. "The Link Between Population Density and Food Stamp Participation." Institute for Research on Poverty, Discussion Paper No. 988–92, University of Wisconsin–Madison.

Rank, Mark R. and Paul R. Voss. 1984a. "AFDC, Food Stamp, and Medicaid Utilization: A Research Note." *Journal of Sociology and Social Welfare* 11: 176–191.

———. 1984b. *Demographic Characteristics of Wisconsin's Welfare Recipients.* Population Series 80–2. Madison, Wis.: Applied Population Laboratory.

Reagan, Ronald W. 1986 (February 4). *The State of the Union: An Address to the Congress.* Washington, D.C.: White House Office of the Press Secretary.

Rein, Martin and Lee Rainwater. 1978. "Patterns of Welfare Use." *Social Service Review* 52: 511–534.

Ricketts, Erol and Ronald Mincy. 1988 (February). "Growth of the Underclass, 1970–1980." Washington, D.C.: Urban Institute.

Rubin, Lillian Breslow. 1976. *Worlds of Pain: Life in the Working-Class Family.* New York: Basic Books.

Ruggles, Patricia. 1989. "Welfare Dependency and Its Causes: Determinants of the Duration of Welfare Spells." Survey of Income and Program Participation Working Paper No. 8908.

———. 1990. *Drawing the Line: Alternative Poverty Measures and Their Implications for Public Policy.* Washington, D.C.: Urban Institute Press.

Rydell, Peter C., Thelma Palmeria, Gerald Blasis, and Dan Brown. 1974. *Welfare Caseload Dynamics in New York City.* New York: Rand Institute.

Sakamoto, Arthur and Meichu D. Chen. 1991. "Inequality and Attainment in a Dual Labor Market." *American Sociological Review* 56: 295–308.

Saks, Daniel. 1975. *Public Assistance for Mothers in an Urban Labor Market.* Princeton, N.J.: Industrial Relations Section, Princeton University.

Sawhill, Isabel V. 1988. "Poverty in the U.S.: Why Is It So Persistent?" *Journal of Economic Literature* 26: 1073–1119.

———. 1989. "The Underclass: An Overview." *The Public Interest* 96: 3–15.

Schatzman, Leonard and Anselm L. Strauss. 1973. *Field Research: Strategies for a Natural Sociology.* Englewood Cliffs, N.J.: Prentice-Hall.

Schiller, Bradley R. 1970. "Stratified Opportunities: The Essence of the 'Vicious Circle.' " *American Journal of Sociology* 76: 426–442.

———. 1989. *The Economics of Poverty and Discrimination.* Englewood Cliffs, N.J.: Prentice-Hall.

Schottland, Charles I. 1967. *The Welfare State: Selected Essays.* New York: Harper and Row.

Schwartz, B. 1975. *Queuing and Waiting: Studies in the Social Organization of Access and Delay.* Chicago: University of Chicago Press.

Sheehan, Susan. 1975. *A Welfare Mother*. Boston: Houghton Mifflin.

Sherman, Gerald. 1989. "Micro-Enterprise Lending: The Grameen Bank–Lakota Fund Experience." *Social Policy* 20: 64–67.

Sherraden, Michael. 1991. *Assets and the Poor: A New American Welfare Policy*. Armonk, N.Y.: Sharpe.

Shryock, Henry S. and Jacob S. Siegel. 1976. *The Methods and Materials of Demography*. New York: Academic Press.

Sidel, Ruth. 1992. *Women and Children Last: The Plight of Poor Women in Affluent America*. New York: Penguin.

Simpson, Patricia. 1990. *Living in Poverty: Coping on the Welfare Grant*. New York: Community Service Society of New York.

Smith, Kevin B. and Lorene H. Stone. 1989. "Rags, Riches, and Bootstraps: Beliefs about the Causes of Wealth and Poverty." *Sociological Quarterly* 30: 93–107.

Soldo, Beth J. and Emily M. Agree. 1988. "America's Elderly." *Population Bulletin* 43: 1–51.

Solow, Robert M. 1990. "Poverty and Economic Growth." *Focus* 12 (Spring): 3–5.

Stack, Carol B. 1974. *All Our Kin: Strategies for Survival in a Black Community*. New York: Harper and Row.

Steinberg, Stephen. 1989. *The Ethnic Myth: Race, Ethnicity, and Class in America*. Boston: Beacon Press.

Strauss, Anselm and Juliet Corbin. 1990. *Basics of Qualitative Research: Grounded Theory Procedures and Techniques*. Newbury Park, Calif.: Sage.

Sudman, Seymour and Norman M. Bradburn. 1982. *Asking Questions: A Practical Guide to Questionnaire Design*. San Francisco: Jossey-Bass.

Susser, Ida and John Kreniske. 1987. "The Welfare Trap: A Public Policy for Deprivation." In Leith Mullings, ed., *Cities of the United States: Studies in Urban Anthropology*, pp. 50–68. New York: Columbia University Press.

Thurow, Lester C. 1987. "A Surge in Inequality." *Scientific American* 256: 30–37.

Tienda, Marta. 1990. "Welfare and Work in Chicago's Inner City." *American Economic Review* 80: 372–376.

Tocqueville, Alexis de. 1983. "Memoir on Pauperism." *The Public Interest* 70: 102–120.

Trattner, Walter I. 1989. *From Poor Law to Welfare State: A History of Social Welfare in America*. New York: The Free Press.

U.S. Bureau of the Census. 1981. "Fertility of American Women: June 1980." Current Population Reports, series P-20, no. 364. Washington, D.C.: U.S. Government Printing Office.

———. 1991. *Statistical Abstract of the United States: 1991*. Washington, D.C.: U.S. Government Printing Office.

———. 1992a. "Poverty in the United States: 1991." Current Population Reports, series P-60, no. 181. Washington, D.C.: U.S. Government Printing Office.

————. 1992b. "Money Income of Households, Families, and Persons in the United States: 1991." Current Population Reports, series P-60, no. 180. Washington, D.C.: U.S. Government Printing Office.

————. 1992c. "Studies in Household and Family Formation." Current Population Reports, series P-23, no. 179. Washington, D.C.: U.S. Government Printing Office.

Vosler, Nancy R., Sally Haywood, and Helen V. Graber. 1992. "An Innovative Policy Practice Model for Building Neighborhood Community." Paper presented at the Annual Program Meeting of the Council on Social Work Education, Kansas City, Missouri, February 29–March 3.

Wachtel, Howard M. 1971. "Looking at Poverty from a Radical Perspective." *The Review of Radical Political Economics* 3: 1–19.

Waite, Linda J. and Lee A. Lillard. 1991. "Children and Marital Disruption." *American Journal of Sociology* 96: 930–953.

Waxman, Chaim I. 1983. *The Stigma of Poverty: A Critique of Poverty Theories and Policies.* New York: Pergamon Press.

Weitzman, Lenore J. 1985. *The Divorce Revolution: The Unexpected Social and Economic Consequences for Women and Children in America.* New York: The Free Press.

Williams, Terry and William Kornblum. 1985. *Growing Up Poor.* Lexington, Mass.: Lexington Books.

Wisconsin Department of Health and Social Services. 1981. "Public Health Statistics: 1980." Madison: Wisconsin Department of Health and Social Services, Division of Health, Bureau of Health Statistics.

Whyte, William Foote. 1943. *Street Corner Society: The Social Structure of an Italian Slum.* Chicago: University of Chicago Press.

Williamson, John. 1974a. "Beliefs About the Welfare Poor." *Sociology and Social Research* 58: 163–175.

————. 1974b. "The Stigma of Public Dependency: A Comparison of Alternative Forms of Public Aid to the Poor." *Social Problems* 22: 213–228.

Wilson, William Julius. 1987. *The Truly Disadvantaged: The Inner City, The Underclass, and Public Policy.* Chicago: University of Chicago Press.

Wiseman, Michael. 1977. "Change and Turnover in a Welfare Population." Berkeley: Institute of Business and Economic Research, University of California, Berkeley.

Wolcott, Harry F. 1990. *Writing Up Qualitative Research.* Newbury Park, Calif.: Sage.

Working Group on the Family. 1986. *The Family: Preserving America's Future.* Washington, D.C.: United States Department of Education, Office of the Under Secretary.

Wright, James D. and Julie A. Lam. 1987. "Homelessness and the Low-income Housing Supply." *Social Policy* 17: 48–53.

INDEX